TOO YOUNG TO DIE

Famed for its nationwide coverage of crime and punishment, *Court TV* is <u>the</u> source for the most up-to-date, in-depth, on-the-scene true crime reporting. Now, for the millions of fans of the acclaimed series, *Crime Stories,* comes the shocking facts about today's most sensational trials.

BABY FACE KILLER—Denver, Colorado neighbors were closer to each other than many families. So why did the teenage daughter of one family kill the daughter of the other in cold blood?

FRIENDLY TERROR—Cambridge, Massachusetts police thought Salvatore Sicari wanted to help them locate a missing ten-year-old boy. Sicari only wanted to make sure the police *didn't* locate the boy's molested body.

THE COED SERIAL KILLER—Gainesville, Florida residents were terrorized as five students were found brutally murdered. DNA evidence was crucial in catching career criminal D̶a̶n̶n̶y̶ ̶R̶o̶llings and bringing him

With si̶x̶t̶e̶e̶n̶ ̶p̶a̶g̶e̶s̶ ̶o̶f̶ ̶p̶h̶o̶tos provided by *Court TV!*

**CRIME STORIES:
THE BEST OF *COURT TV***

TOO YOUNG TO DIE

David Jacobs

PINNACLE BOOKS
Kensington Publishing Corp.

http://www.pinnaclebooks.com

Some names have been changed to protect the privacy of individuals connected to this story.

PINNACLE BOOKS are published by

Kensington Publishing Corp.
850 Third Avenue
New York, NY 10022

All Kensington Titles, Imprints, and Distributed Lines are available at special quantity discounts for bulk purchases for sales promotions, premiums, fund-raising, and educational or institutional use. Special book excerpts or customized printings can also be created to fit specific needs. For details, write or phone the office of the Kensington special sales manager: Kensington Publishing Corp., 850 Third Avenue, New York, NY 10022, attn: Special Sales Department, Phone: 1-800-221-2647.

Pinnacle and the P logo Reg. U.S. Pat. & TM Off.

First Printing: May 2001
10 9 8 7 6 5 4 3 2 1

Printed in the United States of America

CONTENTS

Colorado v. *Tombs:*
"BABY-FACED KILLER"

THE CRIME

On Friday, September 27, 1996, sometime between 10:00 and 11:00 P.M. in Denver, Colorado, Joaquin "Jock" Johnson, twenty-one, weak with stomach flu, rose from a sickbed to answer an urgent wireless summons from his personal pager.

It was only the latest of what had already been a busy night of telecommunicating.

He was being paged by Jennifer Lee Tombs, the fifteen-year-old daughter of the Reverend Madlyn Tombs, pastor of the First Christian Assembly of God Church and its African American congregation. Jennifer, the adopted daughter of single mother Pastor Tombs, had a less-than-heavenly record, including several brushes with the law.

She was also the mother of Johnson's infant son, Jorelle—whom Johnson had never actually seen.

Last summer, Johnson and Jennifer had had a relationship and been intimate, a relationship that cooled when she told him that she was pregnant. She'd told his mom about the pregnancy, too. He'd questioned whether the child was his, and after that, had kind of slipped away from her, out of the picture.

He'd seen her three or four times during her pregnancy, but she hadn't been showing much under the oversize shirts that she wore. After Jorelle was born, he'd been in infrequent communication with her. He'd never had an opportunity to see the baby.

Tonight, there'd been a flurry of messaging between Jennifer and Johnson. Earlier that day, she'd paged him three or four times, adding the number 911, signifying that the call was some kind of emergency. At about 7:00 P.M., he'd called her at her home. She said that she needed to borrow his gun.

Like many law-abiding citizens, Jock Johnson had exercised his constitutional right to own a firearm, a .25-caliber semiautomatic pistol. While he and Jennifer were dating, she'd asked for the loan of the weapon, a request to which he'd acceded. He'd said he'd sell it to her, only she'd never paid him the money, so he reclaimed the gun.

At that time, its clip had been fully loaded, but when she'd returned it to him, it was empty of all but two or three bullets, leaving about eight live rounds unaccounted for.

At 7:00 P.M. on September 27, she said she needed the gun again. Earlier that day, she said, while she'd been visiting her parole officer (she was on probation for auto theft), she'd gotten into a beef with four girls, whom she'd since seen driving past her house and occasionally parking in front of it. She expected further trouble with them.

She was scared, she said—scared for her life. And their baby's, too. She said that baby Jorelle would be coming back to her house at about 9:30 P.M. this night.

Johnson decided to give her the gun. He got into his car, a white 1984 Oldsmobile Cutlass, arriving at Jennifer's Montbello house somewhere between 9:00 and 9:30 P.M.

A handsome house, in a nice neighborhood, it was located only one half block away from the church where Jennifer's mother, Pastor Tombs, officiated. A green car was parked in the driveway.

Johnson called Jennifer on his cell phone and told her to meet him in front of the house. On the passenger side of the front seat lay the gun. The silver-looking .25-caliber pistol was completely unloaded.

Jennifer came outside and grabbed the gun from the front seat. She tucked it under her shirt, in the waistband of her blue denim shorts, and went back inside the house.

Johnson drove away, heading to his brother's house. His brother wasn't home. Minutes after leaving his brother's house, he called Jennifer, checking back with her to respond to the numerous page calls that she'd made on his beeper. Her phone was answered by someone else, a female whose voice he didn't recognize. When Jennifer got on, he told her that she owed him a battery—she'd paged him so much tonight that she'd worn down his pager battery.

She said she'd call him later.

Johnson's mother had asked him to come by, so he dropped in for a visit. He wasn't feeling very well, so he went home, where Jennifer paged him two or three more times. Finally, sometime between 10:00 and 11:00 P.M., he called her back.

Jennifer said she had done something really bad. She couldn't say what it was on the phone, but she wanted him to come over.

"No," he said.

Later, at around 1:00 or 2:00 A.M., Saturday, he got up, still sick, and called her back. Jennifer answered, saying that she was asleep, that baby Jorelle was with her, and that everybody was sleeping.

At 4:30 A.M., she paged him again. Johnson called, asking her what was happening. Jennifer wanted him to come over.

Again he said no.

She said she'd killed somebody, a woman. She said that earlier there'd been a knock on the door, and when she'd opened it, a girl had barged in and attacked her. There was a scuffle, and she'd shot the intruder—shot her five times, emptying the clip into her head. The body was downstairs with a bag on its head.

Johnson didn't believe her. He said, "Call the police and let them handle it."

Jennifer Tombs didn't want to bring the police in, she said, because she was on parole.

Still not believing her, Jock Johnson hung up and went back to bed. There were no further calls for him that night.

Thwarted communication was also the theme that night at the Lavallais [pronounced lah-vuh-lay] family house, where a tense atmosphere of frustration and anxiety thickened with each passing minute as Friday night shaded into early Saturday morning.

Daughter Latanya "Tanya" Lavallais, twenty-three, was out of communication and had been so for some time, worrying the rest of the close-knit Lavallais family.

Tanya, the third youngest of seven children, had attended Aurora Community College and was now working in a real estate office, leasing apartments. Her parents were both former islanders, with step-father Errol Vermont originally hailing from Jamaica, while mother Valeria "Val" Vermont came from Bermuda.

The family was religious. Errol Vermont was an associate minister of the First Christian Assembly of God Church, where he was second in authority only to senior pastor Madlyn Tombs. The Lavallais family had been associated with her from early on in her ministry—Val Vermont had known her for over twenty-six years. The two families were close professionally and personally, frequently socializing and even going on vacations together. Val Vermont had been with Madlyn Tombs on the day she first got Jennifer; the baby girl had been adopted when she was about eight months old.

Since the onset of adolescence, Jennifer's life had been a stormy one. She smoked, drank and skipped school. She liked boys and they liked her. But there were other, more serious problems.

Adoptee Jennifer had set about learning the true identity of her birth mother. On finding out, she'd had the woman's name tattooed on her arm—a heavy statement to her adoptive mother. Her occasional bouts of shoplifting might have been explained away as typical teen troubles, but other actions were less easy to ignore.

Now she had two prior convictions on charges of second-degree auto theft, with a third case pending against her in nearby Arapahoe County. She'd also been arrested on an arson charge, for setting fire to her mother's bed.

She was now on probation for car theft and one of the terms of probation was that she wear an electronic ankle bracelet, which monitored her whereabouts night and day.

Another was that she remain home under parental supervision in a kind of "house arrest," during after-school hours and on weekends, except on special occasions that had to first be approved of by her parole officer.

Now, as Jennifer's probation neared its second level, where the restrictions would be lightened, her adoptive mother, Madlyn Tombs, was called to lead a weekend religious retreat for some of her church members. She wanted to attend, but she couldn't leave Jennifer alone without supervision.

As she'd done before in similar situations, Madlyn Tombs turned to her close friends, the Lavallaises. About a week before September 27, Madlyn Tombs went to Val Vermont's house to have her hair done, telling her of her problem.

Val offered to let Jennifer stay at her house, but Madlyn Tombs had to decline. There was that pesky matter of Jennifer's electronic ankle bracelet, ceaselessly tracking her location. She couldn't leave the house, so they decided to have Tanya stay with her. In effect, Tanya would be baby-sitting fifteen-year-old Jennifer for the weekend. She'd baby-sat Jennifer before. Jennifer called Tanya her "cousin."

The weekend of the retreat was going to be a big one for the Lavallaises, too. One of their sons was going to be married on Saturday, September 28. Jennifer's parole officer had given permission for her to attend the wedding.

Apparently, Jennifer had plans of her own. Earlier in the week, she'd called Tasha at the Lavallais house, asking if her sister Tanya would let her smoke, drink and party this weekend. Tasha said that Tanya wouldn't let Jennifer do anything her mother wouldn't let her do.

Later, Jennifer called back, again asking what Tanya would let her do. Tasha called Tanya on a three-way line, then got off to tend to her son. Ten minutes later, when she got back on the line, she heard Tanya speak, apparently replying to some remark that Jennifer had just made.

Tanya said, "Well, if you fuck with me, I'm gonna fuck you up." She could do it, too, Tasha thought. Tanya was big, weighing about 180 pounds, much more than Jennifer weighed. Tasha joked that party-mad Jennifer was liable to tie up Tanya and lock her in the closet.

On Friday, September 27, Tanya asked Tasha to spend the night with her at the Tombs house. After first picking up Jennifer, Tanya would then pick up Tasha and her young son; then they would all go back to Jennifer's. The next day, they'd all go to the wedding.

Tanya was supposed to page Tasha before picking her up at around eight o'clock. At 7:30 P.M., Tasha paged Tanya from downtown, to no reply. Eight came, but no page. At 8:30 P.M., arriving home, Tasha again paged Tanya. There was still no callback. Tasha paged her a few more times, her anxiety mounting as her pages went unanswered.

At ten o'clock, she called the Tombs house.

No answer.

At 7:30 P.M. on Friday, Val Vermont first began paging her daughter Tanya. There was no reply, no callback. Val paged her a few more times, with no result. By 9:00 P.M., she and husband Errol Vermont were starting to get worried. That's when she first called the Tombs house.

Jennifer answered, saying that Tanya had left the house but would be right back. Val assumed that Tanya had probably left to get something from her apartment. She called Tanya's apartment—no answer.

Later, when she called the apartment again, the phone was answered by Mark Caisey, Tanya's close cousin and roommate. Caisey said Tanya hadn't been there. He himself had started paging Tanya at around seven o'clock that night, also receiving no reply.

In the next few hours, he paged her about six times more without getting an answer. It wasn't like Tanya not to call back.

Aware of the mounting tension, Caisey went over to the Lavallais house and they all sat there by the phone, waiting for Tanya to call, a call that did not come.

Val Vermont called the Tombs house, speaking to Jennifer, asking her why Tanya wasn't answering her pager. Jennifer said that Tanya's pager's battery charge was low, and that she'd given Tanya another battery.

Later, Val called again. The phone was answered this time not by Jennifer, but by her friend Tiffany Lofton. Val was surprised at finding anyone else there. She asked for Jennifer, who got on, explaining that her mother and Tanya had given permission for Lofton to stay over. Tanya hadn't come back yet, she said. Val said she didn't understand why Tanya wasn't answering her pager.

It was getting late. She asked her husband and Mark Caisey to go over.

Concerned about the conflicting stories they were getting about Tanya's absence, Errol Vermont and Caisey went out after 11:30 P.M. and drove to the Tombs house, arriving sometime around midnight.

The house was mostly dark, though a red light was on in a room upstairs. Errol Vermont thought it was Jennifer's room.

The blind was lifted and someone looked through it.

Tanya's green car was in the driveway, and Vermont assumed that she'd just come back from the clubs. He felt the hood. It was cold, meaning that it had been there for some time.

He and Mark Caisey went to the front door, knocked on it. He'd been to the house many times, had been alone with Jennifer in it many times, and had every reasonable expectation that she would let him in.

After a while, the front door was unlocked from

the inside and opened. Jennifer stood there, wearing shorts and a light-colored shirt, opening the door just wide enough for her to stand in it, looking out. Behind her, the room was dark.

Errol Vermont expressed his concern. Jennifer said Tanya had gone out, she didn't know with whom. Vermont and Caisey alternated questions. Caisey asked if everything was okay. Jennifer said yes. Caisey asked if he could come in and look around.

Jennifer said, "You can't come in, you don't have a search warrant."

He said, "I don't need a search warrant, I'm not the police."

He wanted to look around and see what was up. He was determined to go in, to force his way in if he had to. He was all for calling the police.

Vermont resisted, telling Caisey to leave it alone. The police had been called to this house enough times, he said. Later he would recall his feelings as "not wanting to create any more commotion for the pastor."

Frustrated, they left, driving home. While they were still on the road, the phone rang at the Lavallais house. Val Vermont picked up.

Jennifer was on the other end of the line, telling her not to worry. Tanya was okay, Val could go to bed. Jennifer said, "I wouldn't let anything happen to my big cousin."

She added that she hadn't let Vermont and Caisey in because she wasn't appropriately dressed.

Later, when Val Vermont called the Tombs house, all she got was the phone answering machine. Her

last call was made at 3:30 A.M. She never really went
to bed, but eventually she did fall asleep.

When she awoke, it was morning and Tanya was
still missing. She called Tanya's job. Tanya was
scheduled to work that morning, but they hadn't
heard from her.

Earlier that week, Willis Wallace, a seventeen-year-
old high school student, had been invited by his
girlfriend, Tiffany Lofton, to enjoy a shrimp dinner
that would be cooked by her and Jennifer Tombs
at Jennifer's house on Friday, when Pastor Tombs
would be away for a religious retreat. Jennifer's boyfriend, Alan Milliner [pronounced mill-ner], would
also attend, rounding out the group.

Tiffany Lofton, fifteen, had known Jennifer as a
friend since the eighth grade, and Jennifer had
even once lived in Lofton's house for a few months.
Their houses were about four or five blocks away.

On Friday, September 27, however, the evening
plans changed. At 6:30 P.M., Tanya Lavallais arrived
at the Tombs house. Then Tanya and Jennifer ate
pizza. At 8:00 P.M., Tiffany Lofton came over, talking
briefly to Tanya, who was downstairs in the rec
room.

Somewhere between 9:00 and 9:30 P.M., the
guests first arrived. Willis Wallace and Alan Milliner
had brought along two friends, Donald James and
Duvonne [pronounced duh-von] Green. Green,
eighteen, knew Jennifer Tombs casually. James
didn't know Tiffany or Jennifer.

Driving a borrowed Celica, James drove the
group to Jennifer's Montbello house. Tiffany Lofton

came outside on the porch and told them to wait a minute. The group left and came back a little while later, no more than a half hour. On their return, sometime between 9:00 and 9:30 P.M., Jennifer came outside, telling them that Tanya was in the house and that they would have to enter quietly and go to her room. She didn't say that Tanya didn't know they were there.

Duvonne Green recalled later that it seemed like they were sneaking into the house. Willis Wallace never saw Tanya, but thought he heard her as he was going into the house. He heard her talking, so he knew someone else was in the house.

The house had four levels: the ground floor, by which the group entered; upstairs, where the bedrooms were; a level below ground floor, containing a rec room and laundry room; and a basement area.

The four guys and two girls all went upstairs to Jennifer's room, closing the door behind them. The guys had brought a pint bottle of E&J brandy and some wine coolers. It was pretty cramped with six people in the room. People milled around, sitting on the bed and floor. Milliner sat by the dresser, Green beside him. James, Wallace and Lofton sat on the bed.

The guests were told to try to keep the noise down. Jennifer kept popping in and out of the room, waiting for her cousin to leave, she said. Everyone else stayed in the room and didn't go out. Lofton tried to leave the room, but Jennifer told her to go back inside, as she was talking to Tanya.

Jennifer said she was waiting for Tanya to leave

to go to a club, Bernard's lounge, with her boy-friend, whom she said drove "a white Cutlass."

The guys passed the time listening to music, smoking, drinking brandy and shooting craps. Lofton drank wine coolers. Donald James recalled later that marijuana was smoked, though the others later disputed that recollection.

The dice game was played between the bed and dresser. The girls did not take part in the game.

Lofton saw Jennifer with a phone in the hall. She never heard the phone ring, though she heard Jennifer talking on the phone. Jennifer said she was talking to Tanya's unnamed boyfriend, that he was coming to pick Tanya up.

Forty-five minutes to an hour passed by. Milliner was on the bed; James, Green and Wallace were on the floor, and Tiffany Lofton was on the bed by Wallace, close to the window.

Jennifer came in again, telling them to be quiet because Tanya had not yet left, but that she was getting ready to go out. James peeked out the window, but he didn't see anyone coming or going.

Jennifer went back out of the room. A short time later, there was a noise.

To Alan Milliner, it sounded like a backfire—or gunshots. He said so, too, at the time, and asked if anyone else had heard them. He heard muted bangs, "not as many as seven or eight."

Duvonne Green heard three or four booms, not real loud, which could have been gunshots. Willis Wallace heard what he thought were two pops, one low-pitched, the next a little higher. He didn't think they sounded like gunshots, more like a cabinet shutting.

When the sounds came, everyone was in the room but Jennifer.

Not long after, Jennifer came back in the room. She said, "Tanya's gone." Tiffany Lofton never saw a car drive up, never saw or heard Tanya leave the house.

Jennifer seemed "normal," all later agreed. She didn't tell anyone not to go anywhere in the house. Later, Green and Wallace went downstairs to the kitchen to get something to eat. The food was cold, and Green didn't eat any of it. Lofton was with them, leaving Jennifer, Milliner and James upstairs in Jennifer's room.

As Donald James recalled it, about fifteen minutes after Jennifer said that Tanya was gone, his girlfriend paged him. He returned the call, using a cordless phone in Jennifer's room. He, Milliner and Green got ready to leave. Before they left, Jennifer invited Milliner to come back later.

At around 10:40 P.M., three of the guys left. Willis Wallace stayed behind with Tiffany Lofton. The couple went downstairs, two levels down, to the basement level below the rec room. The rec room and laundry room doors were closed.

Jennifer went upstairs to take a bath, a bubble bath. She was quite fond of bubble baths. Later, wrapped only in a towel, she went downstairs to the basement level. Lofton asked, "What are you doing?" shooing her away.

Jennifer went back upstairs and stayed there. Willis Wallace stayed downstairs with Tiffany Lofton until he left the house at 12:45 A.M. He left to go home and had gotten about a block before realizing he'd forgotten his shirt at the house. He went back to get it. He knocked on the door. Lofton came to the door and gave him his shirt and he went away.

Milliner, James and Green stayed at James's girl-friend's house, leaving at about 2:00 or 2:30 A.M. James dropped Milliner at the Tombs house, then drove Green home.

Milliner went with Jennifer to her room, where they had sex for a couple of hours. Tiffany Lofton was in Jennifer's mother's room, watching the movie *Dances with Wolves* on TV before falling asleep.

Milliner left at about 4:00 A.M., going home. Jennifer woke Lofton and they went into Jennifer's room, sharing the bed. Jennifer woke her three or four times that night, asking her if she'd heard anything or smelled anything, and complaining that the room was cold.

The room was cold—so was the rest of the house—about fifty degrees Fahrenheit, because the heat was off.

The next morning, at approximately eight-thirty, Lofton was wakened by Jennifer. Jennifer, hysterical, breathing hard, could say only, "Tanya—Tanya!"

She kept repeating the name. Jennifer then took Lofton downstairs to the rec room. The door was open. Tanya lay on the floor, apparently dead.

As Lofton later told it, Tanya's body lay on the floor. Nearby was a yellow bag with keys. Tanya was wearing the same clothes she'd had on when Lofton had met her earlier, the night before.

She had on one sock and no shoes, with one leg up; her shirt was up, showing her stomach; her pants were unbuttoned. There was blood on the floor.

Lofton didn't try to move the body, and didn't see Jennifer try to move the body. She checked for a pulse, finding none. She saw neither gun nor shells in the room.

She and Jennifer went upstairs. Jennifer went back down, returning a short time later with five empty cartridge shells in her hand, saying that she'd found them. She showed them to Tiffany before setting them down on the kitchen counter.

Jennifer did not call the police or 911. Lofton called her parents' home, getting no answer. She didn't know what to do; this was something she'd never experienced before. She panicked, and Jennifer didn't seem to know what to do, either.

They called the Milliner house, finally getting Alan's father, Benny Milliner. He called for an ambulance.

When police arrived, Lofton was outside—unaware of where Jennifer was, she'd say later in court. She didn't know how long it was before help arrived, but it seemed like a long time.

Someone called 911. When the police came, they separated her and Jennifer. They didn't tell her she was a suspect, but they placed her in a police car by herself, and put Jennifer in the back of another vehicle.

Tiffany Lofton later recalled that when Jennifer woke her up, it sounded like she couldn't breathe. When police arrived, she was plain-faced, as if nothing was wrong.

* * *

Waiting in vain for a call from Tanya, Errol Vermont stayed up "very late" on Saturday morning, until about four o'clock. At 7:00 A.M., his wife said she still hadn't heard from their daughter. He talked to his son and together they drove to the Tombs house, arriving sometime between 7:45 and 8:30 A.M.

Tanya's green car didn't seem to have been moved from where it was parked in the driveway, but it had been interfered with. Items later determined to have been taken from the trunk had been moved to the inside of the car, items that Errol Vermont knew had not been there when he'd last seen the car the night before.

He knocked on the door of the house. Jennifer Tombs and Tiffany Lofton came out, Lofton in tears. He said later that Jennifer "showed on her face that something had happened, but not like Tiffany."

He asked them where Tanya was.

Talking loud and fast, Jennifer said she went downstairs and Tanya had been shot, she didn't say how.

Errol Vermont knew not to interfere with the crime scene. He rushed next door to the house of neighbor Myrna Washington, using her phone to call the police.

Later, Washington told reporters that she'd seen police cars many times before at the Tombs house, and described Jennifer as "troubled. It was always something with that girl," she said. Describing the neighborhood as quiet, she said that she'd heard no sounds like gunshots on the night before.

* * *

Denver police officer Patrick Anderson responded to a dispatcher's call to investigate a shooting with a possible DOA, on Elmendorf Place. He arrived at about 9:08 A.M. The fire department had already been notified and had a unit on the scene. Jennifer Tombs was inside—later he'd be unable to recall her demeanor. Entering by the front door, he went downstairs.

In the subbasement rec room, a young black female lay on the floor, in a pool of blood that appeared to have dried. She looked dead, her head showing evidence of having been shot multiple times.

The body lay diagonally about a foot away from the couch, with its head nearest the couch. The couch had blood on it, along with a white powdery substance. It appeared that attempts had been made to clean the couch and the blood.

An ambulance crew arrived. Officer Anderson was present when the victim was pronounced dead. He stayed until detectives arrived, later taking Jennifer Tombs to police headquarters.

Denver Police Department detective Charles Gudka arrived about 9:15 A.M., finding Anderson in place, talking to Bennie and Alan Milliner in the kitchen. He went downstairs, observed the victim, came up and escorted the Milliners outside. He saw Tiffany Lofton and Jennifer Tombs coming out of a bedroom and escorted them outside. He called for cover cars, to separate all possible witnesses—basic police procedure, to prevent them from agreeing on a story.

He went back in to secure the scene, walking through the entire house to make sure no one was inside.

He returned to the rec room and observed the victim, noting that she had blood on her arm. He noticed the white powdery substance and saw a shell casing under a chair. He left everything where he found it, untouched, later notifying investigators of what he'd observed.

The couch, or love seat, had been moved away from the body. Bloody sheet impressions on the carpet showed traces of what looked like movement. Blood droplets seemed to indicate that the victim had been moved around in this area, or blood had been transported to this area by another.

More bloodstains were found on the stairs on that same level. In a corner near the step lay a sheet with blood on it.

Upstairs, a bathtub was filled with water. In an oversight that would be criticized later, no samples were taken from it.

Denver Police Department homicide detectives Dan Wyckoff and Robert Kraft were working a weekend duty shift when, at a little after 9:00 A.M. on Saturday, Kraft received a call at his desk from the police radio dispatcher, informing him that they had a homicide scene in Montbello. Kraft went to the scene, arriving at the Tombs house at approximately 9:40 A.M.

Already present at the scene were police officers Anderson and Gudka. Anderson indicated that Jennifer Tombs was in the backseat of one of the police cars, where she'd been placed during the separation of the witnesses. Kraft then entered the house, proceeding to the rec room, where the victim lay. He then made a quick walk-through of the house, determining that no other victims or witnesses were present. His focus was on getting enough information on the house so that he could prepare a search warrant for it.

Detective Wyckoff went into the house, finding the victim lying on the tiled floor of the rec room. There were "obvious head defects, brain tissue, blood." The body lay diagonally to the couch and appeared to have been moved.

He walked through the entire house. There were shoes in Jennifer Tombs's bedroom doorway, black Fila tennis shoes.

In the kitchen, he recovered five spent shell casings from the countertop.

The laundry room had an open box of Trend detergent powder.

Kraft took Tiffany Lofton downtown, also ordering Jennifer Tombs transported to the station. At headquarters, Jennifer was given time to speak with her mother in private. Subsequently she was placed in a room, where she was interviewed by Kraft.

In a separate interview, Tiffany Lofton stated that she came over to the Tombs house on Friday at about 8:30 P.M. Already present were Jennifer and Tanya. At about 9:00 P.M., Tanya's mom called and asked where Tanya was and a short time later her father called asking the same. Lofton had gotten this information from Jennifer, as she did not hear the phone ring.

At 9:30 P.M., Milliner, Wallace, Green and James

came over. Jennifer said that Tanya had been talking on the phone to her boyfriend, Michael, and that he told her that he was on the way to get Tanya. Tanya left the house at about 10:00 or 11:00 P.M. to go to Bernard's lounge. A car picked her up.

Jennifer and Lofton then told the boys to leave and waited for Tanya to come to the house. Both then fell asleep.

At the station, Jennifer Tombs wore blue denim shorts and a light-colored T-shirt. Meeting with her and her mother, Kraft advised them of their rights. Madlyn Tombs and Jennifer both consented to Jennifer being interviewed, which state law mandated must be conducted in the presence of a parent or guardian.

According to Jennifer Tombs, on Friday, September 27, her mother had left around 5:00 P.M., Parole Officer Bonnie Brodie had come at six o'clock and had left at about 6:30 P.M., and Tanya arrived shortly after. They'd ordered pizza. Tiffany Lofton then came over. Later, while Tanya had Jennifer running errands, Jennifer had snuck the boys upstairs.

When Jennifer had gone back downstairs, she'd heard Tanya arguing with someone on the phone. Tanya had been wearing a pair of shorts and a T-shirt that Jennifer had given her earlier, but had now changed back into her other outfit because she was going out. Jennifer had come up to the kitchen, and had seen an old white car rolling up the other side of the street. Tanya then said she'd be back. Jennifer had told the others that Tanya had left. Around 11:00 P.M., three guys left, leaving

Willis Wallace with Lofton, the latter two had gone
to the basement. Wallace had left around 12:30 A.M.

Alan Milliner and the other two had returned at
about that same time. Milliner stayed. He'd gone
to Jennifer's room but they hadn't had sex. Lofton
had stretched out on a couch in the living room
and fallen asleep. Milliner left.

At about 2:00 P.M., Errol Vermont and Mark
Caisey had arrived. Caisey, too, had called earlier,
saying that Tanya was not returning her pages.

After they left, Jennifer had called Val Vermont,
telling her that Tanya was not back yet. She'd
woken Tiffany to get in bed with her. She'd told
Tanya she'd leave a key for the front door under
the mat for her.

Sometime later that night, she'd awoken, hearing
the front door open. Tanya had been talking to a
man, arguing with him. At one point, she'd said to
him, "Don't cuss at me, you ain't paying no bills."
Jennifer had heard one person walk in, but didn't
know what time it was. She'd heard heavy breathing
and thought Tanya was drunk.

Jennifer had gone back to sleep. Later she'd
woken up again, hearing booms. She'd woken Tiffany. She'd thought it was Tanya being clumsy.
She'd heard a car drive off—she'd been hearing
cars all night. She then went to sleep.

When she'd woken yet again, the house was cold.
Jennifer had gotten another comforter. Going
downstairs, she'd discovered that the temperature
was down to about fifty degrees.

The top lock of the front door had not been
locked. She'd opened the door and looked under

the mat, finding the key gone. Tanya's car's trunk had been open, so Jennifer had closed it.

She then went downstairs, smelling something funny. She'd put Tanya's work uniform in the dryer—then, through the open doorway of the rec room across the hall, she'd seen a foot.

Tanya lay in the middle of the floor, blood pooled around her head. A bloodstain marred the corner of the couch.

Jennifer had panicked, unable to breathe. She'd gone upstairs to Tiffany, barely able to keep repeating Tanya's name. They then went downstairs.

Lofton had said they should call the police. Jennifer had replied that she wasn't talking to the police until there was an adult present. After a few calls, she'd managed to reach Alan Milliner's dad.

She and Lofton had waited on the porch, until Errol Vermont and Mark Caisey arrived. Tiffany had told them what had happened. Bennie Milliner, Alan's father, then arrived. Jennifer added that she knew that Tanya had called her boyfriend, Michael, whom she knew was an older man, older than Tanya's dad. She and Tanya had once talked about having "boys on the side."

She didn't know whom Tanya had left with, but she'd seen an older white car, one that she'd never seen before.

When she and Tiffany had gone downstairs, she'd picked up the shell casings. She didn't know why.

Trying to pin down the time more accurately, she said that she'd heard Tanya on the phone, arguing, before she'd left around 10:00 P.M. Tanya had left about twenty minutes after the call.

Tanya had asked for a pager battery. She'd been

wearing the pager the night before. Jennifer had seen it on the table this morning.

It was around this point in the interview that Madlyn Tombs interjected herself, telling her daughter, "I want the truth as much as they [the police] do."

Toward the end of the interview, Jennifer said she had seen a weapon on the floor by the victim's leg—a silver gun. A little gun, one she'd never seen before. She feared that the crime would be hung on her and Lofton, especially her, since she had a record.

She said, "Tiffany and I found the gun. I knew if you guys found that gun in my house we were going to get blamed."

She said she'd picked up the gun and some shell casings. She then gave the gun to Lofton to get rid of it, and put the shell casings on the counter. The gun had been thrown away somewhere in a ditch up the street.

At this point, Jennifer Tombs said, "We didn't do it, Mom, I swear we didn't do it. We found the gun."

She also swore she'd never said that Errol Vermont couldn't come in without a warrant. She hadn't tried to clean up the scene, or touch Tanya. She'd picked up the shells, but had never seen the gun before. Jennifer couldn't explain why it looked like someone had tried to clean up the crime scene. Hers and Lofton's fingerprints were on the gun.

Detective Wyckoff executed a search warrant for Elmendorf Place and was unable to find the weapon. The pair of black Fila tennis shoes found in Jennifer's bedroom showed blood on the edges.

Tiffany Lofton denied having gotten rid of the gun, adding that on Friday night, Jennifer Tombs had shown the silver-looking gun to her and the four young men hanging out in Jennifer's bedroom.

Lofton said that Jennifer had brought a gift bag into the room. Standing against the wall near the dresser, Jennifer had reached into the bag and had taken out a box, which she then set on the dresser. Opening the box, she'd taken out the silver gun and had shown it, saying that it was Tanya's and that Tanya was going to take it with her when she went out to Bernard's. Lofton said that the young men in the room could have seen the gun, but she didn't know if they had or not. [Later, Alan Milliner testified that he didn't recall Jennifer Tombs coming into the room and showing off a gun. Duvonne Green, Willis Wallace and Donald James also said they never saw Jennifer with a gun.]

Jennifer Tombs was the prime suspect in the case. Police jailed her on a probation violation as the investigation continued.

On Saturday afternoon, forensic pathologist Dr. James Wahe [pronounced way], Assistant Medical Examiner of Denver, went to the Tombs house to observe the death scene. He estimated that death occurred sometime on the evening of September 27 or early in the morning of September 28. He could not fix the time any more accurately.

The cause of death was multiple gunshot wounds to the head. There were also wounds sustained on the upper arms. He found between six to eight wounds in the brain.

Soot in the wound meant that the murder weapon had been held close to the head when fired. He took possession of a spent bullet that had been found under the body.

On September 29, he performed an autopsy on the body of Tanya Lavallais.

Like an aftershock of Friday night's act of violence, a vandal or vandals preyed on the suburban Montbello neighborhood on Sunday night. Bushes were set afire and a beer bottle thrown through the window of a house on Quentin Street, and a house on East Fifty-fourth Avenue also had a window broken by a thrown beer bottle.

Someone had also used what investigators later determined was either a match or a lighter to set a minor fire, scorching the siding of the Tombs house, leaving a broad sooty vertical mark, like a black plume. Police were unable to connect the vandalism with the murder.

On Monday, September 30, Jock Johnson's mother called him at work, telling him that Jennifer Tombs was a suspect in Tanya's murder. He told his mother that Jennifer had told him she'd murdered someone. His mother called the district attorney. Johnson voluntarily went downtown, where he was interviewed by detectives, including Robert Kraft. He made a written statement and a more detailed video statement.

Johnson said that during their 4:00 A.M. talk, Jennifer had told him that she'd shot a female intruder dead and that her body was in the rec room.

That was doubly interesting to Kraft, since the police had not publically released any information about where the body had been found.

On Monday, September 30, Madlyn Tombs attended daughter Jennifer's detention hearing at the Gilliam Youth Center with her lawyer, defense attorney Kurt Metsger. The Honorable Mel Okamota, Denver juvenile magistrate, ruling that there was enough evidence to find that Jennifer Tombs could be a danger to herself or the community, ordered her to be held without bail.

On Wednesday, October 2, DPD police officer William Fairchild, investigating an unrelated call in the crime scene area, decided to do a little extra searching for the gun. He found a pistol in a sewer grate at the corner of Elmendorf Place and Quari Street and retrieved it—a silver-finish .25-caliber semiautomatic pistol.

Under the terms of the arrest, prosecutors had forty-eight hours to decide whether to file charges against Jennifer Tombs or let her go. In Colorado, the decision to try a juvenile as an adult is made by the district attorney, who may "direct file" against a juvenile in district court for specified offenses. In this prosecutorial venue, virtually all first-degree murder cases involving juvenile defendants over fourteen years of age are filed in district court.

On Thursday, October 3, as the deadline neared, Denver district attorney Bill Ritter filed homicide charges in Denver District Court, accusing Jennifer Tombs of first-degree murder in the death of Tanya by shooting her in the head five times. She was charged as an adult.

If convicted, she now faced the possibility of life without parole. But she was spared the terrors of a capital case, since Colorado law prohibited the death penalty for anyone under eighteen at the time of the crime.

Madlyn Tombs told Jennifer, "Just pray."

One of the youngest girls to be charged as an adult for murder in Denver, Jennifer Tombs was transferred to the county jail. She was the only female juvenile in the jail and was held by herself in the women's section, segregated from other female prisoners due to her age.

On Friday, October 4, on a sunny afternoon, the body of Tanya was laid to rest in a service officiated at by Madlyn Tombs and attended by over 500 people. The service was held at the First Christian Assembly of God Church, Madlyn Tombs serving as a kind of master of ceremonies, bringing on various speakers, with Tanya's brother Carl Lavallais really giving the eulogy. There was much talk that day of "the healing power of forgiveness."

At one point, Madlyn Tombs and Val Vermont walked together arm in arm down the church's long aisle, at whose head lay the bronze casket bearing the body of Tanya.

After Jennifer's arrest, Madlyn Tombs continued preaching from the pulpit of the church.

Rocky Mountain News reporter Linda McConnell's

article of October 13, 1996, described how Pastor Tombs delivered a "fiery" thirty-minute speech at a luncheon supported by the church, occasionally speaking in "tongues" (ecstatic speech rendered in no language known to man).

Madlyn Tombs was quoted as saying, "I'm the mother of the most beautiful, intelligent, loving daughter that a mother can have. Thank God for her."

She was also quoted as saying, "I'm not at liberty to discuss this case. I just want you to know it ain't all out yet."

THE TRIAL

Colorado law defines first-degree murder as causing the death of another "after deliberation and with intent." A class-one felony, it is punishable by life in prison without the possibility of parole.

Second-degree murder, a lesser included offense, is defined as "knowingly" causing the death of another.

The trial would be held at the Denver District Court, in Courtroom 13, the Honorable Warren Martin presiding. A native Coloradan, holding undergraduate and law degrees from the University of Colorado, he was a seventeen-year veteran jurist on the district court bench.

Prosecutor and Denver's Chief Deputy D.A., Henry Cooper had been a prosecutor since 1987, specializing since 1992 in street gang prosecutions. The defendant's youth and alleged casual life-taking fit the pattern of teen gang violence. He would be

seconded by Assistant D.A. Mike Pellow, a D.A.'s
Office veteran since 1988.

For the defense were lead attorney Kurt Metsger
and partner Jeff Timlin, who'd been practicing law
together since Metsger had joined the bar in 1988.
Both attorneys' focus was divided about equally between criminal defense and juvenile law. Timlin was
a former prosecutor in Detroit, Michigan from 1982
to 1984.

The jury included four women and eight men
with one female alternate. Two of the jurors, one
woman and one man, were black.

Trial began on Monday, March 31, 1997, with
Henry Cooper opening for the prosecution. He
first advised the jurors, "You may notice a TV camera over there—*Court TV* is filming this trial. They
will not film the jurors, so you don't have to worry
about how you look."

He went into his opening remarks. "Ladies and
gentlemen of the jury, what you are going to hear
about is a crime that is heinous, senseless and may
even make you ill . . . the murder of a truly innocent victim, Latanya Lavallais.

"On Friday, September 27, 1996, Latanya Lavallais went to the defendant's house on Montbello to
supervise her, to baby-sit her. But this defendant
had made up her mind that she was not going to
be baby-sat that day, that she was going to do as
she pleased. And to reach that end, she put five to
six bullets in the head of Latanya Lavallais at close
range."

He told them something about the victim. "She
worked as a leasing agent for a property company
here in town. She lived with her cousin, Mark

Caisey; she was single; she was a religious woman and a responsible woman.

"No one in the world had anything against Latanya Lavallais, except this defendant. And her animus only grew out of the fact that Latanya was going to watch her, to baby-sit her—and for that particular weekend was not going to let her run wild, as she had become accustomed to doing."

Now he let them know a little something about the defendant. "She was fifteen years old at the time, in high school, but she required strict supervision. During September of last year, she was on probation and had an ankle bracelet, an electronic monitoring device. Basically what this device does is, it notifies the probation department whenever you leave your house, or wherever you're supposed to be, for longer than a few minutes."

Cooper detailed the circumstances that had brought victim, defendant and witnesses together: how Madlyn Tombs was going away for the weekend on a religious retreat and could not allow Jennifer to be alone by herself, so she asked Tanya Lavallais to baby-sit the defendant.

He said, "Tanya was asked to do this because she was a responsible person, a person that could be trusted. And those qualities are what caused her to be in the house that night with a baby-faced killer."

Cooper outlined the background as the prosecution saw it. Earlier in the week of September 27, learning that her mother was going to be out of town on the weekend, Jennifer Tombs "decided she would have a little get-together—a little party. She and a friend named Tiffany Lofton decided they would have a few boys over. That was the plan. But

she didn't realize that Tanya would be there, and
Tanya wasn't going to allow it."

The jury would learn how the defendant had
called Tanya before Friday, September 27, asking if
she would be allowed to get away with having boys
over and partying, and had been told no in no un-
certain terms by Tanya.

Tanya Lavallais went to the defendant's house in
Montbello that night to baby-sit. "She showed up,
she went down to the basement of the house, and
she never left that basement," Cooper said.

The defendant was making plans to obtain a gun,
he said. "You'll hear from a young man named
Jock Johnson, a custodian at an elementary school
in Denver, that he met the defendant a year or so
prior to this murder, that he had kind of dated her
for a while. And a point in time came that the defendant told him that she was pregnant. That was
early in 1996.

"Then, in September of 1996, you'll hear that
the defendant told Jock Johnson that she had a
baby by him—which you will hear is a lie, which
you will hear never happened. You will hear the
defendant never even had a baby."

Cooper described how on the night in question,
the defendant had contacted Jock Johnson, asking
for the loan of a gun. A gun that she'd borrowed
before, and from which the bullets were missing
when she'd previously returned it to Johnson.

"This is the gun that killed Latanya Lavallais,"
Cooper said. "Jock brought the gun over, handed
it to the defendant. She went back into her house
and said: 'I'll talk to you later.'"

Then she went on with her "little party," sneaking four guys into her bedroom. Cooper told of how Jennifer had popped in and out of the room; how Alan Milliner and some of the others had heard what sounded like gunshots, while Jennifer was the only one out of the room; and how she returned, saying, "Tanya's gone."

Cooper echoed, "Tanya's gone . . . Tanya's gone. She was gone—she was dead."

He said that Jennifer had shown Tiffany Lofton the gun. The defendant had given her guests free run of the house, except for the rec room, where the door was closed—because behind that door lay the victim. The boys left, Willis Wallace staying behind with Lofton, when, oddly, the defendant went upstairs to take a bath.

Wallace left around midnight, and soon after, Tiffany Lofton went into Jennifer's mother's room and started watching a movie. "And that's when the defendant starts her botched cover-up," Cooper charged. At 1:00 A.M., she contacts Jock Johnson, telling him: I've done something bad, I've done something real bad. Hanging up, she begins to try to clean up the evidence. Bloodstains on the basement couch are covered with powdered detergent, "detergent that's sitting up in one of the closets down in the basement when the police arrive."

The body's been moved. "It's obvious that the victim was shot on a couch, and she'd been moved to the floor, and an attempt has been made to at least try to drag her out," Cooper said.

"The trunk of the victim's car has been emptied; everything out of the trunk has been piled into the front of the car, in preparation to at least try to move her body."

Later, at 2:00 A.M., Alan Milliner returns to the house, Cooper said. "You see, once this defendant killed Tanya, she was free to ask Alan to just come over, later on tonight—come on in. . . . And at that point, she forgets about the dead body in the basement and goes up in her room with Milliner. They have sex."

After Milliner leaves at about four o'clock in the morning, Jennifer Tombs gets back to work, again contacting Jock Johnson, this time telling him: "I killed a woman. A woman busted into my house and I shot her in the head. I emptied the clip into her head."

She tells Johnson the body is in the basement, and not to tell anyone. Not believing her, he hangs up and stays home.

The next morning, the defendant is back at work with "a series of lies and fabrications that go on all day." She wakes up Tiffany Lofton, who becomes hysterical at the discovery of the body. Later the police find the victim lying on the floor with multiple gunshot wounds in her head. Bloodstains on the couch prove that she was initially shot while lying on that couch. Huge amounts of detergent are spread all over the couch, "in an attempt to clean this mess up."

It appears that somebody was trying to drag the body. The victim's pants are pulled halfway down, indicating that somebody had tried to drag her by her pants. The defendant even admits that she picked up the shell casings.

Cooper told the jurors of Jennifer's interview by the Denver Police Department. "You will hear a convoluted story of a mysterious boyfriend coming over to the house, that nobody saw nor heard. You will hear her talk about things that supposedly happened, that never happened. You will hear her talk about things that didn't happen, that obviously did.

"And you will hear her admit to getting rid of the gun—because, in her own words, she thought she'd get blamed for it."

The gun was ultimately recovered, in a sewer drain near her house in Montbello. Jock Johnson will identify that gun as the one he gave Jennifer Tombs. Tiffany Lofton will say that's the gun Jennifer had. Ballistics has proved that this gun is the murder weapon.

Certain items of clothing taken from Jennifer Tombs will be entered into evidence, including a pair of shorts containing droplets of the victim's blood on them, an identification that DNA testing will verify.

On Friday, September 27, 1996, before taking her bath, Jennifer Tombs wore a T-shirt with a Santa's helper insignia on it—"The shirt she was wearing when Tanya was killed," Cooper said. "And that shirt was tested, and had Tanya's blood on it."

He concluded, the evidence points to one person and one person only as the killer of Tanya Lavallais: the defendant, Jennifer Tombs.

Certainty is a prosecutor's stock-in-trade. The prosecution is certain it has the guilty party, and will prove it beyond a reasonable doubt. Defense's specialty is uncertainty, raising as much doubt, reasonable or otherwise, as it possibly can.

In its effort to raise a reasonable doubt in the

minds of the jurors, the Tombs defense had some potentially critical areas to work with. Foremost was motive. It might be tough to convince a jury that the fifteen-year-old defendant, still showing her baby fat, had cold-bloodedly murdered baby-sitter and "big cousin" Tanya Lavallais execution-style, in order to have her friends stay over to party. The end seems grotesquely inconsistent with the means.

And yet, people are slain every day, all over the world, for such seemingly insignificant trifles, and even less. Sometimes they're murdered for no apparent reason at all. Cold killings happen. But would the jury believe Jennifer Tombs was capable of such inhuman brutality?

The second factor was the presence of others in the house during the time of the murder. Was it reasonable to believe that the victim could have been slain by a pistol being emptied into her head, a few floors below the feet of Jennifer Tombs's five teen guests? Could one of them have had a role in the slaying? If the crime could be parceled out, the defendant's individual guilt would be seemingly lessened by association. Perhaps she was not the killer but an innocent framed for a crime she didn't commit. Or maybe it could be hung on that boyfriend or older man that Jennifer Tombs alleged Tanya had been dating.

Opening for the defense, attorney Jeff Timlin wrapped the case in mystification, telling jurors, "The evidence you're going to hear in this case resembles a mystery novel, like something from a book by Agatha Christie. The only problem with the evidence that you're going to hear in this case is that by the last page, you're not going to know who did this crime. It's not going to be solved."

He spoke of Jennifer's electronic monitoring ankle bracelet, and how she was about to "graduate" to the next, more lenient level in her parole program. "She had no motive to do anything to Tanya that evening—to get time off and to spend [it] with her friends."

The get-together in Jennifer's bedroom with her five friends was simply that, teenagers hanging out on a Friday night. Nothing untoward happened, no gunshots were heard—not until long after the fact, when police questioners were able to refresh the witnesses' recollections.

Tanya Lavallais was planning to go out with some friends that night, Timlin said. "You're going to hear evidence that one of the boys was looking out the window and saw a white car out in front of the house, just at the time in which Tanya left."

Sure, Jennifer took a bath that night—why wouldn't she? She wanted to freshen up to entertain her boyfriend later that night. Why didn't she let Errol Vermont and Mark Caisey in the house when they came looking for Tanya? Because Willis Wallace and Tiffany Lofton were together in the basement, and they weren't supposed to be there. Later, Jennifer found the body and became hysterical, traumatized. That's why she picked up the shell casings, why she got rid of the gun. Because she and Lofton were scared—"scared little girls . . . they didn't know what was happening and what was going to occur," Jeff Timlin said.

"The evidence will show that from the time in which Tiffany Lofton came over, at approximately eight o'clock, until after Mr. Milliner came—after eight-thirty in the morning the next day, on the twenty-eighth—Jennifer was never left alone. She was either with Tiffany or with the boys that were there."

As for the state's star witness, Jock Johnson, there were credibility problems, Timlin said. "He was an ex-boyfriend and possibly a scorned boyfriend. He states that he brought her a gun, but there wasn't any evidence that anyone in that house ever saw him show up at that house and give a gun to Jennifer Tombs."

Also, Johnson couldn't have received as many pages from Jennifer as he claimed, since she hadn't been alone for enough time to have made all those calls. If she had, one of the others in the house would have noticed and made mention of it.

Reminding jurors of the prosecution's burden to prove the case beyond a reasonable doubt, Timlin wrapped his opening: "Ladies and gentlemen, you will determine, when all the evidence is submitted, that the sixteen-year-old little girl that's sitting right at this table did not, in fact, kill her cousin or her sister, as they grew up together."

The state's first witness was Tiffany Lofton. Police and prosecutors were perhaps unsure of how much Lofton might or might not have known, and if she'd told all, but they all agreed that on the morning of Saturday, September 28, 1996, she'd been one frightened individual.

Mike Pellow handled the questioning for the state. Tiffany Lofton, fifteen, a Montbello citizen, identified the defendant, stating that she'd known Jennifer Tombs as a friend since eighth grade, and that Jennifer had lived with her in her family's house for several months. Earlier in the week of September 27, she and Jennifer had made plans for her to spend Friday night at the Tombs house. When Lofton arrived at the house that night, Tanya Lavallais was already there.

Pellow elicited the fact that Tanya had said nothing to Lofton about having plans to leave that night. She told how on Friday, September 27, when the four guys had arrived between 9:00 and 9:30 P.M., she'd taken them upstairs. Later, when Lofton tried to leave the bedroom, Jennifer told her to go back in, because she was talking to Tanya at the time.

She identified a pair of black Fila tennis shoes as ones that Jennifer Tombs had worn that evening.

Pellow established that the music in the room had been playing louder than a normal conversational level. Lofton said that she'd seen Jennifer with the phone, in the hallway, though she hadn't heard the phone ring. The defendant "said she was talking to Latanya's [Tanya] boyfriend . . . that he was coming to pick her up," Lofton said.

Pellow said, "Did she tell you anything about what kind of car he was driving?"

"She told me to look for a white Cutlass on Daytons—on D's." Lofton explained that D's were custom rims, which people put on their cars.

Pellow said, "Did you ever see a car drive up by yourself?"

"No, I did not."

"Did you ever see or hear Latanya leave the house?"

"No, I did not."

After Tiffany Lofton had seen the defendant with the phone, Jennifer had brought something in the room, the witness said—a gift bag, a Christmas-type bag. Lofton said, "Inside the bag was a box; inside the box, there was a gun.

"She said that this is Latanya's gun. She was gonna take it to Bernard's with her."

Then Jennifer left the room, the witness said.

Pellow now showed her what was marked as People's Exhibit #72: a gun. He reassured the court, "For the record, there is a safety device in here, which renders it inoperable."

Tiffany Lofton identified the gun as the one Jennifer had pulled out of the box and showed to her. She was unable to determine how long Jennifer had been absent from the room after showing her the gun. Pellow said, "When she returned to the room, what did she tell you?"

"She told me Latanya's gone," Lofton said.

"Where did she say she had gone?"

"To Bernard's."

Pellow next established that while Jennifer Tombs had been out of the room, the young men in the room discussed hearing what might have been gunshots. "When Ms. Tombs returned to the room, what did you all do at that time?"

Lofton said, "Uh, we went downstairs. We ate pizza. . . ."

No one went down to the family room, where Tanya had been. The room door was closed. Pellow said, "Did the defendant say anything about that room?"

Lofton said, "She told us not to go in there."

After Milliner, Green and James left, Lofton and Wallace went downstairs to the basement. Jennifer said that she felt sick, took a bath and changed clothes. When she came out of the bath, she wore a pair of turquoise-and-white shorts and a short top—different clothes from those she'd been wearing before the bath.

Wallace left about 1:00 A.M., Milliner returned at 2:00, when Lofton went to watch a movie in Madlyn Tombs's room. Later, Jennifer woke her and the two went to bed in Jennifer's room. The defendant woke her several times, asking if she'd heard something, or smelled something, or was cold.

Pellow said, "Did you hear anything that morning that sounded like gunfire?"

Lofton said, "No, I didn't."

The last time Jennifer woke Lofton, the defendant "was like really hysterical," Lofton said. "And she just kept saying, 'Tanya.' "

They went downstairs, to the body. Lofton checked it for a pulse, and did not find one. She saw no shells in the room. After they went upstairs, Jennifer went back downstairs, returning with a handful of shells, which she set down on the kitchen counter. Pellow said, "Did you ever see any shells lying on the floor when you had gone down to that room?"

Tiffany Lofton said, "No."

"What did you do then?"

"I started calling my mom, my cousin—anybody I can get hold of."

"After that night, when Jennifer came into the bedroom and showed you the gun, did you ever see that gun again after that?"

"No."

"Did you ever help her get rid of that gun?"

"No."

"Did she ever ask you to get rid of that gun?"

"No."

When Pellow wrapped up his questioning, it was late in the afternoon, so the judge called a recess, ending day one.

Tuesday, April 1—April Fools' Day—day two of the trial began with defense attorney Kurt Metsger's cross-examination of Tiffany Lofton. He asked her what Jennifer Tombs had been wearing when Lofton came over on Friday night.

Lofton said, "She was wearing tan pants, a white shirt, and some turquoise shoes." Later the defendant had worn the black Filas.

She said that she'd seen Tanya Lavallais once that night, and that Tanya had given permission for Alan Milliner and Willis Wallace to come over to the house. Actually, the guys had come over twice. Once between 9:00 and 9:30 P.M.; then they came back between 9:30 and 10:00 P.M., when they were allowed in and hurried into Jennifer's room.

Upstairs, they weren't quiet. Metsger said, "Tanya could have heard you?"

Lofton said, "Yeah. There was music on, people were talking. You can't help but hear it." Tanya knew that the boys were there, so there was no real reason to be quiet. She'd never heard anything that sounded like gunshots, Lofton said.

Moving in on the time after three of the boys had left the house, Metsger said, "Willis Wallace is your boyfriend, right?"

Lofton said, "Not now—he was then."

"When Jennifer came out of the bath, what was she wearing?"

"When she came out of the bathroom? She didn't have on nothing. She came downstairs, she had on a towel. Me and Willis were still talking. My mother always told me: never let a woman walk around the house with no clothes on. Then she came back downstairs. She had on some bright-colored shorts and a shirt."

"You were downstairs. Jennifer came down with the towel on, and you told her to go get some clothes on."

"Yes."

Then there was the discovery of the body. Metsger said, "You just kept making phone calls, didn't you? And you didn't call 911, right?

"You were trying to call family members and friends, right?"

Lofton said, "Family members and friends—yes."

"Why were you calling them, then?"

"I didn't know what to do."

"Okay," Metsger said. "And you're fifteen years old, and that's probably a good thing—to call your parents first, right?"

"Yeah."

"Okay. Something you've never experienced before, right?"

"No."

"Certainly nothing Jennifer had experienced before."

"I don't know," Tiffany Lofton said.

On redirect, the prosecution went directly to motive. Mike Pellow said, "You said you heard Tanya give permission for these boys to come over. . . . Did she ever say they could stay till four in the morning?"

Tiffany Lofton said, "No."

"Did she ever give Jennifer permission to have sex with Alan Milliner up in her bedroom?"

"No."

When she was upstairs with the boys, Lofton had tried to leave the room. Asked what happened, the witness said, "I went downstairs, to go see why Jennifer wasn't in here entertaining the guests, like normal. And before I can get to the kitchen, she stopped me and told me to go upstairs, 'cause she was talking to Tanya."

"Did you ever leave the room after that?"

"Yes."

"And what happened?"

"The same thing." Lofton said that two or three times she'd tried to leave the room, but Jennifer wouldn't let her go downstairs.

The prosecution had a stipulation read into the record, stipulating that People's Exhibit #74 was a white T-shirt with a Santa's helper emblem on the shirt; that Jennifer Tombs was wearing the shirt on Friday evening, September 27, 1996; and that the chain of custody of the shirt was solid and unbroken.

Defense counsel Kurt Metsger agreed to the stipulation, and the judge ruled it into the record.

On recross-examination, Metsger told the judge he only had a few brief questions. He didn't know that he was about to walk into a classic courtroom trap: asking a question to which you don't already know the answer.

He said, "When you had the discussion with Tanya about the boys coming over, she didn't tell you what you could do or couldn't do, did she?"

Lofton said, "No."

"She didn't say [that] the boys have to leave at midnight, did she?"

"Yes."

"She did say that?"

"Yes."

"What'd she say?"

"She said [to] just have 'em gone before twelve o'clock. I remember her saying [that]," Tiffany Lofton said.

"No further questions."

The state's next witness, possibly its star witness, was Jock Johnson, with Henry Cooper on direct. Johnson, twenty-one years old, was a custodial worker at Smith Elementary School. He told of meeting Jennifer Tombs about a year prior to September 27, 1996, at a movie theater, after which they began seeing each other from time to time, perhaps two or three times a month at most. He said he didn't consider her his girlfriend, and that he was seeing other women at the time, and she was seeing other men.

Cooper said, "Ultimately, did a time come that she told you that she was pregnant by you?"

Johnson said, "Yes." She'd told him in late January 1996.

"And when she told you that, what went through your mind?"

"It was a question of whether it was mine or not . . . 'cause she was seeing other people."

"Okay," Cooper said. "Once she told you that she was pregnant, did you still see her on the same consistent basis?"

"No," Johnson said, "I kind of faded away."

After she'd told him of the pregnancy, he'd only seen her three or four times. "We discussed what she was gonna do, and how was it gonna be taken care of—and, you know, just like how she was doing, pretty much."

"Did she tell your mother that she was pregnant?"

"Yes."

"Did a time come when she told you, the defendant told you, that she had actually given birth to a baby?"

"Yeah. It was like September tenth or the thirteenth, one of those days."

"She tell you what the baby's name was?"

"Yes. Jorelle."

In a vivid bit of business caught by *Court TV*'s camera, Jennifer Tombs's reaction to Johnson's statement was caught as she broke up laughing, quickly putting her hands to her mouth to cover it, her eyes wide and gleeful, delighted with her own mischief.

The questioning continued. Cooper said, "Was she still maintaining that it was yours?"

"Yes."

"Okay . . . did you ever see this baby?"

"No. She said it looked just like me."

"Have you since found out that the defendant never did have a baby?"

"Yeah," Johnson said.

Moving on to the murder gun, the witness told how after Jennifer had told him she was pregnant, she'd borrowed his gun, telling him that her mother was going away for a week and she wanted something with which to protect herself. He told her he'd sell it to her for fifty dollars, but she hadn't come through with the money, so he'd taken it back.

Cooper said, "When she returned the gun, was it still fully loaded?"

Johnson said, "No."

"How many bullets did she give you back?"

"Uh, like maybe two or three."

"And how many did the gun hold?"

"Eight—one in a chamber."

"After she gave you the gun back, did a time come that she asked for the gun again?"

"Yes."

"And when was that?"

"Uh . . . the night of the murder."

Johnson told how she'd paged him early that night, with 911 attached to the pages. Cooper said, "What does that mean, when somebody pages you and they put 911 on it?"

"Emergency." Johnson related how Jennifer Tombs had told him that while on the way back from seeing her parole officer, she'd had a confrontation with some girls. She said they were parking in front of her house and driving around it.

Cooper said, "Did she indicate whether or not she was scared of these girls?"

"Yeah," Johnson said. "She said, uh, the baby was coming back [to the house] around nine-thirty."

"This is supposedly your baby?"

"Yes. Her grandparents are supposed to be bringing it back around nine-thirty. And she was afraid for her life and his."

"What did you do once she told you that?"

"I kinda debated."

"Debated what?"

"Whether or not to give her the gun back."

"Ultimately, did you decide what to do?"

"Yes. I decided to give it to her."

The witness told of driving to Jennifer Tombs's house that night in his car, a 1984 Oldsmobile Cutlass, white with a blue vinyl top. Cooper said, "And did you have any type of special rims or tires on that?"

"Yeah, some high-polished chrome spoke rims."

"Did they look like a type of wheel called Daytons?"

"Yes."

"People also call them D's?"

"Yes."

When he arrived at Jennifer's house, Johnson said, he saw a green car parked in the driveway. He called Jennifer on his cell phone and met her in front of the house. "I told her it [the gun] was on the seat. She grabbed it, and I told her to call me—

you know, just call me—let me know what was going on.

"And I drove off."

Johnson went to his brother's house, but he wasn't home. He went to his mother's house on thirty-sixth and Kearney, ate something, socialized awhile with her and her friend, and went home. He felt sick to his stomach and vomited.

Jennifer paged him a couple of times and he called her back, between ten and eleven o'clock. "She just told me that she had did something really bad."

Cooper said, "And what did she say?"

"She said she can't say on the phone, 'cause she didn't know if the phone was tapped or something. . . . I asked her, but she just wanted me to come over, so she could tell me."

"And what did you do?"

"I just told her: no—you know, I don't feel good, and I ain't coming back over there."

"What did you do at that point?"

"She hung up. I laid back down."

But that wasn't the last time he'd spoken with her that night, the witness stated. Waking up about 1:00 or 2:00 A.M., he'd called Jennifer. "I was, like, so are you gonna tell me what happened? She was—well, she was just telling me that she was asleep."

"Okay, so she wouldn't talk to you when you called at that point in time. Did you say anything about the baby at that point?"

"I asked her where the baby was, and where everybody else was. She said the baby was right here, asleep . . . and everybody else was asleep. That's pretty much all she said."

He'd hung up, he said. Later she'd paged him between 4:00 and 4:30 A.M., and he'd called her back. "I just asked her what was up. She just said she wanted me to come by again, around that time. And I was, like, no, I ain't coming around, you know, that early in the morning. I was asleep—I didn't feel well."

Cooper said, "What's the first thing she told you about what happened?"

"She started off, 'Well, you know, I did something really bad.' And I said, 'What?' And she killed somebody.

"She said it was a knock at the door. And when she opened it, the girl barged in and attacked her.

"She said they got in a scuffle. She said she shot her five times in the head. She unloaded the clip in the head—that's what she told me."

Cooper said, "She said she unloaded the clip in her head?"

"Yeah."

"When she told you that a person barged in her house . . . did you believe her?"

"No, not really."

"So she told you this woman barged in and she emptied the clip in her head. Did you then ask her where the body was?"

"Yes. She said it was downstairs."

"Did she tell you anything about what she did with the gun?"

"She said she threw it in some bleach or something."

"Did she say anything about the shells?"

"Uh, yeah. I asked her where the shells was, and she said they was on the counter."

"Did she say anything else about a bag or anything being present?"

"She said she had put a bag over the . . . the victim's body—the head of the victim's body."

"When she told you all this, what was your reaction?"

The witness made a sound indicating disbelief. "I didn't have one. You know, at four o'clock in the morning, somebody tell you something like that—you know, I didn't really believe her."

"Did you ever tell her what she should do?"

"I told her she should call the police—you know, let them handle it. . . . She said, no, she didn't want to bring the police in, 'cause she was already on parole."

"And what was your response to that?"

"Uh . . . pretty much we jumped off the phone, I went to sleep. That was the last I heard of her."

He hadn't read any newspapers or watched the news for the rest of the weekend, so it wasn't until Monday, September 30, that he'd learned what had happened, when his mother called him at work. She called somebody from the D.A.'s Office, and he went downtown to make a statement.

Jock Johnson then identified a .25-caliber pistol as being his gun because it had the same serial number.

On cross-examination, Jeff Timlin emphasized that Jock Johnson had seen the defendant only a few times after she'd told him that she was pregnant. Moving to the first time the witness had loaned her the gun, Timlin said, "When she gave you the gun back and you only saw that two or three bullets were in the gun, did you ever ask her where the other bullets were?"

Johnson said, "The question was brought up, but it was kinda like brushed off."

On Friday, September 27, 1996, when he'd brought Jennifer Tombs the gun, there were no bullets in it, Johnson stated. Jeff Timlin said, "When the gun was on your passenger's seat, it wasn't in anything, correct?"

"Yes."

Defense counsel asked, if Johnson had been sick with stomach flu, why had he gone to his brother's house and mother's house?

"Well, my mom told me to come by, because a friend that she had over there wanted to see me. So I went over there," Johnson said.

Timlin said, "How many times did she [the defendant] page you between seven o'clock and the time in which you arrived at the house?"

Johnson said, "Between about fifteen or twenty times."

Timlin pointed to Johnson's written statement to the police on September 30, 1996, which showed no mention of those pages.

He asked why Johnson had dragged himself from a sickbed at 1:00 A.M. Saturday to call Jennifer Tombs. "Why were you so concerned about Ms. Tombs? When, in the last four or five months, you hadn't had maybe two or three conversations with her?"

Johnson said, "Well, she seemed like she was upset about something—something had happened. So I just was calling back to see what had happened."

"But you didn't care much about her well-being, did you?"

"I mean, undoubtedly, I was. I tried to give her something to protect herself."

"Well, if she had told you that she was pregnant back in January of 1996, you sure weren't around much in that last nine months if you really cared about her well-being, did you?"

"Well, I mean, her life wasn't in danger or nothing, so . . ."

After a recess, Timlin tried to pin Johnson down on how he was so readily able to identify the weapon as his gun. Johnson said he recognized it because of the serial number's first three digits, which were 1, 2, 3.

On redirect, the prosecution established that unlike Jock Johnson's written statement, his more detailed video statement did indeed show him stating that Jennifer Tombs had paged him more than thirty times that night.

Denver Police Department police officer Patrick Anderson took the stand, testifying that he was the first police officer to arrive at the crime scene, that he was present when the victim was pronounced dead, that he secured the scene for the detectives, and that he drove defendant Jennifer Tombs to the station. He could not recall her demeanor at the scene.

His testimony was followed by that of Officer Charles Gudka, the second police officer to arrive at the scene. He told how he'd separated the witnesses and walked through the house, observing the victim, noting blood on her arm, white powder on the bloodstained couch, and a shell casing on the floor. On Metsger's cross, the witness said that he hadn't taken a sample of the tub full of water in the upstairs bathroom, and could not recall if it had looked red.

Denver Police Department homicide detective Dan Wyckoff testified that he'd found the black Fila shoes in the upstairs bedroom doorway, and established the chain of possession of evidence for the court. He identified the five shell casings that he'd found at the scene, on a kitchen countertop; also identifying the spent shell casing that had been collected from the rec room floor and the slug that had been found under the victim's body.

On Metsger's cross-examination, the defense suggested that police might have done a more thorough investigation. They did not check to see if the family room door would close with the body in the position in which it was found, and they didn't test the water found in the tub for blood.

Wyckoff's partner in the investigation, Denver Police Department homicide detective Robert Kraft, stated that on Saturday, September 28, he'd arranged to have defendant Jennifer Tombs transported downtown, while in a separate car, he'd transported witness Tiffany Lofton to the station.

After conferring privately with Jennifer's mother, and after both had been advised by Kraft of their rights, including the right not to talk to him, they "freely and voluntarily" agreed to talk to him.

Henry Cooper said, "During that interview, what exactly did the defendant say about a weapon—finally, at the end of the interview?"

"She said that she saw a weapon laying on the floor, next to the victim's leg," Kraft said. "She said that she picked up the weapon and gave it to Tiffany Lofton, and instructed her to dispose of it. . . . She said it was at the end of the street, in some sort of drainage ditch, or concrete ditch. Some type of a drainage system."

"And was a weapon found in a ditch near her home?"

"Yes."

"How far from the Tombs home was this weapon found?"

"From the front door to where the weapon was located—approximately 535 feet."

Cooper next tackled the issue of the Fila shoes. "Did you also talk to the defendant about whether or not she had shoes on the morning she found the body?"

Kraft said, "She said that she had stepped on an earring post, or something, at the bottom of the steps, and that it hurt her foot. And I made a comment: you were barefoot. And she said yes."

Cooper nailed that down. "She indicates she was barefoot when she found the body?"

"Yes."

That was important to the state's case, since if

the defendant said she'd been barefoot when finding the body, then the blood must have gotten on the Fila shoes at another, earlier time, indicating that the defendant had been aware of the corpse at a time prior to when she said she'd found it—meaning she was lying.

Kraft was shown People's Exhibit #75, a bag containing denim shorts, which he identified as the shorts that were taken from the defendant by a female police officer at the station on Saturday, September 28. He said that at that time, a light-colored T-shirt was also taken from the defendant.

Cooper then questioned him about his interview of Jock Johnson, during which Johnson had told of the 4:00 A.M. Saturday phone call he'd had with the defendant, in which she'd told of shooting a female intruder in the head and that the body was downstairs in the rec room. Kraft stated that he'd released no information about where in her body the victim had been shot, and that a review of the newspaper articles dealing with that killing in the pre-Johnson interview time frame had made no reference to such information.

The implication was that the defendant had known such facts because she was the killer.

People's Exhibit #84 was introduced into evidence. It was a copy of Kraft's videotaped interview with Jennifer Tombs on Saturday, September 28.

The tape was then played for the jury. Lengthy and of poor audio quality, it remained the only personal account of the night of the murder that the defendant had given. Present at the interview were Jennifer Tombs, her mother, Robert Kraft, Lamar

Sims of the D.A.'s Office and Sgt. John Priest of the Homicide Unit.

In the video, Jennifer Tombs begins by claiming that Tanya Lavallais gave her permission to have a couple of boys over, but directed her to keep them quiet and upstairs. She says she was running back and forth between Tanya in the rec room and her friends upstairs.

Jennifer Tombs says, "I gave her [Tanya] a pair of shorts and a T-shirt. When I came back downstairs and she was on the telephone, she had changed back into what she had on. She had her blue jeans on and her shirt again. So I thought she was going to leave. I was, like, cool, cool, she's about to go. . . . She had came upstairs and I was, like, by the microwave doing my pizza.

"This is in the kitchen . . . and there's an opening and you can see out the front door . . . and we have a big old pine tree in front of our house. And a white, it looked to me like a Cutlass, an old white car rolled up on the side of the pine tree."

Kraft: Is it dark out?
Tombs: Yes. It's dark. It's like ten o'clock. And she [said] "All right. I'll be back," and I [said] "All right, 'bye."
Kraft: Tanya told you that she would be back.
Tombs: Yeah, she was just, like, "I'll be back." So I went upstairs and I was, like, "she left" and everyone was, like, "cool, cool," you know,

so we was all kicking it and whatnot, having
fun, cracking jokes. . . .

Tombs says that Milliner, Green and James left at
around 11:00 P.M., returning "around one," with
Milliner staying while Green and James departed.
Wallace left at around 12:30 A.M.

Kraft: And what happened when Alan stayed?
Tombs: We just went up to my room and we
were talking. We were making out and stuff,
but we didn't have sex.

Milliner left to go home at about two o'clock,
she says. "And so at around two, I was, like, 'you
gotta bounce,' you know what I'm saying, because
Tanya, I don't know when she's going to come
home. 'If you're over here this late, she's going to
try and trip.' So he was, like, all right. We called a
cab. The cab came and got him."
Tombs says that Errol Vermont and Mark
Caisey—"Tanya's dad and her cousin"—then came
over, Caisey having called earlier that night, trying
to find out why Tanya wasn't returning his pages.

Kraft: About what time was that?
Tombs: Twoish?
Kraft: About two? After two this morning?
Tombs: Yeah. And so he was, like, "Well,
Tanya's car is here; why isn't Tanya driving her
car?" [So] I don't know, she just, she just
bounced. She said she was gonna come
back . . . and so I assured them that I'd tell
Tanya to call them as soon as she came in the

door. So they said fine. After that, I went upstairs. I called Miss Val, her mom, and said, "Miss Val, Tanya is not home yet . . . but I will tell Tanya to keep on calling; when Tanya comes in to call you guys. And she said, "Well, I'm going to keep on calling until I talk to her because this is unusual."

Jennifer Tombs goes on to say that prior to Tanya's leaving the house, she'd told her she'd leave her key under the doormat for her, because she didn't want to leave the door unlocked. She'd put the key under the mat and locked the door.

At about 2:45 A.M., she woke Tiffany Lofton and they went to bed in her room, she says. "Tiffany and I had fell asleep. And we were woke up by something. I was woke up first because I heard the door open. I was, like, "Tanya's home." And I heard somebody come in the house. And I didn't tell the police this earlier because I was afraid. Because he has my key, whoever. Tanya's dead."

Kraft: Why do you say he?
Tombs: Because the last person she was talking to was a man.
Kraft: Okay. Did she say it was a man? Or how do you know it was a man?
Tombs: Because I can hear him. They were arguing. She was telling him, "Don't cuss at me, you don't pay no bills, and when you start paying bills, that's when you can cuss at me." And he said something. Whoever came in the house and they were breathing hard.
Kraft: Okay.

Tombs: And I'm thinking, all right, Tanya is in here drunk. Tanya came home, you know, drunk. She might have been out partying, whatever.

Kraft: Okay, what did you hear after that?

Tombs: About five minutes after that, I hear like a [here the defendant thumps on the table with her hand] boom noise. Three of them. And I went, "Tiffany! Did you hear that?" I said, "Somebody is in the house." And we heard it again. And it was [defendant thumps on the table with her hand] like that. Like something was booming on something. And Tiffany was, like, "Well, what is it?" And I was, like, "I don't know—Do you think Tanya is home?" She was, like, "I don't know." And I was, like, "I'm not going down there to see." She was, like, "Well, neither am I." Because we just thought it was Tanya being clumsy.

Kraft asks her about "going down to see," and Jennifer says she was positive that the noise came from there.

Tombs: I don't know what it was. It was just a boom. Tiffany heard it. I heard it the first time; then I woke her up—A couple minutes later, I heard a car drive off. I've been hearing cars up and down my street all night. . . . So I hear a car drive off and I'm, like, "Whatever, cool, she's home." I go to sleep.

Tombs says that she woke up at around 7:50 A.M. and found the house cold. Going downstairs, she saw that the heat was off and bumped the thermostat up to seventy degrees Fahrenheit. That's when she saw that the top lock on the front door was unlocked, while the bottom was locked.

Tombs: I don't have a key for the top lock, I just have a key for the bottom lock. So I'm, like, "Dang, did Tanya even come home?" So I open up the door, look under the mat . . . on our porch, and my key's gone. And I look up and see Tanya's [car] trunk open. So I go over there and I shut her trunk. And it was like just a bunch of bags and stuff, I guess she had in the trunk and they were sitting in the front seat.

She shut the trunk, Tombs says, trying unsuccessfully to rouse sleepy Tiffany Lofton from bed for some breakfast. She went to the kitchen and made herself some breakfast cereal, then went downstairs to put Tanya's work uniform in the washing machine.

Tombs: I go downstairs. I start to smell something real funny. . . . So I go in the wash room; put her uniform in the dryer, and I turn around and I see Tanya's foot. Now when I went down there—after Alan left, I went down there because her light and her TV was on [in the rec room]. I turned all that off. She was not home.
Kraft: And what time—
Tombs: This was before her dad came.

Tombs resumes telling about the finding of the body. She was in the laundry room, directly opposite the rec room. "So this morning I look over and I see her foot and she's like laying in the middle of the floor. . . . And I see her foot and I went in there and I see her laid down on the floor with a bunch of blood around her head at the top. I panicked, I couldn't breathe. And I stayed there for a minute and just looked at her. Until I could finally get the energy to run upstairs and tell Tiffany."

Kraft: Okay, and what did you tell Tiffany?
Tombs: I said, "It's Tanya. You gotta come downstairs." 'Cause I couldn't get nothing else out.

She and Tiffany went downstairs, she says. "So we sit there and we look at her for a minute and try and think what to do. And she [Tiffany Lofton] was, like, 'We gotta call the police.' And I was, like, 'I'm not calling the police until an adult gets here, 'cause I can't be answering no questions without an adult present. She's my baby-sitter.' So we called Tiffany's mom. Her mom doesn't answer. I call Tanya's house. The line is busy. I call my grandma's house. The answering machine comes on. So finally we call Benny Milliner."

Kraft: Who's that?
Tombs: Alan's dad.
Kraft: Then what happened?
Tombs: Then when me and Tiffany were on the porch waiting for him to show up, Brother Errol and Mark Caisey drove up and said,

"Where's Tanya?" And Tiffany told them what happened.

Kraft: All right.

Tombs: And then Mr. Milliner came. Gave us instructions of what to do and what not to do as far as talking to people goes, and then the police put me in the car and took me away. And they got a statement from me but they couldn't use it because I ain't over eighteen.

Kraft changes the subject, saying, "Let's go back a little bit here, um, now, when Tanya was talking on the phone to this male voice, who was she talking to?"

Tombs: I don't know. I know she had called her boyfriend Mike . . . Michael.

Kraft: Okay. What's his last name?

Tombs: I don't know. All I know is he's older than she is.

Kraft: Where does he live?

Tombs: I don't know. I don't know anything about him. She just told me about him. But me and Tanya had also talked about us having like boys on the side and stuff. I don't know who she was talking to, I just know she was arguing with somebody.

Tombs says that Tanya had once told her, "He's [Michael] old enough to be your dad."

Kraft: Okay. Well, as far as you knew, she left [the Tombs house] with some guy named Michael.

Tombs: I don't know who she left with. I just know that that's her boyfriend and she was trying to get in touch with him. But I don't know who she was on the phone arguing with.

Kraft again changes course. "There's another thing, too, that I'm kind of curious about. You never mentioned the shell casings."

Tombs: Oh, when I picked up the shells? That was when me and Tiffany had both went down to look at the body. . . . I picked them up and I set them down on the [kitchen] counter.
Kraft: Why did you do that?
Tombs: I don't know. I just said, "Tiffany, look," and before she could say anything, they were in my hands. She was, like, "Your fingerprints are on them now." I was, like, "Dang." So I told Mr. Milliner I picked up the shells and he said to make sure I told the police. But I did pick them up.
Kraft: Let's go back a little bit to the couch. There was blood on the couch. And what was around the blood, when you saw the blood?
Tombs: Some white stuff.
Kraft: Some white stuff? What was that?
Tombs: I don't know. I didn't touch it. It was just white and it was, like, thick. It wasn't real thick, but it was like globbed on there, so I don't know what it was.

Then Kraft offers a first, indirect challenge, but a challenge no less. "Why would someone try to clean up the blood off the couch?"

Tombs: They were trying to clean the blood up?

Kraft: Mmm-hmm. Why would somebody want to do that?

Tombs: I don't know.

Kraft: Is it because the couch was damaged, soiled by the blood, and you wanted to get it cleaned up before your mother got home?

Tombs: No.

Kraft: Well, somebody tried to clean it up.

Tombs: I don't know, Officer. I just saw the white stuff, I didn't touch it. The only thing I touched was the shells.

Kraft: If you didn't try to clean it up, who was there that would want to clean it up?

Tombs: I don't know. I didn't see any water stains or anything like that, any wash towels, any bleach. I just seen the white stuff on it. I didn't even know what it was. It didn't look like any Clorox or any Tide or anything like that.

Tombs repeats that at 2:00 A.M., she'd gone into the rec room to turn off the TV and lights, then shut the door. Now Kraft offers a second, slightly more direct challenge.

Kraft: Your times don't add up, because you said that Errol Vermont and Mark Caisey came by after two o'clock, when, in fact, they came by before midnight. Why do we have a two-hour difference there?

Tombs: They couldn't have come by before

midnight because they came right after Alan left.

Kraft: They told me they came by at midnight.

Tombs: No.

Kraft: And you met them at the door.

Tombs: I did meet them at the door, but they came by after Alan left.

Kraft: What did you tell them at the door?

Tombs: I told them Tanya wasn't there . . . and I didn't know where she was at. She would be back.

Kraft: What else?

Tombs: That's all. I'd have her call them.

Kraft: I talked to them this morning. In front of your house. And I have a written statement from him [Errol Vermont]. You told him he couldn't come in the house without a search warrant.

This is a direct challenge in the form of a discrepancy between witness testimony.

Tombs: I did not tell him that, sir, I swear to God I did not tell him that. He never asked to come inside, not once did he—

Kraft: Why did he tell me that? Why would he tell me that out of the blue, that you refused to let him into the house when he came over to see where Tanya is?

Tombs: He never asked to come in the house, ever.

Kraft: And you never said he couldn't come in the house.

Tombs: I never said anything.

Kraft: He's making this up? Why would he . . . ?

Tombs: He asked me where his daughter was. I said I didn't know. I said I'd have her call him as soon as she got back. He never said, "Can I come in and check things out?" Brother Errol knows I would let him in. I didn't know the other dude. I didn't know Mark.

Kraft: Well, he [Errol Vermont] was upset because you wouldn't let him come in the house.

Tombs: I'm telling you, officer, he never asked me. He didn't. He didn't say, "Can I come, can I look around?" Nothing. He said, "Where's Tanya?"

Kraft: And you never said he couldn't come in without a—

Tombs: I never said he couldn't come in the house without a search warrant.

Kraft: Now why would he tell me that?

Tombs: I don't know. Why would he need a search warrant?

Kraft: Why? Why would he?

Tombs: I don't know. He wouldn't. Brother Errol knows he can come in the house. Him or Miss Val.

Kraft then asks why none of the young men who were upstairs in the bedroom saw the white Cutlass that came to pick up Tanya. "They said they were tired of waiting in the room, because all they did was listen to music and play dice, and they kept looking out the window because they wanted to come out of the room, and they never saw a car."

Tombs: There was a car. Ask my neighbors. One of them had to see it.

Kraft asks her if she moved the body after she found it. Jennifer Tombs denies it. A little later, Kraft turns the questioning over to Sims from the D.A.'s Office. Sims asks about Tanya's alleged phone calls, in which the defendant claims she heard Tanya's end of the conversation, arguing with an unidentified man.

Nearing the end of his questioning, Sims asks Madlyn Tombs, "Mrs. Tombs, is there anything that you want either the detective or me to talk with your daughter a little more about that we haven't talked about?"

Mrs. Tombs: I wouldn't know where to begin. This is my first experience with something like this and it's very difficult. . . .

Sims: I understand, ma'am. Do you have any questions regarding the conversation that you and the detective had about Jennifer understanding what's going on? That this is a voluntary conversation?

Mrs. Tombs: I do understand that. I'm not afraid of the truth. If my daughter killed Tanya, then we all need to know. Tanya's dead. I've known Tanya since she was little, so I'm struggling. But I want to know the truth. I don't want their family to not know the truth. At the same time, my daughter knows that I stand for the truth and I'm willing to tell the truth, the whole truth and nothing but the truth, and she also knows that I stand with her as a mother, so I want the truth as much as they do.

Sims asks Jennifer Tombs if she knows where they could find the murder weapon. Jennifer says she doesn't know. Kraft says, "Tiffany told me about a half hour ago, before we started this interview, where we might be able to find the gun. Now, why would she know where the gun is?"

Tombs: I don't know.
Kraft: You know, in these cases that we investigate, when a person dies, sometimes it was not because it was intended. Sometimes we find out it's an accident, that no one was trying to harm another person, but accidents do happen. Now, there's a difference between an accident and an "on purpose." And usually when someone takes another person's life, and there's a reason for it, there's a motive. And a lot of times, it's an obvious motive. Other times, it's not, but we find out later on what it is. If it's an accident, there's no motive, it's just simply an accident. Accidents happen. We have no control over accidents. And if that's the case, then we need to know now.
Tombs: I didn't do it. Tiffany didn't do it. But I did not tell you guys about something.
Kraft: Okay, we're here to listen. I'm sure your mom wants to hear it, too.
Tombs: Tiffany and I found the gun. And I knew if you guys found that gun, and Tiffany knew if you guys found that gun in that house, that we were gonna get blamed. So Tiffany and

I decided to go put it in the ditch up the street and that's where it's at.

Jennifer Tombs says that she found the gun near the body: "Silver and black. It was a little gun. It wasn't a big gun, it was a little gun."

Kraft: Have you seen it before?
Tombs: No.
Kraft: Did Tanya ever show you the gun?
Tombs: Unh-uh [no].
Kraft: Did she keep it with her?
Tombs: Unh-uh [no]. I've never seen it before. I just seen it because her purse was laying half-way open—
Mrs. Tombs [interrupts]: Can I talk to you a minute? [To defendant] Obviously, they know something, okay. And they're going to pull it out of you.
Tombs: Mom, I'm telling—
Mrs. Tombs: Hold on. Listen, listen to me. You can either tell it now, or you can drag this whole thing out.
Tombs: Mom, I'm telling—
Mrs. Tombs: Just a second. Just a second. We were in here for quite a while. You assured me that you told me everything you knew. And you didn't. Now I'm hearing about a gun. Okay. And I'm, uh, hearing . . . you say you called Mrs. Vermont. You didn't tell me that. Okay, so now I want the truth and I want the whole truth. Okay. Did you and Tanya struggle? Did you accidentally kill Tanya?
Tombs: Mom, no.

Mrs. Tombs: Okay, did Tiffany accidentally kill Tanya?

Tombs: Mom, no. We didn't do it. I swear we didn't do it, Mom. We did not do it. We didn't. We found the gun.

Mrs. Tombs: Okay, what else did you not tell us?

Tombs: Nothin'. I told her to go put the gun somewhere. She said, "All right." But we didn't do it, Mom.

Mrs. Tombs: All right.

Tombs: Mom . . . if one of us had shot Tanya, don't you think somebody else would have heard it?

Mrs. Tombs: Could be, but I didn't hear about the gun before, so I'd really like to know the truth.

Tombs: Mom, we didn't do it. We just found the gun. I promise you, we didn't do it.

Mrs. Tombs: Lying to these gentlemen is—

Tombs: Mom, I know.

Mrs. Tombs: —is not going to help you any. . . . See, there's two ways to make a mistake, through omission and commission. Commission is actually doing. Omission is by not telling, okay? And the things that you don't tell, you're just as guilty for. Best thing for you is to tell it all now.

Tombs: Mom, I am telling it. . . . We found the gun.

Mrs. Tombs: Okay, but you didn't tell me that before, so what else is there?

Tombs: Nothing. I never said Brother Errol couldn't get in without a search warrant. I didn't try and clean the blood up. I didn't touch her. I picked the shells up. We found the gun. Tiffany and I both touched the gun.

Kraft: Jennifer, I've got to tell you, standing from afar and looking at the situation, you know, and it doesn't look good for you. Okay, there's two people in the house. Started out last night with three people in the house. This morning, there's two people. Now you've told us about the weapon. You picked up the shell casings. There's an obvious sign of someone trying to clean up that couch.

Tombs: I never touched the couch. I didn't touch her.

Kraft: How do you explain all this powder around the body? And it looked like somebody had scrubbed to try and clean it. How do you explain that? Jennifer, there's one thing you've got to understand. . . . This isn't the first case I've ever worked on, and it's not the first homicide scene I've ever gone to, and it's not the first body I've ever looked at. But this is the first time I've seen somebody try to clean a crime scene. You eliminate the gun, you clean up the shell casings. Somebody, you don't know who, tried to clean the blood up off the couch. And you tell me you don't know anything about this and you don't call 911. Which most people do when they find somebody hurt or dead on their floor.

Tombs: We didn't call 911—

Kraft: See, you've got reasons for all these things, you know, "I'm not supposed to talk to an adult without my family or parents present," or whatever the case may be, but it doesn't wash out because your actions aren't normally the way people act. You see someone on the floor, My God, I'm going to call 911, I'm going to call somebody over here, I'm not going to stay and clean up the shell casings, I'm not going to get rid of the gun. Why? Who cares? Why would you care? That the gun is laying there . . .

Tombs: Because I thought if you guys found the gun in the house that you guys were gonna assume Tiffany and I did it, which now I see you guys do, or me or whoever. We both panicked. We both agreed to get rid of the gun.

Kraft: If you were a boat, you'd be leakin' and sinkin' right now because you didn't do what a person would normally do under those circumstances. You tried to change a crime scene. You tried to eliminate the weapon. That doesn't mean anything, you know, we've got a person that's full of bullets. That doesn't mean we won't find out the person was shot.

Tombs: I know.

Kraft: So why get rid of the gun, it's not going to change anything.

Tombs: I don't know.

Kraft: Because your fingerprints are on that gun.

Tombs: My fingerprints were on the gun?

Kraft: Mhm.

Tombs: Tiffany and I both picked up the gun.

Kraft: You both picked up the gun.

Tombs: When we found it, yeah.

Kraft: Then why get rid of the gun? Give me

a reason, a logical reason why you wanted to get rid of it.

Tombs: We just thought that if you guys found it, you guys were gonna take us to jail and we'd be in a lot of trouble. That's why we got rid of the gun.

Kraft: It doesn't make sense. Here we have a body laying on the floor. What difference does it make whether the gun was there or not, unless it's something that you used?

Tombs: I don't know.

Kraft: If it's an accident, tell us.

Tombs: I didn't do it.

Kraft: Understand, things do happen. But you've done things that people don't normally do. There's no reason for it. Unless you give me a good reason, I have to think the worst. I have to think that you did it. So let's clear this up now. Get it off your chest.

Tombs: I didn't do it. Officer, I swear I didn't do it. I didn't kill Tanya.

Kraft: Jennifer, I want to believe you, I really do, but you haven't been exactly easy with the truth. Okay. We've had to tug and pull and get the truth out of you. That doesn't help you.

Tombs: I'm not used to walking downstairs in my basement and seeing somebody lying there. That scared the hell out of me and I didn't know what to do. Especially her. I been knowing her since I was little. I had Tiffany in the house with me, I had Alan and them in the house with me. I didn't know what to do. Fine, I tried to get rid of the gun, but I didn't do it. I didn't try and clean up the couch.

Kraft says that the blood on the crime scene floor was not fresh, but old: "The times aren't working out here. . . . This didn't happen early in the morning, at two, or three, or four o'clock in the morning. That is dried blood and from what I've learned the last few years of working this business, that was around midnight, or before midnight. At the earliest. I think it happened before midnight. Whatever happened. And you had to do some serious thinking. And Tiffany was involved. Scared to death, but involved."

Tombs: We didn't do it.
Kraft: "We didn't do it." Then tell us who did.
Tombs: I don't know. I swear to God, we didn't do it.
Kraft: Who did?
Tombs: I don't know, Officer.

After an inconsequential moment or two more, the interview ends.

The videotape had featured minimal visuals and abominable sound quality, but its effect was riveting, and potentially damaging to the defense, especially the sequences where Madlyn Tombs questions her daughter's honesty and implores her to tell the truth.

Resuming direct examination, Henry Cooper asked Kraft about a conversation regarding the gun he'd had with Tiffany Lofton prior to the interview with Jennifer Tombs.

Kraft said, "I said, if the gun is somewhere where

a small child can get it, they could be hurt. I tried to play on her emotions. I said, 'We need to know where that gun is,' and she said, 'You might try in the backyard of the house—of the Tombs house.' " But a search of the area failed to yield the weapon. Cooper said, "When she told you to look in the backyard of the house, was she guessing, or was she telling you something that she had observed?"

"She was guessing. She said maybe it might be there," Kraft said.

At this point, Judge Warren began to give the witness a hard time about the shaky quality of the videotape's audio track. "Detective Kraft, is that the sound recording system owned by the Denver Police Department?"

"I'm afraid it is."

"Would you suggest to [the chief of police], on my behalf, that if he has any discretionary income, he ought to spend it on some new recording system. It is positively painful to listen to, and these people have [had] to listen for an hour and a half."

"Absolutely—I totally agree. And we have replaced that system," Kraft said.

"Okay," Judge Warren said.

On cross-examination, Kurt Metsger said, "When you had the interview with Ms. Tombs, was she wearing an ankle bracelet at that point of time?"

"I believe she was," Kraft said.

Metsger pointed out that while the witness said he monitored the news clippings about the case in the papers, he hadn't watched all the videos of every news station that covered the story. "So you don't know what they covered, or who they talked to, do you?"

"No, I don't," Kraft said.

"There were a lot of people that knew what had happened, and you don't know if any of that got out to the news media—the television news media—do you?"

"No, I don't."

"Okay. When you were interrogating Ms. Tombs, you were saying that a lot of things didn't add up," Metsger said. "Well, let's take a step back. Ms. Tombs at that point in time was a suspect, right?"

Kraft said, "In my mind, yes."

"And one of the tactics you use is to lie to who you think is a suspect, to try and draw them out—isn't that correct?"

"Yes, it is."

"And when you told her that you'd recovered the weapon and found fingerprints on it, that also was a lie, wasn't it?"

"Yes, it was."

"Once again, all those things that you were telling her, even though they were lies, they're ways of getting information out, correct?"

"That is correct."

"Specifically, you didn't have the gun in your possession, did you?"

"No," Kraft said. "At that time, we weren't aware of where the gun was."

Metsger said, "And there were no fingerprints of Ms. Tombs found on a gun, were there?"

"No."

"And Tiffany Lofton hadn't told you where the gun was, had she?"

"She had not, no."

Metsger moved on to the issue of the shell casings. "You state that [the defendant] cleaned up shell casings. Well, in essence, she didn't clean them up, did she?"

"No," Kraft said, "she just merely cleaned them off the floor."

"Is it uncommon for people to touch crime scenes before the police get there?"

"Well, actually, it is kind of uncommon for them to disturb a weapon, or pick up shell casings—things like that."

"Okay. But people do it, don't they?"

"Yes, they do," Kraft said. "But it's not a common practice for people to clean up a crime scene, or spruce up a crime scene. Especially a family member—they're usually too distraught to even think about doing things like that."

Metsger said, "Okay, but in terms of picking them up—picking up shell casings and moving them . . . essentially from the basement to the kitchen—that's not cleaning—well, it's not hiding those shell casings, wouldn't you agree?"

"Highly unusual. But why would you move 'em from one room to another? There's no reason for it."

"There's no reason for it because you're gonna find 'em anyway, right?" Metsger said. "I mean, if they were sitting in the kitchen, obviously when you came, or the rest of the department came, they're gonna find 'em."

Kraft said, "Eventually, yes."

"Well, they were pretty obvious on that counter there, weren't they?"

"Yes, they were."

The witness was excused.

* * *

Mark Caisey, cousin and roommate of Tanya Lavallais, took the stand for Mike Pellow's direct. He told of trying to contact her on the night of Friday, September 27, 1996, with about six pages that went unanswered. "If you paged Tanya, she'll call you back in five minutes, at the most."

Worried about Tanya, he went to the Vermont home, arriving at about 11:20 P.M. He and his uncle, Errol Vermont, went to the Tombs house; Caisey drove. Pellow said, "Approximately what time did you get there?"

Caisey said, "Eleven thirty-five, eleven forty-five."

"Are you positive it wasn't as late as two o'clock?"

"No, it wasn't that late."

"Was it before midnight?"

"Correct."

At the house, Caisey knocked on the door, which was answered by Jennifer Tombs. "Well, she said Tanya's not there. And we checked the car . . . and the car was cold—not like it was moved. I said, was everything okay, you know? And she said, 'Yeah, everything's fine.' I said, 'Can I come in and check it out?' And she said, 'No—you don't have a search warrant, do you?' And I said, 'I'm not a police officer—I don't need a search warrant.'

"And my uncle said, 'Come on, Mark—leave it alone.' "

Pellow said, "Are you sure that you asked to go into the house?"

"I'm positive."

"Did she say why you couldn't come in the house?"

"I don't have a search warrant."

"And why did you want to go inside?"

"Check around—see what's up, you know?"

On cross-examination, Jeff Timlin suggested that given the witness was a stranger to Jennifer Tombs, plus his demeanor, might have influenced her decision not to allow him into the house. "She's looking at a face at eleven-thirty that she doesn't know, correct?"

Caisey said, "Mr. Vermont was standing right next to me."

"The question, Mr Caisey—she's looking at your face and she didn't know who you were, did she? At eleven-thirty at night."

"Yeah, I guess so."

"At that point in time, were you getting angry? Were you threatening when you said you wanted to come in?"

"No . . . not at all."

"She never told you you needed a search warrant, did she?"

"Did she tell me I needed a search warrant?"

"Yeah."

"Yeah," Caisey said. "And that made me kinda think: Why are you asking me that?"

Timlin said, "And the conversation was over?"

"Pretty much."

"Didn't that make you suspicious?"

"Of course."

"Why didn't you just go in? You're bigger than her."

"Why should I do that, when I have my uncle standing next to me, telling me, 'C'mon, Mark—let's go'?"

"Well, if you think that Tanya's in danger in that home, and then [Jennifer] says something as suspicious as, 'Do you have a search warrant?'—don't you think that maybe you ought to go in, no matter what she says?"

"Now I do."

"But you didn't then, correct? You just thought, 'Oh, well—we'll just go home and come back tomorrow.'"

Caisey said, "No, not come back tomorrow. We're gonna go home, and we're gonna call. 'Cause she said Tanya might have gone to a club. So we figured the club lets out at three, any club—or two-thirty. We figure we'll wait and see what happens."

Timlin said, "So you weren't too worried, that you didn't think it was necessary to just go in anyway, and then you just left."

"I was very worried."

"But not worried enough to go in the house anyway—correct?"

"No, not worried enough to make a mistake and regret it later."

On redirect, the prosecution moved to nail down the reason why Mark Caisey had not been more insistent on gaining entry or pressing the matter. "Mr. Caisey—did you want to call the police?"

"Yes, I did."

"Why did you not call the police?"

"My uncle and aunt said, 'What if Tanya is at a club? We don't want to cause so much grief.'"

"Your aunt and uncle talked you out of it?"

"Right."

"And were you worried enough to where you wanted to call the police, though?"

"Correct."

Errol Vermont, stepfather of the victim, family friend of the defendant and professional church associate of the defendant's mother—tragic, dignified, carrying a weight of worldly sorrows on his shoulders—took the stand for Pellow's direct examination.

Pellow said, "Mr. Vermont, what do you do for a living?"

"Well, right now I have a business—a plumbing business—that's what I do for a living," the witness said.

"Are you involved in the church that Pastor Tombs is involved in?"

"Yes, sir. I'm one of the associate ministers at the church."

Vermont told of the tensions and ever-mounting concern for Tanya Lavallais's well-being on Friday night, September 27, that prompted him and nephew Mark Caisey to go to the Tombs house. "My wife also started calling the phone number to Jennifer, and she told me she's been getting conflicting answers. So she started getting alarmed about it, and I started getting alarmed at the same time—and we determined that I should go over there and see, really, what's going on."

"And about what time did you and Mark Caisey go over there?"

"It was between eleven-thirty and twelve o'clock."

"Are you positive it was not later than that?"

"Oh, I'm positive about that."

"It was not as late as two o'clock in the morning."

"No, sir—no, sir."

Vermont said that he'd been to the Tombs house many times before, that the defendant knew him very well and had never had any problem letting him in the house. Pellow said, "Had she ever denied you entrance to that house before that night?"

"No, sir—no, sir," Errol Vermont said. He told of seeing Tanya's car in the driveway, of touching the hood to see if it was warm from being recently driven, only to find it cold. When he returned the next day, Saturday morning, the first thing he noticed was that items of Tanya's, which had not been in sight last night, were now on the seat of the car.

He said, "I was alarmed about that. When I came here the night before, I didn't see all these things on the seat of the car. So I said, 'Somebody has been in the car.'"

He told of his and Caisey's meeting with Jennifer Tombs the night before. "We chatted for a few minutes. And we were concerned. We asked her, 'Where was Tanya?' She said, 'Tanya went out. . . .' And I said, 'Went out? Who did she go out with?' She said she did not know. I said, 'You mean, somebody's gonna leave your house, go through this door, and you didn't even come to the door and see—to lock the door back and see anything?' She said, 'No.' And I told her, I said, 'You know, that's— that didn't sound right to me.'

"Mark Caisey said to her, 'Well, can we come in and take a look?' And she said, 'No.' Well, Caisey was more determined to go in and take a look. And

I just say, 'Mark, don't—let's keep calm about this thing here.' And he said, 'Okay, let's go call the police.' And I said, 'No, don't call the police—don't call the police.' And he asked me why I don't want to call the police and I told him that the police have been to that house before, and I didn't want to create any more commotions for the pastor. And I said, 'That's the reason why. Let's just wait.' "

Asked if he'd heard the defendant tell Mark Caisey he needed a search warrant to come in the house, the witness said that he hadn't heard all of it, but he had heard her say "Well, you can't come in, because you don't have a search . . ."

Pellow established that the above phraseology was what Errol Vermont had written in a statement he made to police shortly after the murder.

Pellow said, "Did you basically talk Mark Caisey out of trying to go into the house?"

"Yes, yes," Vermont said. "He was determined to go into the house, to find out what was going on—because I think he became suspicious at that time, when we asked her if we can come in. I became suspicious myself, because I've been to the house several times . . .

"She [the defendant] said, 'I'm not gonna let any men in the house this time of the night.' That's what she said. And I said, 'Well, you know, I've been here before, Jennifer—you know who I am. You know, I'm not a stranger to you—you know from the church. So even if I'm with somebody, I wouldn't take a criminal here to do any wrongs.' "

Pellow said, "What time did you go back to Jennifer Tombs's house the next morning?"

Vermont said, "I would say between seven forty-five and eight-thirty—around that area there."

"Why did you go back over there?"

"Well, we stayed up that night until very late, because I know for sure we were up after two. I think we stayed up until about four o'clock, waiting for a phone call. Because we were told that, as soon as Tanya returns, that a message would be delivered to her and she would call us. So we were waiting for a call.

"Well, at seven o'clock that morning, I asked my wife, 'Have you heard from Tanya?' And she said, 'No.' I said, 'Okay, I have to go back over there.' "

His son Mark Treadwell came over to the house, and the two of them went to the Tombs house, the witness said. Pellow said, "Did you see Jennifer Tombs at that time?"

Vermont said, "Yes, sir. We knocked on the door that morning, and Jennifer Tombs and Tiffany—they came out almost at the same time. And Tiffany was in tears, and crying. And Jennifer wasn't. . . . She showed in her face that something had happened, but she wasn't giving the same emotional reaction as Tiffany."

"She wasn't crying?"

"No. But she was talking, loud and fast, that something had happened, yeah."

"And do you recall what she was saying when she was talking loud and fast?"

"Yeah. We asked her, 'Where was Tanya?' And it took a few minutes for us to get the words out. She said she went downstairs and Tanya had been shot."

"Did she say anything about how it had happened?"

"No, no."

"Did she tell you anything about an intruder coming into the house?"

"Not at that time—no, she didn't," Errol Vermont said.

On a brief cross-examination, Jeff Timlin suggested that Vermont did not ask to go into the house and that he had the authority to enter without Jennifer's permission. A hairsplitting digression about Vermont's interchangeable use of the words "we" and "I" in his statement prompted Timlin to complain about laughter coming from the gallery.

Following that, court recessed for the day.

April 2, 1997, day three of the trial, began with the testimony of Denver Police Department detective William Fairchild, describing how, on October 2, 1996, he'd gone to the corner of Elmendorf Place and Quari Street, discovering the murder weapon in a storm drain, in several inches of standing water, in plain sight. He went down into the drain, recovering a .25-caliber semiautomatic, which then went first to the police property department, then to ballistics. The witness identified the gun in court and testified that he'd measured the distance from the drain to the Tombs house, which was approximately 500 feet.

There was no cross-examination.

At this point, the courtroom was cleared for testimony from a witness about the operation of the monitoring ankle bracelet the defendant was wearing the night of the crime. It was established that, due to the computer-based operating system of the ankle bracelet monitor, a potential window of opportunity did exist for the defendant to have gotten rid of the gun in the storm drain up the street and still have made it back to her house in time to avoid tripping the alarm.

Next was Alan Milliner, now eighteen, the defendant's boyfriend at the time of the murder. Henry Cooper, on direct, said, "I want to direct your attention back to the late summer of last year. Had you been seeing Jennifer Tombs or dating her at the time?"

Milliner said, "We were hanging out."

"What do you mean? Tell the jury what you mean by hanging out."

"Um, we were just kicking it," Milliner said, looking at the jury and smiling. "We were seeing each other once in a while."

"Would you characterize her as your girlfriend at that time?"

"No."

"Would she have characterized you as her boyfriend?"

"Not that I know of."

"How often were you kicking it with her?"

"Couple times a week," Milliner said.

Cooper directed the witness's attention to the events of Friday, September 27, 1996. Milliner said that earlier that week, on Monday or Tuesday, he and the defendant had made arrangements for him to go over to her house. Cooper said, "What did she tell you or ask you?"

Milliner said, "Um, that her and Tiffany were gonna cook dinner. They wanted us—wanted me and Willis Wallace to come over."

"She say anything about whether her mother would be there?"

"No, she said she was out of town."

"She said her mother would be out of town?"

"Yes."

The witness described how, on that Friday night, arriving at the Tombs house with James, Green and Wallace, they'd been told to be quiet and go straight upstairs to Jennifer's room, making him feel as if they'd been "snuck in."

Cooper said, "Did she [Jennifer Tombs] tell you why she wanted you to keep it down?"

Milliner said, " 'Cause her cousin hadn't left yet."

"Did she tell you her cousin was leaving?"

"Yes . . . she said her cousin was going—her boyfriend was coming to pick her up and was going to the club."

"You remember what she said the boyfriend's name was?"

"No."

"Did she say anything about the type of car the boyfriend was coming in?"

"A white Cutlass."

The four young men were hanging out, drinking, smoking, shooting dice in the upstairs bedroom. Tiffany Lofton stayed in the bedroom, while Jennifer Tombs ran in and out of the room, saying she was waiting for her cousin to leave.

Cooper said, "I want to direct your attention to the last time Jennifer left the room, before she came back and told you that Tanya was gone. When Jennifer was in that last time, did she do anything to the music?"

"Um, she turned it up a little louder than it was."

"Did she leave the room?"

"Yeah."

Cooper said, "Did a point in time come, right after Jennifer turned up the music and left the room, that you heard something unusual?"

Milliner said, "I heard a noise, but I didn't know what it was."

The witness seemed evasive on what he'd said to the others in the room when the noise sounded, so Cooper pinned it down. "Mr. Milliner, didn't you say, when you heard the noise, 'That sounded like gunshots'?"

"I couldn't tell what it was."

"Right now I'm not asking what you thought it was. I'm asking you what you said. And what you said at that point was, 'That sounded like gunshots,' correct?"

"Yes."

"After saying that, did you think any more of it?"

"No."

"And then Jennifer came back in the room?"

"Yes."

"What did she say?"

"That Tanya was gone."

"Told you Tanya was gone?"

"Yes." The witness said that he'd never seen anybody come to the house, had heard no car drive up nor people downstairs, nothing that would make him think that Tanya had left with someone.

Cooper said, "After Jennifer said, 'Tanya's gone,' what happened next?"

Milliner said, "Um, she just opened the door and

turned the music up a little louder, and told us we could get something to eat downstairs."

About an hour or so later, he got ready to leave with Green and James. Cooper said, "And when you left, did Jennifer ask you about anything later that night?"

"To come back," Milliner said.

"And when she asked you to come back to the house, did she say anything to you about being concerned that Tanya may be back?"

"No."

The witness stated that he did, indeed, come back, somewhere between 2:00 and 2:30 A.M. Cooper said, "And when you and Jennifer went into her room, what did you do?"

Milliner said, "Had sex."

"Had sex?"

"Yeah."

"And how long were you in the room?"

"Couple hours."

He'd left about 4:00 A.M., going home, the witness said. The next morning, he'd received a phone call from Jennifer Tombs and Tiffany Lofton, indicating that there was a dead body in the house.

Cooper said, "And do you recall after hearing about this on the phone, saying something out loud in relation to maybe what caused this dead body to be in the house?"

"No," Milliner said.

"Do you ever recall saying, 'I thought I heard something'?"

"Yes."

"And your father heard that, didn't he?"

"Yes."

On Jeff Timlin's cross-examination, Milliner denied ever having seen Jennifer Tombs bring a gift bag into the room, taking from it a box that held a silver gun and displaying it to the others. Timlin said, "Did you see a gun at any time that evening?"

"No," Milliner said.

He said that the noises sounded like a car backfire, that there weren't as many "booms" as seven or eight, but "maybe a couple at most." He'd been around guns enough to know the smell of gunpowder, and hadn't smelled any gunpowder on Jennifer Tombs when she'd returned to the room.

Timlin said, "Now, did you notice anything unusual about the clothes she was wearing? Did you see any blood on the clothes?"

Milliner said, "No, I didn't."

Timlin noted that the defendant's demeanor was normal and unchanged after she'd returned to the room after the noises. "And when she came up and said, 'Tanya's gone, you can all come out of your room' . . . she was still acting the same way, correct?"

Milliner said, "Yes."

"Was there any emotional change, was she anxious, stressed, nervous?"

"No."

Timlin moved on to the events of the morning of Saturday, September 28. "The next morning, Mr. Milliner, you received a call from Tiffany Lofton. . . . And you found out that something had occurred at the house, and you made that statement that, 'Well, I thought I heard something yesterday.' You still didn't know whether those were gunshots, did you?"

"No."

"You didn't believe they were gunshots at that point in time, did you?"

"I didn't want to," Milliner said.

Timlin said, "Pardon me?"

"I didn't want to."

"But you're not sure they were?"

"No."

"And it surely wasn't five or six gunshots, was it?"

"No."

"You surely would have heard a gunshot if it shot six or seven times, correct?"

"Probably."

On redirect, Henry Cooper said, "You've indicated that the sounds that you heard, you don't know if it was gunshots, or it may have sounded like backfires, you didn't tell everybody in the room and they didn't hear you say that sounded like backfires, did they?"

Milliner said, "No."

"What they heard you say was, 'That sounded like gunshots,' right?"

"Yeah."

"Jennifer Tombs is your friend, right?"

"Yes."

"You indicated you didn't want to believe you heard gunshots—you still don't want to believe that, do you?"

"Yes."

Alan Milliner's friend Duvonne Green, eighteen, took the stand, stating that when he went to the

Tombs house on Friday, September 27, 1996, he'd never met Tanya Lavallais and didn't know she was there; that he was told she was there by Jennifer Tombs; that Jennifer had said that Tanya was getting ready to leave to go to Bernard's lounge, but that he'd peeked out Jennifer's bedroom window and had never seen anyone come or go.

He recalled that Milliner had said that the noises sounded like shots and asked if anybody else had heard them, and that he personally had heard three or four booms, "not real loud," that could have been gunshots. About ten minutes later, the defendant entered the room, saying, "Tanya's gone."

On Kurt Metsger's cross-examination, Green testified that he never saw the defendant with a gun and certainly didn't hear six or seven noises. He stated that the defendant never told him not to go into any part of the house.

Tasha Lavallais, the victim's younger sister, testified that on Friday, September 27, 1996, she'd spent the day with her mother and Tanya, and she'd planned to spend the night with her sister at the Tombs house. She'd expected Tanya and Jennifer to pick up her and her son later that evening.

She said that Tanya was a very responsible person, a very caring person, always willing to help friends or family members when they needed her. Henry Cooper said, "Directing your attention to the twenty-seventh of September, the night she was killed, was she, in fact, helping a friend of the family on that date?"

Tasha Lavallais said, "Yes, she was."

She told how, earlier that week, on Wednesday

or Thursday, Jennifer Tombs had called Tasha to find out if Tanya was going to let her "smoke, drink and party" when she supervised her over the weekend.

"And I told her no. My sister won't let her do anything that her mother wouldn't let her do. Which she already knew," Tasha Lavallais said.

Cooper said, "And when you told the defendant that, did she appear disappointed, or anything like that?"

"Yes, she did."

So upset that, later that day, Jennifer had called Tasha Lavallais at home, causing Tasha to arrange a three-way call, which included Tanya. "I told Jennifer, 'Here, I'll let you talk to Tanya, and you guys discuss that,' " Tasha said.

After which, she'd put down the phone, to attend to her son, picking it up ten minutes later, just in time to hear the end of the conversation.

Tasha Lavallais said, "I heard my sister say—excuse me, parents—'If you fuck with me, I'm gonna fuck you up.' "

Cooper said, "What did you interpret that to mean, knowing your sister?"

"I interpret that as Jennifer was asking her, could she have company? Or could she drink? What could she get away with? What could she do that her mother wouldn't let her do? And being the way my sister was, she would say, 'If you plan on misbehaving, then I'm gonna have to handle it.' "

That Friday, the witness recalled having first started paging Tanya early in the evening, growing worried as her pages went unanswered. Responding to the prosecutor's questions, she described Tanya as the type of person who'd go out to a club "once every blue moon," and that "she didn't drink at all."

Cooper said, "Knowing your sister the way you did, is it conceivable that she would leave Jennifer's house, while she was baby-sitting her, and go out to a nightclub?"

Tasha Lavallais said, "No—absolutely not. Tanya knew how Jennifer was—she wouldn't leave her alone."

On cross-examination, the defense suggested that the defendant was close to the victim and had no reason to harm her. Jeff Timlin began, "You've known Jennifer for pretty long, haven't you? Your family and her family are pretty close?"

Tasha Lavallais said, "Yes."

"You all call each other cousins?"

"Used to—yes."

Valeria Vermont, the victim's mother, took the stand, describing Tanya as "wonderful" and very responsible. Henry Cooper said, "How long have you known the defendant and her family?"

Val Vermont said, "Since her mother got her."

"You say, 'Since her mother got her.' What do you mean by that?"

"She was adopted. I think she was maybe seven—between seven and nine months."

Moving to the events preceding Friday, September 27, 1996, Cooper said, "Was there any discussion made as to whether or not Jennifer should come over to your house and stay, or whether Tanya should go over there?"

Val Vermont said, "I suggested that Jennifer can stay with me. But her mother says she had the ankle bracelet on."

"So it was decided that Tanya would go over there."

"Tanya would go there."

"That's Friday. What type of plans did your family have for that Saturday?"

"My son was getting married."

"And I assume everybody was going to the wedding."

"And Jennifer had permission to go."

Val Vermont said that she began paging Tanya about 8:00 P.M. Friday, and started calling Jennifer Tombs at about 9:00 P.M. After she sent her husband and Mark Caisey over to the defendant's house, but before they came back, she received a phone call from Jennifer.

"She [the defendant] says, 'Don't worry—why don't you go on to bed. Tanya's okay. And, first of all, I wouldn't let nothing happen to my big cousin,' " Val Vermont said. "That's exactly what she said to me."

Cooper said, "And, at this point, was she telling you Tanya's whereabouts?"

"No. She told me she was not there. She says, 'Well, if I go to bed before she gets in, I will leave a message on the refrigerator for her to call you immediately.' "

"Did she make any reference to Errol and Mark's visit to the house during that phone call?"

"Yes. She said she didn't let them in because she wasn't dressed appropriately."

* * *

Willis Wallace, a seventeen-year-old high school student, was dating Tiffany Lofton in September 1996, and was one of the guys who was at the Tombs house on the night of the murder. The prosecutor said, "How do you know Tiffany Lofton?"

Wallace said, "Um, I used to be in a relationship with her."

"Was she your girlfriend?"

"Yes. Currently we're not together."

He said that early in the week of September 27, 1996, Tiffany Lofton had invited him to the Tombs house for dinner that Friday. Willis Wallace, Tiffany Lofton, Alan Milliner and the defendant would be present, though by the time he went to the house that night, the group had grown to include Green and James.

Arriving at the house, he and the others were rushed upstairs. He neither saw nor spoke with Tanya. He recalled hearing Milliner say he'd heard gunshots, and he'd heard noises himself, but he didn't know if they were gunshots or not, or from where they had come. At the time, Jennifer Tombs had been out of the room. Lofton was inside the room.

Cooper said, "After you heard these gunshots, did Jennifer make it back to the room?"

Willis Wallace said, "Yes."

"Did she say anything?"

"That . . . that, you know, that that girl was gone."

"Okay. What did you guys do then?"

"Left," Wallace said. "Well, I went downstairs and went to the kitchen to eat. 'Cause, you know what I'm saying, it was supposed to be like a little dinner, you know. And it was just cold pizza—and I was just eating on that while Duvonne Green was down there, too. Donald James and my other friend stayed up in the room."

"Had you been promised a different type of food?"

"Yes—shrimp."

"Shrimp? And it ended up with cold pizza," Henry Cooper said, tsk-tsking.

The witness said that after a while, the other guys left while he stayed behind with Lofton and they went down to the basement, two levels below the kitchen. They did not go into the rec room. Jennifer Tombs went upstairs to take a bath.

Later, Cooper asked, "Now, you say you were drinking. Were you drunk, or just . . . ? What was your state of sobriety?"

"Still in my right mind, but buzzing," the witness said. The prosecution had no further questions.

On cross-examination, Metsger said, "Did you ever see a gun that night?"

Wallace said, "No."

"So if Jennifer would have come in and pulled out a gun, and showed it to Tiffany, you would have seen that, wouldn't you?"

"Yes."

"Now, you said that Alan at some point said he thought he heard a couple of pops. Did you hear a couple of pops?"

"Yes." Wallace said he'd heard about two pops, not seven or eight, and that they hadn't sounded like gunshots. He said that he'd thought they sounded like a cabinet shutting. He hadn't seen any blood on the defendant during the time they were in her room, hadn't noticed any smell of gunpowder on her, and thought that both before and after the noises sounded, she'd seemed "normal."

After the other guys left, he and Tiffany went downstairs, into the basement. The door to the rec room was closed. There was no blood on the wall or stairs. Jennifer Tombs came down in a towel once and went back upstairs.

On redirect, the prosecution elicited from Wallace the admission that it was possible that Jennifer could have shown Tiffany something, such as the gun, without him seeing it.

Donald James told essentially the same story as his other three buddies, except to say what the other three had denied, that there'd been marijuana-smoking in Jennifer Tombs's bedroom. That might be important, since the combination of cigarette and marijuana smoke could have been powerful enough to mask the smell of gunpowder.

He said that he'd heard noises, but they hadn't sounded like gunshots to him, but conceded they might have been. He didn't see or hear Tanya leave. About fifteen minutes after Jennifer said Tanya was gone, he, Green and Milliner left. About 2:00 A.M., they dropped Milliner back at the Tombs house.

On cross-examination, James testified he never saw Jennifer Tombs with a gun, didn't see any blood and didn't smell gunpowder. To him, Jennifer seemed to be acting normal.

After the lunch recess, Michael Hosely, Tanya Lavallais's boyfriend, testified he had talked to Tanya on Friday morning and knew she was going to be baby-sitting that weekend. He tried to page her twice the night of the murder, but he did not talk to her at the Tombs house and did not take her out that night. He said that neither he nor Tanya drank or liked to go to clubs.

Next came the technical experts.

Denver Police Department detective Frank Kerber, a ballistics expert, testified that he'd tested the gun recovered from the storm drain to determine whether it was the murder weapon. He concluded that the bullets that killed Tanya were fired from that gun. On cross-examination, he testified that if eight shots were fired from this gun, it would create a heavy smell of gunpowder and could probably be heard easily in the next room.

Dr. James Wahe, Assistant Medical Examiner for Denver County, had performed the autopsy on Tanya Lavallais. He described the wounds that had killed her—multiple gunshot wounds to the upper arms, head and brain—between six and nine wounds. On cross-examination, he acknowledged that he could not determine the time of death.

Tom Griffin, a bloodstain pattern analyst, testified that he found blood both on the inside and outside of the denim shorts taken from the defendant at the police station, and on the soles and sides of the black Fila shoes found at the house. He'd found blood on the back of the Santa's helper emblem T-shirt identified as having been worn by the defendant Friday night.

He also testified that there was nothing in the room inconsistent with the victim having been shot on the couch, then later moved to the floor. He also found nothing inconsistent with a person dressed in the shorts and black Filas moving the body.

On April 3, 1997, day four of the trial, the prosecution called Greg Leberge, who had done serology and DNA tests on various items of evidence from the scene. DNA tests were done to compare blood found on the black Fila shoes found at the scene, the denim shorts taken from the defendant at police headquarters the next day, and the Santa shirt the defendant was wearing on the night of the murder.

He concluded that the blood found at the scene and on the defendant's clothing was consistent with the victim and inconsistent with the defendant.

On cross-examination, the defense elicited that the stains were small, the spots on the Santa shirt were on the back, and there were no stains on clothes taken from the defendant at the police station, except on the shorts.

The state rested its case.

After a recess, the defense began presenting its case. Their first witness was Bonnie Brodie, a pretrial case manager who had been supervising the defendant in September 1996. At that time, Jennifer Tombs was in the program because she had violated probation on an earlier, aggravated motor-vehicle theft charge. Under the program, the defendant wore an ankle bracelet that registered her absences from her home.

In the early evening of Friday, September 27, 1996, the witness had a home visit with the defendant and her mother. Jennifer Tombs had been doing well on the program and was ready to move to the next, more permissive monitoring level. Brodie stated that on Friday, the defendant's electronic ankle bracelet registered her as being out of range only once, from 6:19 through 6:34 P.M., and was not out of range anytime thereafter before 10:45 A.M. of the following day, Saturday.

On cross-examination, Henry Cooper established that because of the way the system works, there is some time lag before the computer registers that the transmitter is out of range. The witness also conceded that during her home visit on Friday, September 27, 1996, the defendant hadn't said anything about, as Cooper put it, "inviting four boys over for dinner, about having those boys in her room smoking weed and shooting craps, and having another boy spend the night."

Roland Martin, the defendant's tracking officer, testified that Jennifer Tombs was told the monitor would register if she left the house. He said he emphasized to her that "out the door was out of range."

Defense expert witness Robert Burroughs, a forensic scientist with the Denver crime lab, reviewed the results of gunshot residue (GSR) tests in this case. He testified that all of the people in the Tombs house on the night of the murder were later tested, but gunshot residue was found only on the victim. On cross-examination, the state pointed out that negative results may not mean anything, because gunshot residue can be removed by washing or by the passage of time. The tests were not done on the defendant until the morning of Saturday, September 28.

The defense's last witness was the defendant's mother, Pastor Madlyn Tombs. Describing the arrangements for Friday, September 27, 1996, she said that she'd told Tanya Lavallais that, except for family, Tiffany Lofton was the only person who could come over that night, and that there'd been no discussion with regards to Tasha Lavallais and her son coming over and staying overnight.

People's Exhibit #73, the pair of black Fila tennis shoes with blood on them, was identified by the witness as belonging to her. To her knowledge, Jennifer Tombs had no pair of black Fila shoes.

On cross-examination, Cooper said, "Why is it that you wanted a baby-sitter for a fifteen-year-old woman? Or girl?"

Madlyn Tombs said, "Well, it was my custom. And as I was raised, until you reach a certain age, you're provided with supervision. And so I intended to raise my daughter as I was raised."

"Was it, in fact, that you didn't trust her, that was why you asked that a baby-sitter come over?"

"It was that I wanted to provide the best possible care for her that I could."

"Did you trust her?"

"As a parent, I trusted my daughter as any other parent trusted their daughter."

Cooper pressed, "You didn't really trust her, did you?"

"I answered your question already," Madlyn Tombs said stiffly. "She was my daughter; she was on a pretrial release program; she needed supervision; I was giving it to her. And to the degree that she had earned credits, she was already earning that trust."

"Ma'am, isn't it a fact that you have told people that you didn't trust your daughter to the extent that you would lock your own bedroom door at night, and wear your jewelry, to keep her from coming in and getting it?"

"There was a point in time when I made some assumptions, in reference to whether my daughter would do as I asked her to do, just as any parent. Yes."

"And didn't you, in fact, have to put in special security measures in your house—bars, locks on doors—to either keep the defendant from coming in or out?"

Defense objected that the prosecution had gone outside the scope of the questioning, an objection that the judge sustained. Cooper then showed Madlyn Tombs a crime scene photo. "That was her [the defendant's] bedroom on the twenty-seventh, correct?"

Madlyn Tombs said, "Yes."

"It wasn't your bedroom."

"No."

"And in her bedroom, do you see the two black Fila shoes?"

"Sure do."

"Let me ask you this, ma'am. You didn't wear

those Fila shoes anywhere in the proximity of Tanya Lavallais's blood, ever, did you?"

"I never was in the house when Tanya's body was there."

There were no further questions and the witness was excused.

The defense rested its case.

They hadn't put Jennifer Tombs on the stand. Prosecution attorney Henry Cooper later commented, "A common feeling amongst defense lawyers is that if you get a statement of your client in evidence, through the prosecution or whatever, and her statement was brought in through the videotape, why put her on the stand to say the same thing over again and expose her to cross-examination? So I think it was a sound decision, based on trial tactics."

Before charging the jury with their predeliberation instructions, Judge Warren Martin made a humorous reference to the dimness of the courtroom lighting. "Good afternoon, ladies and gentlemen. We used to have light in this courtroom so you could see. Now it's in the dark. They filmed the *Perry Mason* series in here for a while, and they gussied it up with chandeliers and drapes and fancy paint—and it was nice of 'em to leave the stuff."

Then he read the jurors the law that they must apply to the case. "The elements of the crime of murder in the first degree are: that the defendant, in the city and county of Denver, state of Colorado, between and including the dates of September twenty-seventh and September twenty-eighth, 1996, with intent to cause the death of a person other than herself, and after deliberation, caused the death of that person and another person.

"The elements of murder in the second degree are: that the defendant . . . knowingly caused the death of another person."

Mike Pellow delivered the closing for the prosecution. Reminding the jurors of what they'd sworn to during voir dire, he said, "Is there anyone who believes a sixteen-year-old, attractive young woman could *not* commit murder? And all of you said: No, I don't believe that upfront. I need evidence to decide.

"Well, we all talk the talk in jury selection—and now, as they say, it's time to walk the walk. Because not only can a sixteen-year-old young woman commit murder, but *this* sixteen-year-old young woman, right here, *did* commit murder. And it's time to say so; it's time to hold her accountable for it."

Pellow addressed the seeming inconsistency between Tiffany Lofton's testimony that Jennifer Tombs had shown her the gun and that of the four guys who said they hadn't seen it.

"Now, four boys were in the room and said, 'Oh, I didn't see that gun.' Why? Well, what were the four boys doing? Playing dice for money; gambling; drinking; smoking weed, said one of them—Donald James said. They weren't paying attention to these girls the whole time they were in there."

Tanya Lavallais was no drinker, no devotee of the club scene, and with her strong sense of responsibility, she'd never have gone out partying while leaving Jennifer alone in the house. "She took that job seriously, supervising the defendant," Pellow said. "She was supposed to have her sister and nephew come over and stay the night with her. Why would she get up and leave? She's supposed to go to her brother's own wedding the next afternoon. . . .

"She wouldn't have gone out until four in the morning, and she did not go out at all. She lay dead on the couch in the rec room, until the defendant came down, at some point, and dragged her off the couch onto the floor."

Pellow reminded jurors of a promise made early in the trial by the defense, a promise not kept. "You heard, in opening statement, the defense attorney said, 'There was somebody watching her at all times.' No, there was not—no. She was in and out; music is on; conversations are going; people are talking with each other; they're drinking."

Why didn't anyone in the upstairs room smell gunpowder on the defendant when she came in and said, "Tanya's gone"?

Pellow said, "Gunpowder smell you heard talked about—two floors down this gun was shot. Doors closed. Twenty-five-caliber—doesn't require as much gunpowder for bigger guns . . . it wouldn't be like smoking a cigarette—you couldn't smell it on a person like that.

"And what, according to Donald James, were people doing in that bedroom upstairs? Smoking weed, he said. Anyone on the jury ever smell burning marijuana? Better tell the others. You ain't smelling gunpowder or *anything* else with that marijuana burning in that room.

"And people in the room didn't see blood on

her, either, but there was blood on that Santa Claus shirt."

There was the phone call confession to Jock Johnson. "And finally, about four, four-fifteen, four-thirty, in the morning, she says, 'A woman broke into the house. We had a scuffle. I emptied the clip in her head. She's dead in the basement. I put a bag on her head. I picked up the shells. . . .'

"She confessed to this crime. But there wasn't any scuffle, and it wasn't a woman who broke in. It was Tanya Lavallais lying dead in the basement, with the full clip emptied in her head, with the bag under her head."

The prosecutor spoke of the defendant's "botched cover-up," saying, "Clean up a couch? Why would an intruder, breaking into somebody else's house, kill an occupant in that house—why is that person going and getting detergent out of the laundry room, and trying to clean up the couch?

"Why? That person is trying to beat feet—get out of there as fast as he or she can. They're not staying around, trying to clean up a couch."

And what about the bloodstained black Fila shoes?

"There's blood on the carpet from those shoes," Pellow said. "Her mom's shoes—walking around, down there in the basement, with a dead body, with her mama's shoes on. Now, who else put blood on those shoes? Pastor Tombs wasn't wearing 'em. She wasn't walking around in there in blood. Nobody else was wearing 'em. And they were recovered in that house—there's a photo of 'em in the defendant's bedroom."

Pellow addressed some more evidentiary matters.

"You heard the testimony of the ankle bracelet guy—535 feet away is that storm drain . . . the defendant's got four minutes [window before alarm triggers] to get down there, throw that gun in there. Why get rid of a murder weapon? Why get rid of it?

"Take the stuff out of the trunk of Tanya's car and put it in the front seat—so you can try to put the body in the trunk. She's calling Jock over to help her, 'Help me get rid of the body.' "

He tackled the issues of deliberation and intent that made the killing a case of first-degree murder, Murder One. "She calls a man for a gun, 'Bring me a gun.' She waits for the gun. She gets the gun. She takes it in her house. She loads the clip and puts it in the gun.

"She goes into the rec room. Tanya, most likely from the evidence . . . [is] sitting or lying down. She's got her arms over her head. And the defendant—this young woman right here—shoots her six times in the head, four of which would be fatal. Puts it up to her head. One was so close there was *soot* in that wound. She executes her.

"All that time, thinking about getting the gun, thinking about killing her—shooting her in the head with the gun. Deliberating, intending to do it.

"Call it what it is, folks. Whether it's a thirty-eight-year-old, tattooed, bearded, one-eyed man, or a sixteen-year-old young woman—you call it what it is.

"It's cold-blooded, it's premeditated murder—it's first-degree murder. And it's your duty, as jurors, to hold the killer—Jennifer Lee Tombs—accountable for that murder," Mike Pellow concluded.

Now it was Kurt Metsger's turn to close for the defense. Reminding the jurors of prosecution's requirement to prove the defendant guilty of the crime beyond a reasonable doubt, he argued that the state's theory of the case was impossible.

Calling the murder a "tragedy," he said, "You cannot compound that tragedy by finding somebody guilty that is innocent."

Tiffany Lofton testified that Tanya Lavallais had given permission for the guys to come over that night. The guys were all consistent in saying that they never saw a weapon.

"Why would you show a gun if you intended on using it? It makes absolutely no sense. And the reason is, 'cause there was no gun," Metsger said.

He pointed out that no one claimed to have heard as many as seven noises—Alan Milliner, the only one who thought it sounded like shots, heard three sounds; Willis Wallace said it sounded like a cabinet door; and James said it sounded like a knock on the door.

When Jennifer Tombs came back to the room, she was wearing the same clothes, with no blood on her and no smell of gunpowder, and acting perfectly normal, her demeanor unchanged.

Metsger said, "Tiffany and Willis Wallace are down in the basement. Jennifer takes a bath. Now, how are you supposed to take a bath and not be concerned that there's two people in the house that could discover the body?"

He argued that it made sense only because Tanya was gone—gone out to the clubs with an unknown male friend or associate.

Then there was the matter of the unreturned pages all evening. Metsger said, "The D.A. wants you to believe that Tanya wasn't returning her pages because she was dead, that [otherwise] she was *always* returning her pages. And that's what everybody's testimony was.

"But listen to when they said they started paging her—they started paging her at six-thirty in the evening. They paged her five, ten, fifteen, twenty times an hour, from everyone that was paging her.

"Why didn't she return the pages from six-thirty to nine-thirty? We all know she was around then. She had to have been. Tiffany saw her. Willis Wallace heard her at nine-thirty. For three hours she didn't bother to return anybody's pages. Maybe her pager wasn't working—I don't know. I don't know why she didn't, and that's an unanswered question in this case."

Metsger noted that all the GSR residue tests came up negative on all six people in the house. The coroner had been unable to determine the time of death. "Had the police done their job and not waited until four-thirty in the afternoon to call out the coroner in this case, we might have been able to solve this case. . . .

"But they don't bother—and the reason they don't bother is because, 'Heck—we've got Jennifer Tombs. She's in the house. We don't need any other suspects. Who cares if there were five other people in the house?'"

Defense counsel slammed the police for not taking a sample of the bathwater found in the tub, which according to the prosecution's theory that the defendant did it, might have had gunshot residue or blood traces in it.

He asked, "How reliable is Jock Johnson as a witness?" He argued that Johnson had a "peripheral relationship" with the defendant. "She doesn't talk to him anymore; there is no baby—he's not the father of her child; she's having a relationship with Alan Milliner; she has sex with Milliner that night. . . .

"Jock Johnson never dropped off a gun, and we don't know where that gun came from."

Kurt Metsger hit hard at what he characterized as the defendant's lack of motive for killing the victim. "There is no motive for this—it wasn't party time. And whether or not she decided to have sex at two o'clock in the morning has nothing to do with anything in this case. If Tanya would have been back—yeah, Tanya probably would have nixed it.

"But she [Jennifer Tombs] wasn't planning, 'Hmm—I'm gonna have a party that's okayed, but I really want to have sex with Alan tonight. So I think I'll call Joaquin [Johnson], get a gun over here, kill Tanya, and then Alan can come back at two o'clock.'

"It's absurd! The way they want you to run this is absurd, ladies and gentlemen. Where's Tanya? I don't know. Where'd Tanya get killed? I don't know. Who did it? I don't know. And we wish we did."

Defense counsel scoffed at the notion of a botched cover-up. "There is no botched cover-up by Jennifer Tombs. She admits she hid the gun; she admits she moved the shell casings. The white detergent—what sixteen-year-old girl apparently tries to clean up something with dry detergent?"

Metsger pointed out that the victim weighed 180 pounds, arguing that it would not be possible for Jennifer Tombs to move the body without leaving bloody drag marks in the room and getting blood all over her clothes. While there was a little blood on the shorts she wore Saturday, there was no blood on the pants she wore that previous evening and only a couple of drops on the back of her shirt.

He argued that Jennifer and Tanya grew up together, and that it was not possible that the defendant could shoot her seven times in the head with no emotion.

Summing up, he argued, "The fact of the matter is, is that Jennifer Tombs didn't do this. The district attorney is relying on one person, and that's Jock Johnson, and he is unbelievable. Jennifer Tombs didn't have the time, the motive, the energy or the ability to kill her cousin. She didn't do it, she's innocent—and I beg you to come back with an innocent verdict."

Delivering the state's final close, Henry Cooper said, "The people are not relying on one person in this case—we're relying on Jock Johnson; we're relying on Tiffany Lofton; we're relying on Greg Leberge—we're relying on all the witnesses. . . .

"They [the defense] argue that because everything that happened around this crime is so strange, or so illogical, that means the defendant couldn't have done it. Well, this crime is illogical—

this crime is crazy. And only a person with some type of demon in their head would do this type of crime—somebody that's not thinking clearly all the time, somebody that would put detergent on a couch and think they could get blood out. Somebody that would try to move a body, somebody that would try to open a trunk, and call a friend to come over and help get rid of the body. That's the kind of person who would do this—and that's this defendant."

He described Jennifer Tombs's videotaped interview with the police as "sorry, convoluted, contradictory." To believe the defendant's story, one would have to believe that all the other witnesses were lying.

Credibility?—"Let's look at Jock Johnson," Cooper said, "a young man, a working man—he works as a custodian. Met Jennifer, kind of dated her—but it wasn't an exclusive thing. At a point of time, she tricks him into having a baby—and Mr. Metsger asked, 'Well, why would she have Jock come over to the house to help clean up, instead of Alan?'

"Jock was a sucker—he was a sap. He had believed all along that she had this baby, and she didn't even have one. She knew if there was one guy she could get over there to come help, it was Jock.

"What about Tiffany Lofton? A young girl, friend of the defendant. Why would she come in here and lie? Why? Is there any reason? She's got nothing against Jennifer—she even took Jennifer in at one point in time and let Jennifer live in her house."

It was the defendant who was lying, Cooper argued. "She tells a story that is utterly unbelievable.

She says an unknown person came in the house; does not come, does not blow the horn; no one sees or hears this person—but Tanya leaves with this person—disappears—but doesn't tell anybody where she's going.

"Tanya—a homebody person that doesn't go out, doesn't drink really, responsible to a fault—leaves Ms. Ankle Bracelet, Ms. Probation, Ms. Juvenile Delinquent, at home by herself and goes out partying, and stays out for about six hours—then comes home, drunk and clumsy. . . .

"She [the defendant] goes to bed, and once again this unknown person—that nobody hears, nobody sees—but this defendant comes back in the house—and kills Tanya. She hears booms and thumps that nobody else hears. And this unknown person goes into the laundry room, grabs a box of Trend detergent, puts it on these bloodstains—this intruder does this, then places the box carefully back, up in the laundry room.

"Then, after going to all this trouble to clean up, decides he's gonna leave the gun. Or she's gonna leave the gun. That's what the defendant wants you to believe; that's the story she expects you to believe.

"Then, after all this happens, Errol Vermont, Mark Caisey, Val Vermont, Jock Johnson, Tiffany Lofton—all get together and lie to the police. She says Errol lied, Val lied, Mark lied, Jock lied, Tiffany lied. Everybody lied—it's a huge conspiracy to get her. Poor Jennifer."

Cooper finished by urging the jury to hold the defendant accountable. "It's time to tell this defendant, 'You have committed the most heinous crime known to man. It was motivated by anger, selfishness—an evil desire to do what you wanted. You killed an innocent, truly innocent, beautiful person.

" 'And we, as jurors in this community, are not going to stand for it, and we are going to hold *you* responsible."

In the end, that was what it came down to, the two sides of the coin, angel or devil? Was Jennifer Tombs an innocent victim of the legal process or a baby-faced killer?

The jury received the case at about 3:15 P.M. on Thursday, but they took a walk before beginning their deliberations. They were sent home at about five o'clock that night, returning at 9:00 A.M. on Friday, April 4. They reviewed the defendant's taped interrogation until about 10:45 A.M., worked through lunch, and announced they had reached a verdict at about 2:30 P.M. The total time for deliberations, discounting breaks and review of the tape, was about four hours.

The jurors returned to the courtroom, giving the verdict to the bailiff, who gave it to Judge Martin to read aloud for all to hear:

"Verdict reads as follows: We, the jury, find the defendant, Jennifer Tombs, guilty of murder in the first degree."

The courtroom spectators stirred, clamoring, some applauding. Jennifer Tombs, who'd pretty well kept her cool throughout the trial, crumbled as the verdict sank in. First she looked stunned, then began sobbing, gasping.

She kept sobbing as the sentence was read: life in prison without parole.

A juror later told *Court TV*, "Each one [juror] had something that clicked for them, that convinced them that she was guilty. And for me one of the things was that she tried to clean up the evidence. A killer who comes in off the street and would shoot somebody isn't gonna clean up after himself and try to hide the evidence, and leave the dead body there. . . . They're not gonna just try to clean the bloodstains off the couch and make it look nice, and then leave."

"I got some sort of read into that," the interviewer said. "That she figured out how to tell her mother about the murder, but she couldn't figure out how to get off the hook with her mom 'cause she messed up the sofa."

Defense attorney Kurt Metsger commented afterward, "I think the big deal to the jury was the video statement made by Jennifer. I think they [the prosecution] hinged their case on that. I think that that evidence is what convicted her . . .

"And I think she came off as cold."

Defense attorney Jeff Timlin told an interviewer, "We truly believed, with the investigation that we conducted during the trial, that it was virtually impossible for one person to commit that murder—and we still believe that today.

"We think that someone other than Jennifer committed the crime, but we also think that that wasn't done by one individual person, necessarily.

That there was some assistance at some point in time during that episode.

"Her friends that came in and partied through that evening, and different people that came in and out of the house—what role they play, I'm not so sure we'll ever know. I believe they played a bigger role than anyone wants to admit. It was virtually impossible for one person to commit that murder."

Cocounsel Metsger agreed. "There are certain facts in the case that, if Jennifer was involved in any way, don't add up to her being the sole participant in this. . . .

"I think if it was someone else in the house that killed her, I think it comes down to a bunch of teenagers not thinking. And that that's the type of thought process that they have—We're going to get in trouble—and reacting to it, on impulse."

Prosecutor Henry Cooper later told *Court TV*, "I would describe Jennifer Tombs as a sociopath, manipulative, a cold-blooded killer.

"There was a point in the trial where I just looked at her and I said [to myself] she has this baby face, and look what she did. I mean, she shot a family friend in the head multiple times. You know, the irony was just amazing. . . .

"That's why I think she's a sociopath. She's a person that is morally bankrupt; killing another human being does not make her feel bad. Her only remorse to this day is probably the fact that she got caught.

"She never showed any remorse, and she stated that she was innocent up until the second the verdict was read—and then she was shocked, I think, when she was found guilty."

How did she get that way?

"I don't know," Henry Cooper said. "Maybe she was—maybe some people are just born that way. Maybe it's just something in their brain. . . ."

Val Vermont wept as family and friends tried to console her, finally being escorted from the courtroom flanked by her husband, Errol Vermont, and daughter Tasha Lavallais. Since the murder, Val Vermont's health had collapsed, ultimately leading to the loss of both kidneys, a collapse that she blamed on her daughter's death and its aftermath.

The Vermont family would need to seek elsewhere for spiritual peace. In the months leading up to the trial, Pastor Madlyn Tombs's preaching from the pulpit about her daughter's innocence in the case, and asking the congregation to pray for her acquittal, had alienated the victim's family, causing them to leave the congregation.

Sobbing, handcuffed, Jennifer Tombs was escorted from the courtroom by security officers, one of her lawyers walking beside her. Madlyn Tombs stood outside the courtroom, waiting. Composed, very calm, as she walked beside her weeping daughter, Madlyn Tombs said, "Don't make a statement. . . . And it's not over."

"Yes, it is," Jennifer said.

"It's not over. Remember the day—"

"I don't want to talk about it."

"Okay, let's not talk about it just yet."

Massachusetts v. *Sicari:*
"FRIENDLY TERROR"

THE CRIME

On Thursday, October 2, 1997, in Newton, Massachusetts, police were notified of a developing situation at the local Honda Village car dealership out on the highway. Newton Police Department detective sergeant William Byrne got the call at 5:10 P.M., arriving at the site at about 5:30. Also present on the scene were Newton police officers McCarthy, Cahoon and Garry.

A half dozen or more young white males in their late teens and early twenties were gathered in front of the dealership building. As Byrne later described it, there were "raised voices—confusion, commotion."

The group, whose members came from neighboring Cambridge, Massachusetts, was angrily confronting Honda Village employee Charles Jaynes, twenty-two. Angriest and most confrontational were brothers Robert "Bobby" Curley, twenty, and Shaun Curley, eighteen, whose kid brother, ten-year-old Jeffrey Curley, had been missing since midafternoon of the previous day, and was now the object of an extensive missing person search back in their home turf of East Cambridge.

The object of their animosity, Charles Jaynes, a light-skinned black male, oversize and pudgy, weighing over 250 pounds, was the son of Edward Jaynes, the owner and operator of Cojack's car reconditioning studio, a part of Honda Village. Worried about the increasingly volatile confrontation, someone at the dealership had called the police.

The Curley brothers yelled at Jaynes, demanding to know what had happened to their missing ten-year-old brother, Jeff. As near as the investigating officers could tell, the Curley brothers and their friends thought Jaynes knew something about the disappearance.

Prominently featured in the fracas, taking so active a part that police at first thought he, too, was a Curley relative, was Salvatore "Salvy" or "Sal" Sicari, twenty-one, a short, wiry man with black curly hair and beard, wearing a blue hooded sweatshirt. Sicari, part of the Cambridge crowd, had spent a good part of his early years growing up in the house next door to the Curley family, and he now lived two blocks away. They all were part of a tightly knit neighborhood, though in the past there had been no love lost between Sicari and the older Curley brothers. But past differences seemed to have been forgotten in the current crisis.

Cambridge, Massachusetts, is the site of two of the most prestigious learning centers in the world: Harvard University and the Massachusetts Institute of Technology (MIT). But there are other parts of the town unrelated to academia, such as the blue-collar, working-class neighborhood of East Cambridge.

Here lived Robert Curley Sr., a firehouse mechanic, his wife Barbara, and their three sons: Bobby, Shaun and Jeffrey. The parents had separated a year earlier, with the three Curley boys living with their mother. Jeff's big brothers tried to keep an eye on him and so did others in the neighborhood. Robert Curley continued to work nearby as a mechanic in the local Inman Square firehouse.

Jeff Curley, four feet seven inches, with red hair and bright blue eyes, was a fifth-grader at nearby Charles G. Harrington school. He played catcher for the Little League–champion Marlins, and also played hockey and basketball. He seemed to be a normal, ordinary kid, maybe more streetwise than some. He spent a lot of time hanging out in the street. He loved riding his bike. This summer, he hadn't had much luck with bikes—three of them had already been stolen from him, and his mother was in no hurry to reward what she thought of as his "carelessness" by replacing them with another. He'd told some of his pals that he thought he knew how to get a bike.

On Wednesday, October 1, 1997, early in the afternoon, Jeff's brothers were leaving the house to go get a car part. He wanted to tag along, but they told him to go hose down the family dog, a rottweiler, which was now staying around the corner at the house of their grandmother Muriel Francis. Jeff went there and washed the dog, using a garden hose.

At about 3:00 P.M., he'd said to his grandmother,

"I have to go do something—I'll be back in a little while."

That was the last she saw of him. That was the last time any of his friends and relatives saw him.

He didn't come home for dinner. Robert Curley Sr. called all of Jeff's friends, with no result. His brothers and their friends scoured the neighborhood for him, also coming up blank. Concern deepened from anxiety into fear. At about 11:30 P.M., Barbara Curley phoned Cambridge police to report that Jeffrey was missing.

A large-scale search was organized. An integral part of the effort to find Jeff Curley involved distributing flyers bearing a picture of his face. Night passed with no news of the missing boy, no release of the ever-grinding tension.

Arriving at the station for the day shift on Thursday, October 2, Cambridge Police Department sergeant Lester Sullivan first learned that a ten-year-old boy was missing. Dressed in plainclothes attire and driving an unmarked car, Sullivan went to the Curley family residence on East Hampshire Street in Cambridge, arriving at about 9:35 A.M. Speaking to family members, he learned that the missing boy still had not yet been found. He searched the house, contacted Jeff Curley's school, made arrangements for hospitals to be called, and had investigators canvass the area to see if they could locate the boy.

Sullivan went to a mobile command post that had been set up nearby to coordinate search efforts. Concerned friends and neighbors were out in the street, passing out flyers with pictures of the missing boy. The most asked question, "Anything new about the kid?" continued to be answered only in the negative.

At 11:15 A.M., Sullivan returned to the Curley house. Inside, in the hallway leading to the living room, stood a group of family and neighbors, among them Sal Sicari. Clutching a handful of the Curley boy's missing-person flyers, Sicari approached the officer. His demeanor was upbeat, enthusiastic and helpful.

Sal Sicari was a neighborhood guy, an unemployed house painter living in a house on Market Street with his mother, sister and younger brother, Bobbie. In school, they used to call Sicari "Pigpen." His friends called him "Salvi." He had two different children by two different mothers. He knew the Curleys. Years ago, when they'd been next-door neighbors, there'd been some bad blood between then.

Now, Sicari jumped into the search. Going to the Curley house earlier this morning, he'd kissed Barbara Curley, grabbed a stack of flyers, and gone outside to distribute them, handing them out to passersby.

Sicari told Sullivan he had information regarding the missing child. For reasons of privacy and confidentiality, Sullivan asked him to accompany him outside to his unmarked police vehicle.

Seated inside the car with the plainclothes cop, Sicari said that he'd seen Curley yesterday, sometime in midafternoon. In fact, Sicari said, young Curley, walking the dog, had threatened to sic it on him, causing him to jump a fence to get away. Sicari had then picked up a brick and told Curley to keep the dog off him or he'd mess him up. Curley had then pulled the dog to heel and walked away.

Shortly thereafter, Sicari had encountered one Charles Jaynes, standing near his parked Cadillac. Jaynes wasn't from the neighborhood, but he'd been hanging around a lot lately. In summer and September 1997, he'd been hanging out with Jeff Curley; they'd been seen driving around in Jaynes's car and Jaynes had promised to buy Jeff a bike.

Sicari and Jaynes had then gone to the Boston Public Library and they'd hung around together for the rest of the day and night. Sicari said he'd last seen Jaynes this morning.

This was the information told to Sullivan by Sal Sicari. Sicari next attempted to beep Jaynes from Sullivan's phone and gave him the number. Jaynes was paged but didn't answer. After ten minutes, Sicari and Sullivan got out of the car. Sullivan had his phone with him, but Jaynes didn't return the page.

Sullivan walked with Sicari to the latter's residence on Market Street, a five-minute walk. They went inside, where Sicari again paged Jaynes. Sullivan waited about ten minutes for a call that never came, then left.

Immediately after departing, Sullivan contacted Cambridge Police Department sergeant Patrick Nagle, assigned to the Homicide Unit. Proceeding to the locale, Nagle found Sal Sicari standing in the middle of the street, handing out missing-person flyers. He took him aside and they spoke for thirty to forty minutes, Sicari essentially repeating what he'd already told Sullivan. He, too, found Sicari helpful and enthusiastic. Sicari gave Nagle Jaynes's beeper number.

Nagle returned to the station. At about 12:55 P.M., he first contacted Charles Jaynes, speaking to him on the telephone, telling him that he wanted to ask him some questions about a ten-year-old boy named Jeffrey Curley. Jaynes said that he didn't know any Curley.

Nagle called Sal Sicari around 2:10 P.M., asking him to come downtown. Sicari was agreeable, so Nagle sent two detectives to pick him up and give him a ride to the station. Sicari went to the third-floor detective bureau, and at about 3:10 P.M. once more retold his story about yesterday's meeting with Jeff Curley and his dog. After meeting up with Charles Jaynes, he said, they had gone to the Boston Public Library so Jaynes could meet with his girlfriend, Laurie Pistorino. Afterward they drove to Honda Village, staying there from 4:40 through 8:40 P.M. They went to a liquor store, then drove to New Hampshire.

Sicari said that he'd met Jaynes two years ago when he lived in Brockton, Massachusetts, and that for the last few months they'd been hanging out quite a bit. He said that he'd seen Jeff Curley with Jaynes in his car about two weeks earlier, and that he'd told Curley to go home and that he shouldn't be hanging with older people. Then he told Jaynes that it didn't look right—him driving young kids around in the car.

The interview ended at 3:45 P.M., Nagle thanked Sicari, who declined the offer of a ride home and left the station.

Now later that same day, Sal Sicari was once again in the foreground, this time with the Curley brothers. In fact, it seemed as if he was the one who'd brought them down here, to confront Charles Jaynes in an encounter fraught with potential violence. Only the timely arrival of the local law had helped cool down the scene.

While sorting out the participants' various stories, police learned there were a number of outstanding default warrants on Jaynes—he was wanted for passing some seventy-five or so bad checks. He was arrested and advised of his rights.

Jaynes was transported to the Newton police station. "Pursuant to department policy" that the vehicles of all arrested persons be impounded and towed to the station for an inventory search, Jaynes's gray Cadillac was hauled to the station house garage by Towie's Towing Service.

At Honda Village, Sgt. Byrne decided that "because of the large traffic jam and the yelling, I would ask everyone to proceed back to the police station so we could sort everything out."

Arriving at the Newton police station, Byrne went to the detective bureau on the second floor, where he was soon joined by Sal Sicari and the Curley brothers. Later, Sgt. Byrne went with Officers McCarthy and Aucoin to search Jaynes's gray Cadillac. As McCarthy did the search, Aucoin noted down the contents, and Byrne observed.

The search of the car yielded among other things a wallet, found in the glove compartment, containing a driver's license made out to one "Anthony Scaccia." But the face on the thumbnail-sized ID photo was that of Charles Jaynes. A library card and video store card were also made out to Scaccia.

Also in the wallet were four receipts, all for items purchased with the credit card of Edward Jaynes,

Charles Jaynes's father. Ominously, in view of Charles Jaynes's alleged linkage with the missing boy, the items were: a receipt from Bradlees for a Rubbermaid container; a receipt from a Home Depot for bags of cement and lime; a receipt for a bicycle purchased from International Bicycle; and a receipt from an Osco Drug Store for cigars and No Doz pills.

All of these purchases were made on October 1, the day of Jeff Curley's disappearance.

The search also yielded a pamphlet from NAMBLA, the North American Man-Boy Love Association.

When questioned, Jaynes said that he'd spent Wednesday, October 1, with Sal Sicari, and that he did, in fact, know Jeffrey Curley, but denied ever seeing him on that date. When asked about the receipted purchases, he asked for a lawyer.

Meanwhile, as the hunt for Jeffrey Curley continued, the Cambridge police station was a hive of activity. The State Police had gotten involved, and so had the FBI.

While Sicari was at the Newton police station, Cambridge homicide investigator Sgt. Nagle spoke to him on the phone. Sicari said he wanted to talk to Charles Jaynes. Nagle said, "Jaynes is under arrest and would you like to talk to me?"

Sicari said yes. Nagle sent a patrol car to pick him up, taking him to the station. He was not under arrest and could have left anytime, but he chose not to. As before, he was enthusiastic about helping out, and still cooperative.

He arrived at the Cambridge police station on October 2 at about 7:00 P.M., where he waived his Miranda rights and began to speak. He talked readily, without a lawyer, as he continued to deny knowing anything about Curley's disappearance. The questioning continued, off and on, for five to six hours.

Sicari finally even agreed to take a lie detector test. But the polygraph test didn't work out well—the results indicated deception. Sicari was starting to "breathe hard," according to one observer.

He hid his face in his hands, sobbing. At about 12:30 A.M., October 3, he was confronted with the fact that police knew about the receipt for concrete and lime that was bought at Home Depot. At this point, those present agreed he said something like "Fuck it, you might as well lock me up." Later, individual recollections of what exactly he'd said would differ.

Sicari fell silent, remaining so for a half hour, after which he began talking again. Now he had a different tale to tell—a ghastly one. Charles Jaynes was a pedophile, he said. On Wednesday, October 1, 1997, at about 3:30 P.M., he and Jaynes had picked Jeffrey Curley up at his grandmother's house in Jaynes's Cadillac. Jaynes drove; Sicari was in the front passenger seat. Curley got in, believing he was to receive $50 and a bicycle from Jaynes.

Sicari said he ducked down as Curley entered the car, for fear that Curley's grandmother would see him.

The ten-year-old had been hanging around a lot with both men lately, especially with Jaynes. Sometimes they'd go to Honda Village, where employees had observed the boy alone with Jaynes, and sometimes together with Jaynes and Sicari. "They were buddies." They'd horse around in the new cars and go down into the basement garage.

Jaynes had been promising that he'd buy Curley a bike ("If I do something for him," Curley had told others). Curley had gone out riding with both Jaynes and Sicari many times, so there was no difficulty in coaxing the boy into the car on that Wednesday afternoon.

The three drove from Cambridge to the Boston Public Library, where Jaynes's girlfriend worked. While Jaynes went inside, Sicari said that he told Curley to stay away from Jaynes and forget about the bike and the $50—that he, Sicari, would get him the money and the bike.

When Jaynes returned, they drove to a Newton gas station for a fill-up. Sicari said he saw Jaynes surreptitiously soak a rag with gasoline while filling up at the self-service pump. Next they went to a parking lot behind a hardware store, to relieve themselves. All three got out of the car to urinate.

The next he knew, as Sicari told it, Charles Jaynes had grabbed Jeffrey Curley and was forcing him into the backseat of the car. Sicari dashed around the vehicle, closing all four doors. He got behind the wheel, zooming off.

In the backseat, the 250-plus-pound Jaynes lay atop the seventy-seven-pound youngster, crushing him. The assailant held a gas-soaked rag covering the boy's nose and mouth, forcing him to inhale the fumes soaking the rag. According to Sicari's version, Jaynes said, "Don't fight it, kid, don't fight it."

Sicari was afraid of getting caught, especially when he noticed in his rearview mirror a police car coming up behind him. Apparently, the police car was still a long way off and was uninterested in the gray Cadillac, for Sicari said he put on a burst of speed, distancing the car and losing it.

Sicari kept driving around while the scene played itself out to its lethal conclusion. It took about twenty minutes for Curley to die, he said. Jaynes rose up into view from behind the backseat, saying, "The kid's not going to con a conner—he thought he was going to get a bike and fifty dollars for nothing."

They drove to another parking lot, where Jaynes made Sicari get in the backseat while he drove. The car stopped at a hardware store, where Jaynes bought some rolls of duct tape and a 9' x 12' canvas tarpaulin.

Returning to the parked car, Jaynes used duct tape to secure the gas-soaked rag over Curley's nose and mouth. At about 4:40 P.M., Jaynes went to work at his job at Honda Village's Cojack's reconditioning studio. Usually, he'd drive his car down the ramp and into the garage area, parking it there. This time, he went against his usual pattern, parking his car out on the street.

While Jaynes was at work, Sal Sicari toiled over the body, rolling it up inside the tarp and placing it in the Cadillac's trunk. He waited outside for Jaynes to return, which he did at about 8:30 P.M. They then drove to several stores to purchase items needed for disposing of the body. Each of these purchases was made with Jaynes's father's American Express card.

The two first went to a Bradlees in Watertown, Massachusetts. They didn't go to the nearer local Bradlees in Somerville—Barbara Curley worked there as a store supervisor. Here they bought a fifty-gallon Rubbermaid container to hold Curley's body. Sicari said that while in the store, Jaynes said "he *would* spend the forty dollars on the kid [after all]".

At a Home Depot in Somerville, they bought bags of lime and cement. An Osco Drug Store yielded cigars and No Doz pills. That was their last stop in Massachusetts.

Jaynes drove, with Sicari on the passenger side, arriving at about midnight at Jaynes's apartment in Manchester, New Hampshire, on Elm Street, an apartment that Jaynes had taken under a phony name. Jaynes carried the bags of lime and cement upstairs, Sicari carried the container, and they both carried the body up to the apartment.

The place was furnished with *The Lion King* posters and pinup posters of teen-boy TV stars. The duo put the body on the kitchen floor, opened the tarp, and then Charles Jaynes stripped Curley's body naked. Jaynes then defiled the child's corpse, fondling the dead boy's penis, performing anal sex on him, and inserting a lubricated beer bottle up his rectum.

Sicari said the sight of it made him ill. When he ran to the bathroom, Jaynes said, "Don't be a baby. Come out here and help me—he's [Curley] starting to stiffen up."

Souvenirs were taken: a jeans label and button, cut off from Curley's jeans. Cement was mixed and poured into the bottom of the Rubbermaid container; then the body was stuffed inside, limbs folded and cramped. Sicari said he heard bones snap as the corpse was crammed into the box.

They put lime on the boy's face, his eyes and mouth, to hasten decomposition and unrecognizability. The lid was put into place and secured with strands of duct wrapped around it.

Around 2:00 A.M., the container with the boy's body in it was loaded into the trunk of the Cadillac as Jaynes and Sicari prepared to get rid of it. Not right away, though. They saw two women coming out of a bar and talked with them, Sicari trying to persuade one of them to come back with him to Jaynes's apartment. But Jaynes's "rudeness" and attitude turned the girls off, so they left.

Now, at 3:00 A.M., Jaynes and Sicari got back to business. Sicari said that Jaynes pulled out a map, pointed to a location with a red line on it, and said, "There's water here. . . . We'll dump the container there."

At 3:15 A.M., with Jaynes at the wheel, they began the drive into Maine. Sicari became disoriented, losing his sense of direction, but he remembered seeing a state symbol on a sign that "looked like a badge."

At about 4:15 A.M., they stopped at a Bickford's restaurant near a Howard Johnson's, where they got out and dumped the empty bags of lime and cement and some of Curley's clothes in a Dumpster.

Somehow, they managed to lock themselves out of the car, and Jaynes had to go inside and borrow a wire coat hanger with which to unlock the door. Sicari stayed outside, out of sight. They unlocked the car and drove away.

At about 4:30 A.M., they pulled into an Exxon

station in Portsmouth, New Hampshire, where Jaynes hailed a truck driver, calling him over to the car to ask him if he knew of any cheap motels along the route. The trucker said no.

Jaynes and Sicari drove some more, finally coming to a two-lane bridge over a river out in the woods somewhere. They pulled over to the side of the road and then came back to the bridge. It was sometime between 5:15 and 5:30 A.M.

Sicari and Jaynes popped the trunk, got out of the Cadillac, lifted the container out of the trunk, and rested it on the bridge's guardrail. They tipped it over the edge and let it drop into the waters below. There was a big splash, and a light came on in a nearby house—had they been heard?

Nobody came out to investigate. The duo got in the car and drove back toward Cambridge. Twenty minutes later, Sicari entered the local Doverpoint variety store, which had just opened up, and bought a pastry. He was their first customer of the day.

Sicari said that before Jaynes dropped him off at his house, he suggested that Sicari stop by Curley's mother's house "and ask her where Jeffrey is," so as to torture her. By 11:00 A.M., he was back in Cambridge at Curley's house, with a stack of missing-person flyers, handing them out to passing cars. He also began focusing attention on Charles Jaynes.

At the conclusion of his statement, at about 3:00 A.M., Sal Sicari was charged with murder and ordered held without bail.

On Friday, October 3, the search for the missing boy became a search for a missing body. The night before, while making his statement, Sicari had cockily said that he should get a few years off his sentence for leading them to the body. Trouble was, now he couldn't find the locale, claiming he'd been disoriented and confused on the night of the body-dump. He drove around with detectives for several hours that morning, visiting several rivers in Maine, but was unable to identify which if any was the Great Works River. The body remained unfound.

Also that day, Charles Jaynes's Manchester apartment was searched by New Hampshire police. The search was videotaped. Investigators found Jeff Curley's football jersey (with gasoline on it), a button and label from his jeans, and the label from a Rubbermaid container. Also found were several rolls of duct tape, both used and unused; a stirring spoon with cement residue on it; and a Coors Lite bottle and petroleum jelly. The bottle was used to molest the dead body, according to Sicari.

State Police detective sergeant Greg Foley, a twenty-four-year law enforcement veteran, whose last sixteen years had been as an investigator, was supervisor of the Jeff Curley case. Now that it was officially classed as a homicide, it fell under the jurisdiction of the State Police and the District Attorney's Office.

The FBI, too, was involved, policy being that the Bureau gets called in on missing child and exploited child cases. The boy was actually reported missing on Wednesday night, October 1. The FBI was called in the following morning and began to assist the Cambridge Police. Later that afternoon, with certain developments indicating that there could be foul play involved, the State Police and D.A.'s Office were called in to assist.

Foley supervised the search for Curley's body, a tri-state five-day team effort. He had five children himself. As he later told *Court TV*, "This was a heinous, heinous crime. It was brutal. It's every parent's worst nightmare. It's every police officer's worst nightmare.

"We were involved in the search for six of the seven days. For five of those days, we searched day and night.

"It was an all-out effort by the Massachusetts State Police, the Cambridge Police, the Newton Police. When we crossed the state line into New Hampshire, we got unbelievable cooperation from the New Hampshire State Police, the Portsmouth Police Department and several others. And the Maine State Police also joined in that investigation.

"We used numerous divers from all three states, we used helicopter pilots from all three states, canine units. We had command posts and command personnel there to search the banks of the rivers [in case the body had washed up on shore]. We covered numerous waterways, numerous bridges and roadways."

Police searched from Friday, October 3, through Sunday, October 5, in numerous New Hampshire and Maine waterways. On Sunday, they did a test drop of a container similarly rigged to the one described by Sicari, lining it with cement, adding a bag of lime, plus seventy-five pounds of dry cement to simulate Jeff Curley's body weight. They then rolled duct tape around the container several times.

It was tossed off a bridge on Route One in Kittery, Maine.

The drop was much longer than the South Berwick bridge where the body-dump had taken place, and the water was moving fast. When the box hit the water, the top blew off. The box filled with water, sinking about twenty-five yards from the bridge itself. Investigators figured the container with Curley's body would do likewise.

"It was an exhaustive, exhaustive—and at times frustrating—effort," Foley later recalled. "We went three days around the clock. And at the end of the third day, we were actually in the right location . . . in South Berwick, Maine. We had our divers go into that water, and they only went about twenty-five to thirty yards from the bridge, which is where we were hoping and expecting to find the container."

It was late in the day. The divers had been at it for three days, nonstop, for eight to ten hours a day. Searchers called it a day, sending the divers home for some rest. They took the fourth day off to strategize; then on Tuesday, October 7, they had a full Maine State Police dive team go into the waterway in the Great Works River.

Foley said, "It was a beautiful day. It was sunny and bright and warm. Most of us were in shirt sleeves. It was a beautiful fall day. The leaves were starting to turn, and the leaves were falling into the water. It was a beautiful fall day."

Diver Matthew Grant was in the water when he felt a tug on his line—nestled on the bottom of the river was the Rubbermaid container. About 150 feet away from the bridge, a tree with submerged roots had caught the box that held the body of Jeffrey Curley.

Unlike the test demo, the shorter drop from the bridge had kept the container from coming open. There was a bit of a current and the box had a bit of buoyancy, causing it to travel a little farther than investigators had expected.

"It was a stressful and frustrating search at times, and that was the culmination of it, and most people were very relieved to have found him," Foley said.

Curley family members, grandmother Muriel Francis, a couple of aunts and cousins, were right there, standing on the bridge over the waterway, when the container was found. They became emotional, hugging each other.

Curley's parents were back in Cambridge, where the news was broken to them by D.A. Tom Reilly.

Crime scene technicians were very careful about taking the container out of the water, not wanting to disturb any possible evidence, including maybe even evidence inside the water that was in the container (i.e., fingerprints, hairs and fibers that might've gotten caught up on the sticky part of the tape). Six to eight divers in the water were assisted by numerous persons on the riverbank. The container was put on a grate and lifted up out of the water, while being photographed in and out of the water.

It was loaded onto a Massachusetts State Police dive team truck and was transported to Augusta, Maine, to the Maine Medical Examiner's Office, where it was tested and analyzed from the outside-in, ultimately being opened to reveal the body of Jeff Curley.

Performing the autopsy on Curley, in Augusta, Dr. Henry Ryan, the state of Maine's Chief Medical Examiner, found that the cause of death was gasoline poisoning by inhalation. Remnants of concrete clung to the boy's body and there was lime in his throat.

The Curley's East Hampshire Street house became a kind of shrine, where hundreds of friends, neighbors and strangers came to express their solidarity with the grieving family.

Jeffrey Curley's funeral was held that Saturday.

Much later, Robert Curley Sr. told *Court TV*, "I remember him [Sal Sicari] growing up. He was always an oddball and actually I felt kind of bad for him. . . . He just seemed odd, everybody in our neighborhood was involved in some type of activity and he never seemed to be involved in anything.

"It struck me as odd . . . you just can't imagine something like this, somebody being this far out of the ordinary."

Prosecutors charged Sicari with first-degree murder and kidnapping. Massachusetts's joint venture doctrine applied in this situation. Although the commonwealth believed that Sicari did the actual killing, it conceded that it could not prove definitively that he was the killer. However, if Jaynes was the killer, Sicari was still guilty of first-degree murder as a joint venturer—that he shared the intent to kill, aided in the commission of the murder, and thus was just as responsible for it as Jaynes.

Not long after the arrests, Jaynes and Sicari became the poster boys for a legislative attempt to reinstate the death penalty in Massachusetts. Robert Curley and the rest of the family were strong advocates of the restoration bill, which was instantly engulfed in fierce public debate and controversy.

On October 21, 1997, the state senate debated the bill for six hours, while the Curleys watched from the gallery. The next day, in a rally in front of the State House, the family presented acting governor Paul Celluci, another powerful advocate of the measure, with a pro–death penalty petition with 8,600 signatures.

On November 6, 1997, the measure was defeated by one vote, the result of a last-minute defection from the pro–death penalty camp by Rep. John Slattery (D-Peabody), producing an 80–80 tie that doomed the bill, dashing its supporters' hopes.

At the December 17, 1997, joint arraignment of the two suspects, both Jaynes and Sicari pleaded innocent to the charges. The proceedings were disrupted when Bobby Curley, believing Sicari had "winked" at him, began swearing at the defendant, and had to be removed by court officers.

Later in December, Bobby and Shaun Curley were arrested for going to Sicari's sister's house and brandishing a hammer and baseball bat. Both were charged with assault with a dangerous weapon.

THE TRIAL

The trial would be held in Middlesex Superior Court, not far from the East Cambridge neighborhood where the victim had lived. Sicari defense lawyer Arthur Kelly made a motion for a change of

venue, requesting that the proceedings be moved
to the western part of the state, arguing that pretrial publicity had made it impossible to empanel
a fair and objective jury that was not prejudiced
against his client.

Judge Judith A. Cowin denied the motion. Earlier, also appearing before the judge, Kelly had argued that Sicari's confession had been obtained by
coercive means, after he'd first stopped talking for
a half hour, and should be thrown out. That motion, too, was denied.

Sal Sicari was charged with the kidnapping and
first-degree murder of Jeffrey Curley. Two lesser
charges were added, namely, second-degree murder
and felony murder second degree (with the under-
lying felony of kidnapping). Joint venture theory
would apply to the lesser included charges as well.

A conviction for first-degree murder carried an
automatic sentence of life imprisonment without
possibility of parole.

Second-degree murder carried a sentence of life
imprisonment with parole possible after fifteen
years.

Kidnapping was a felony punishable by a maximum sentence of not more than ten years.

Sicari's and Jaynes's trials were severed, with each
to be tried separately, under the law that states that
if two codefendants are charged with a like offense
and one defendant has made inculpatory statements about the other, then the cases are tried
separately, so the statement doesn't come in against
the other defendant.

As the trial's start date in late October 1998 approached, both the prosecution and defense had

their strategies in place. The Commonwealth of Massachusetts alleged that Sicari killed Curley and tried to blame it on Jaynes. Assistant District Attorney David Yanetti further maintained that, in any case, it didn't matter who actually did what to Curley. Under the theory of joint venture, both were equally culpable, and Sicari shared with Jaynes the intent necessary to dispose of Curley's body.

The prosecution argued that Sicari was a joint venturer by his own statement, when he'd said that when Jaynes grabbed Curley, he'd closed all the car doors, gotten in and driven away, further seeking to evade a police car nearby—clear evidence that Sicari aided Jaynes in the commission of the murder. Yanetti also claimed that Sicari and Jaynes jointly decided that they were going to seduce Curley weeks before the killing—that they planned it. He claimed that the purchase of a bicycle prior to the killing was proof of the above, that it was bait with which to lure Curley into the car on October 1, 1997. Other witnesses would testify that Sicari and Jaynes had made statements indicating their sexual interest in Curley.

Honda Village employees would testify that on multiple occasions, Sal Sicari and/or Charles Jaynes were seen palling around with Curley at the dealership. Sicari and Jaynes were cohorts, and their actions on October 1, 1997, and the next-day aftermath were one and the same.

Prosecutor Yanetti opined, "I think it's fair to say, in the weeks leading up to October 1, 1997, there is evidence to show that Sicari exerted some type of control over Jeff Curley and that that was his mind-set when he and Jaynes picked up Curley on October first.''

The commonwealth also alleged that Curley was molested before and/or after he was dead, by Sicari and/or Jaynes.

Defense attorney Arthur Kelly denied that Sicari was a joint venturer as to the killing, claiming that he in no way cooperated with Charles Jaynes or shared any intent to harm Curley. Sicari was telling the truth in his October 3, 1997, statement to police. Sicari did not kill Curley and had no idea that Jaynes was going to do so.

Sicari conceded that he did nothing to prevent the killing, and that he helped Jaynes cover it up by assisting in preparing the body for disposal and throwing it in the river, but that he was not responsible for the boy's death.

Charles Jaynes, an overt pedophile and member of NAMBLA, was alone in planning to seduce and perhaps even murder Curley. There was nothing to support prosecution's claim that Sal Sicari was a pedophile—rather, he was a "well-adjusted" heterosexual male with former girlfriends and who had always treated kids well.

The defense would produce witnesses to testify that it was not Jaynes and Sicari who were hanging out with Curley at Honda Village in the weeks preceding the boy's disappearance, but rather, Charles Jaynes alone with Curley. The bicycle was a gift for another, much younger boy, Sicari's ex-girlfriend's son; it had training wheels and would have been inappropriate for a veteran rider like Jeff Curley.

Shawna Clemens, an old acquaintance of Jaynes's, would claim that long before Jaynes knew Sal Sicari, he'd said to her that if he ever killed someone, he would dispose of the body by putting it in a container with cement and dumping it in a river.

The defense also claimed that there were insufficient grounds to warrant the kidnapping charge. Kelly said Curley had been in Jaynes's Cadillac many times previously, and there was no evidence to suggest that Curley didn't voluntarily enter the car on October 1, 1997.

The trial of Sal Sicari began at the Middlesex County Courthouse on Monday, October 26, 1998.

Opening for the prosecution, Assistant District Attorney David Yanetti said, "This is about seduction that led to murder—two grown men seducing a young boy with a bicycle and trying to have sex with him. When he refused, they murdered him."

On Wednesday, October 1, 1997, at 3:15 P.M., Jeffrey Curley was alive when he was picked up by the defendant and Charles Jaynes in the latter's Cadillac, Yanetti said, continuing, "We will prove that within one hour, Jeffrey Curley was dead—his skin blistered and burned by gasoline—vapors of gas going into his lungs, then in his vital organs and bloodstream—so he couldn't function and then he died."

The seduction began weeks before. "During the month of September 1997, there were many witnesses to the unnatural relationship between these two men and this ten-year-old boy. . . . This unnatural relationship meant giving him [Curley] rides and bringing him to the car dealership and letting him play with cars, and taking him to dinner and promising him a bicycle."

Witnesses would testify about incidents where defendant Sal Sicari body-slammed young Curley into a car hood, and another time when he locked the boy in the trunk of Charles Jaynes's car and revved the motor until neighbors made him desist.

Fabio Selvig, an employee of International Bicycle, would tell how on Friday, September 26, Jaynes and Sicari came in to make a final payment on a boy's bicycle.

"That brings us to October 1, 1997, a Wednesday," Yanetti said. "Tashika Ellis will say that on that day she was in the neighborhood, at two-thirty in the afternoon, taking a walk with Sal Sicari, when they ran into Jeff Curley and a confrontation took place between Curley and Sicari. Curley pretended to sic his dog on Sicari and Sicari got angry and yelled at Curley, and then Sicari and Ellis walked on.

"They went around the corner and then saw Charles Jaynes in the neighborhood, leaning against his Cadillac."

Sicari stayed to talk with Jaynes, while Ellis walked on, returning ten minutes later to find the two males still talking. They gave her a ride home to her Market Street house next to Sicari's. She saw them drive away in the direction of the playground.

"Jeff Curley told his grandmother he would be back in a little while," Yanetti said. "Sicari and Jaynes pulled up on his grandmother's street and we will prove they picked up Jeffrey Curley, and

Jeffrey Curley never returned to Cambridge alive again."

Later, when Jaynes went to work, he broke his usual custom of parking his car in the basement of the dealership. Yanetti said, "His Cadillac was on the street instead. They did that because they didn't want anyone to find the body in the trunk of the car."

Jaynes and the defendant went to Bradlees in Watertown, where they bought a Rubbermaid container to dispose of the body. "There was a video camera on the counter where they bought their purchase," Yanetti told the jury, promising, "You will see both of them on videotape. We will prove they needed that container to dispose of Curley's body.

"Then they went to the Home Depot in Somerville. There was also a video camera there, at the counter where they bought their purchases. . . . You will learn that Jaynes and Sicari bought concrete and lime.

"They needed a container to put Curley in it and needed lime to put it in Curley's mouth to prepare him for burial."

At Osco Drug Store, the two bought cigars and No Doz—"Because they had much more work to do that night."

While they were making those purchases, they made pay-phone calls, including one that Sicari made to his girlfriend, Charlene LeTourneau. She'd been immunized and would testify about what had been said during that call.

Returning to Cambridge after the body-dump, Sicari began a cover-up, which soon collapsed, Yanetti said. "Sicari told police in early evening [of October 2] that he knew Jaynes wanted to have sex with Curley and that he promised Curley fifty dollars to have sex with him.

"At twelve-thirty in the morning, Sgt. Lester Sullivan said, 'Tell us about the bag of lime and concrete you bought.' Sicari put his head down for thirty minutes, he was silent for thirty minutes—we will prove he needed that time to think about his next move, and the next words he said were, 'I'm guilty, but I didn't kill Jeffrey, Charles Jaynes did.' Then he told another story."

The sealed box hauled out from the Great Works River was taken to Augusta, Maine, where it was opened under the direction of Chief Medical Examiner Ryan. "Inside, they found the body of Curley—contorted in cement and water—lying naked, dead, skin reddened, burned and blistered from gasoline," Yanetti said.

"Two men picked him [Curley] up on October 1, 1997, at three-fifteen—two men bought the instrument of his death, gasoline—two men murdered him—two men tried their best to cover it up, but two men got caught and two men are guilty.

"At the close of this trial, I will ask you to find one of those men, Sal Sicari, guilty of murder in the first degree and nothing else," Yanetti said.

In his opening, defense attorney Arthur Kelly tried to inoculate his client somewhat from the heinousness of the crime by conceding in so many words that Sal Sicari was indeed a dirty, no-good louse, but that whatever else he was, he was not the killer of Jeff Curley.

Kelly said, "The actions of Sal Sicari on October first and second are reprehensible—he could have prevented this death—and his actions were disgusting, despicable, inexcusable and criminal, *but he did not kill that child.* . . .

"He was there, he didn't stop it, *but he did not kill that child.* He purchased the concrete and the lime and he helped dispose of the body, *but he did not kill this child.*"

Not Sicari but his friend Charles Jaynes was the killer. "Jeffrey Curley was a loving ten-year-old boy and in the summer of 1997 he was befriended by a three-hundred-pound monster—Charles Jaynes.

"Jaynes took him to Honda Village many times when Sicari wasn't present. People thought it was unnatural.

"What Mr. Yanetti didn't tell you is that a parade of witnesses will say that Charles Jaynes was a pedophile—preys among young boys for sex, boys ages ten to eighteen. And from the beginning, he seduced Curley and he used Sal Sicari to some extent. . . .

"Jaynes said he wanted to do that kid. You will hear about his apartment in Manchester, New Hampshire . . . on Elm Street . . . you will see kids' toys and posters on the wall from *The Lion King.* He was a member of NAMBLA: the North American Man-Boy Love Association.

"No one will say these things about Sicari—just about Jaynes."

Jaynes was the killer. "The medical examiner will say inhalation of gas killed him [Curley] and that someone sat on the child and killed him—that was Charles Jaynes—he's a three-hundred-pound monster. He sat on Jeffrey Curley and killed him."

The opening statements delivered, a morning recess followed. When court resumed, the prosecution called its first witness, Barbara Curley, the victim's mother. She said that she knew Sal Sicari from around the neighborhood, and identified him in court. Questioning established that Jeffrey Curley had had three bikes stolen from him during the summer of 1997.

The witness said, "He [Jeff Curley] said a friend of Salvy's was going to give him a bicycle."

Yanetti said, "And what did you tell him?"

"That no one gives you a bike without wanting something in return and that he was not going to take that bike."

On October 1, 1997, at some time between 2:30 and 2:45 P.M., she saw Jeff Curley leave the house to go wash the dog at his grandmother's. "He was wearing a football jersey, maroon, with the number twenty-two—it said Boston College—and dungaree jeans," she said.

Yanetti showed her a maroon football jersey that had been entered into evidence. "Mrs. Curley, tell the jury if you recognize this. . . ."

"This was Jeffrey's shirt."

"Was this the shirt that he was wearing when he left your house on October first between two-thirty and two forty-five?"

"Yes, it was."

She said that the jeans he'd been wearing that day were Bradlees Exchange brand jeans, and identified the label and a button from the shorts marked with the name-brand logo.

Yanetti said, "Now, ma'am, after Jeffrey left your house that afternoon, did you see him again that night?"

"No, I didn't."

Barbara Curley said that she'd called the police about her missing child, that she hadn't slept that night, that the next day the family had had missing-person flyers made up with Jeff's picture on them, and that the flyers were passed out around the neighborhood.

Yanetti said, "I direct you to eleven o'clock on October 2, 1997—did someone arrive at your house at that time?"

She said, "Yes, Salvi Sicari."

"Had he ever been in your house before, to your knowledge?"

"No."

"Did he have anything in his hands?"

"Some of the flyers we were passing out."

"And that day or any other day, did you ever see Jeffrey alive again?"

"No."

There was no cross-examination.

Next up was grandmother Muriel Francis, telling how Jeffrey Curley had finished washing the dog at about 3:00 P.M., then came into her house. "He just said, 'Nanna, I have to go somewhere, and I will be back in a little while.' "

Yanetti said, "And when Jeffrey walked out of your house at five past three, did you see him again, ever?"

"No."

Again, no cross-examination.

Tashika Ellis, neighbor and friend of Sicari's, told of seeing him "palling around" with Jeffrey Curley in the summer of 1997. "I used to see him [Curley] around with Salvy and Salvy's younger brother [teenager Robert Sicari]."

Yanetti said, "And how often would you see Jeff Curley with Sicari?"

"Like every day, because Jeff was out every day, too, so once a day or so, he would be with him for a little while."

"Now, Miss Ellis, during that summer, did you also begin to see someone who was not from the neighborhood hang around there?"

"Yes—I forget his name."

"What did he look like?"

"He was a heavyset guy who wore glasses."

The prosecutor showed her a photo of Charles Jaynes, whom she identified as the individual in question. She said, "I saw Salvatore sometimes with him, or Jeff, or sometimes all three would be together."

"How often was Sicari with him [Jaynes]?"

"Like every day—that was his friend. . . ."

"How often would you see all three together—Sicari, Jaynes and Curley?"

"Like a couple of days out of the week, all three would be together . . . sometimes driving in the car, or sitting out in front of the houses."

"When you say the car, do you mean the Cadillac?"

"Yes."

The witness said that on October 1, 1997, at about 2:30 P.M., she asked Sicari to walk with her to Izzy's, a local Spanish restaurant. Walking on Market Street toward the park, they saw Jeff Curley standing in the bushes just outside the park, with his dog on a leash.

Yanetti said, "And what happened?"

Ellis said, "He tried to sic the dog on us. . . . He was telling him to get us."

"And did Sicari have a reaction to that?"

"He was calling him a little punk and stuff like that. . . ."

"Speaking loudly or softly?"

"Loudly."

"How long did it last?"

"Just a couple of minutes."

"Then what?"

"We walked off to Izzy's."

While walking, they came across Charles Jaynes, standing next to his car. Sicari said he was going to talk to Jaynes for a minute and walked across the street. She continued to Izzy's to get something to eat. When she returned, she got in Jaynes's car and they gave her a ride back to her house, then drove off at about 3:15 P.M., driving in the direction where Curley had gone.

On cross-examination, defense counsel Kelly asked if there were many times the witness had seen Curley alone with Jaynes in his car.

"Yes," Ellis said.

"About ten times, right?"

"Yes."

"And just a couple of times did you see Curley and Sicari and Jaynes in a car together?"

"That's right."

Ellis said that Curley had told her that Jaynes was going to give him a bike. Kelly said, "Did he ever say Sal Sicari was going to get him a bike?"

She said, "No, it was always Jaynes."

"And he said he had to do something for him?"

"Yes."

"Did you ask what that was?"

"No."

Donna Ellis, the witness's sister, followed, testifying that she'd seen both Jaynes and the defendant with Curley. "Jeffrey was usually around Salvy a lot."

Yanetti said, "Of the times you saw Sicari that summer and fall, how many times was Curley with him?"

"He was around him a lot."

She said that on October 1, 1997, she'd seen Sicari and Jaynes drive toward the park in Jaynes's car.

On cross-examination, Arthur Kelly underlined the fact that the witness had heard Curley say that Jaynes was going to get him a bike, but that she'd never heard him say that Sicari would get him a bike.

Robyn Kneil, twenty, from Brockton, Massachusetts, had seen Charles Jaynes around as she was growing up in the neighborhood (though he lived on the other side of town), and had become his girlfriend around 1994 to 1995. She also knew

Victim Tanya Lavallais, 23.

Lavallais was shot 5 times in the head.

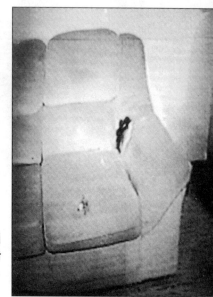

Detergent sprinkled on couch did not remove bloodstain.

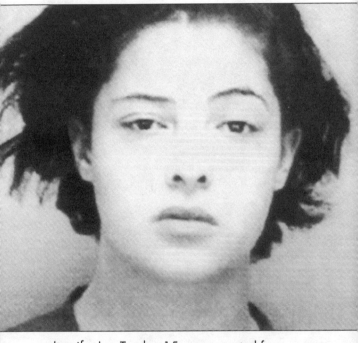
Jennifer Lee Tombs, 15, was arrested for
the murder of Lavallais.

Tiffany Lofton, 15, testified about Tombs's activities the night of the murder.

Jock Johnson, 21, loaned Tombs his .25 caliber semi-automatic pistol.

Tombs laughing in court as Johnson testifies.

A police video of Detective Kraft questioning Tombs was played in court.

Tombs hearing verdict of life in prison without parole.

Victim, Jeffrey Curley, 10.

Charles Jaynes, 22, was arrested for the
murder of Curley.

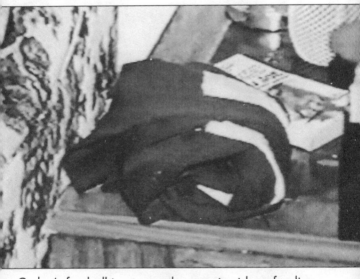

Curley's football jersey can be seen in video of police search of Jaynes' apartment.

Salvatore Sicari, 21, was charged with the kidnap and murder of Curley.

Barbara Curley holds up her son's jersey during her testimony.

Victim's family reacts to the guilty verdict.

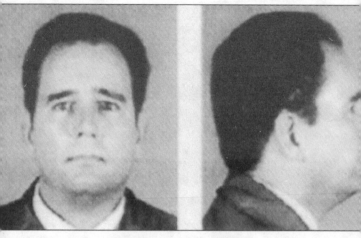

Career criminal Danny Rolling, 36, was arrested for the murders of five students.

Rolling (*fourth from left*) during police interrogation.

While in prison, Rolling became engaged to crime writer Sandra London, 45.

Florida attempted to seize the advance and royalties from *The Making of a Serial Killer*, which London and Rolling wrote together.

Granted permission to address the court,
Rolling began serenading London instead.

Florida electric chair where Rolling's death penalty
sentence for the five murders will be carried out.

Charlene LeTourneau, and through her, she knew Sal Sicari.

That wasn't all she knew.

Yanetti said, "What did you learn about Charles Jaynes?"

"That he was a pedophile," Kneil said. In his room, she'd seen something—"a book about young boys and sex."

"Did you have conversations with Jaynes about that?"

"Yes, he told me it was something he liked to look at but not something he would ever act on."

Yanetti pressed, "What did he like to look at?"

"Young boys having sex," she said.

"He made no secret of this?"

"No."

On September 11, 1997, Jaynes picked up Kneil at her house. Kneil said, "He was with someone."

"Who?"

"Jeff Curley."

Jaynes had dropped off Curley on Hampshire Street, close to his house. On Friday, September 12, Kneil and two female friends met Jaynes at Honda Village, the group then going to Cambridge to pick up Sal Sicari.

When they met him, Sicari came to the car's passenger side door, speaking across the witness to Charles Jaynes.

Kneil said, "Sal said he would ride his bike around the block to see if he could find J.C."

"Did you know who he was talking about?"

"Yes, because Charlie had called him J.C. at that time, too—I didn't know him as Jeff." Sicari went looking for Curley, but couldn't find him, so the group went to Jaynes's Manchester apartment without him.

Kelly didn't waste any time getting to the meat of it on cross-examination. "In July of 1996, you found out that Charles Jaynes was a pedophile?"

Robyn Kneil said, "Yes, I saw a book in his room."

"Did you find other evidence that he was a pedophile?"

"Just books and movies . . . movies of young boys having sex."

"Did you see a purple and aqua container in his room [at his parents' Brockton home] back then?"

"Yes."

"What did he keep in it?"

"His books and movies."

"And he fastened a lock to it?"

"Yes."

"Did you ever look inside it? What was in it?"

"Books and movies of young boys having sex."

"And to the best of your recollection, this was when?"

"Probably August of 1996," the witness said.

Kelly focused on September 11, 1997, when Robyn Kneil had seen Jaynes with Curley, whom he had introduced to her as J.C. "Now, you knew he was a pedophile?"

Kneil said, "Yes."

"And you knew the age of the boy in the car?"

"Yes."

"Did that cause you concern?"

"No."

Kelly moved to Jaynes's alias. "Do you know Anthony Scaccia?"

"I knew that Charlie used that name before," the witness said.

"So when you knew him, he didn't always go by the name Charles Jaynes, did he?"

"Well, as far as friends talking to him, he was Charles Jaynes, but he also used the name Anthony Scaccia."

The commonwealth's Witness #6, Jeff Donovan, an employee at Honda Village, knew both Edward Jaynes Sr. and Charles Jaynes, as well as Sal Sicari, who'd worked at Cojack's reconditioning business at the car dealership. He'd seen Jeffrey Curley at the dealership three times.

Sometime in September 1997, he'd seen Curley with Sicari and Jaynes, horsing around some new cars under protective plastic sheets, vehicles awaiting reconditioning. Kelly on cross-examination said, "How do you recall that Saturday so well?"

Donovan said, "I thought it was a strange group—to see the three together was quite odd."

"So when you saw Curley that third time, [it was] only then you thought it odd, since Sicari was with them?"

"I thought it odd to see the three of them together."

So ended day one. Day two, Tuesday, October 27, 1998, began with the testimony of Henock Desir, originally from Haiti, and presently employed as a lock manager at Honda Village. He knew Charles Jaynes—"Cojack's son"—and Sal Sicari from the job. On Friday, September 26, 1997, he'd seen Jaynes and Jeffrey Curley standing around talking at the dealership's front reception desk.

Desir identified a photo of Curley as the boy he'd seen that day. He'd seen the boy before, he said, on the previous Friday, September 19, when he'd gone into the dealership basement while making his usual rounds.

Yanetti said, "Did you see something unusual?"

Desir said, "Yes, I saw Charles Jaynes carrying Curley on his shoulders, and then he said to him, 'I am going to drop you—I am going to throw you away,' and Curley said, 'You can't do that.' "

"Did they seem to be playing?"

"Yes."

"When this went on, did you see someone else approach them?"

"Yes, Sicari," the witness said.

"Did you pay attention to them after that?"

"No."

On cross-examination, defense attorney Kelly said, "When you saw Jaynes pick up Curley and put him over his head and turn him around—did you see Sicari touch Curley in any way?"

"No," Desir said.

"And when Sicari came over, did Jaynes stop what he was doing with Jeffrey over his head?"

"Yes."

Commonwealth witness William Pelligrini testified that he'd met Charles Jaynes during the fall of 1995, at a meeting of the Boston Alliance of Gay and Lesbian Youth. They'd become friends. He'd seen Jaynes about four or five times, and each time, Sal Sicari was with him.

Yanetti said, "In April of 1997, did you learn something about Charles Jaynes?"

Pelligrini said, "Yes, I found out he was a pedophile."

"How did you find out?"

"He said he found younger teenagers attractive; then it became younger boys."

"Did he give an age range?"

". . . Around twelve or younger."

In April 1997, Jaynes had told the witness that he was a member of NAMBLA. Yanetti said, "What did he show you then?"

"It was a Swedish film with a young boy in a shower."

"When you were a friend of Jaynes's, how openly did he discuss being a pedophile?"

"He discussed it freely—all his friends knew he was a pedophile."

"No secret, then?"

"No, none."

In the first week of September 1997, wanting to show off his new place, Charles Jaynes drove Pelligrini and his friend Sarah Wetterhahn to New Hampshire. Yanetti said, "Did you have a strange conversation with Jaynes?"

Pelligrini said, "Yes, when we were past Boston."

"What happened?"

"He told me he had been talking to some friends—specifically, Sal and his younger brother."

"Did Jaynes say that Robert Sicari [the defendant's brother] was going to hook him up with a boy?"

"Yes."

"Did Jaynes talk about the boy he was going to get fixed up with?"

"He said there was a boy in Cambridge with chubby cheeks and red hair that he was going to fix him up with. He said he was going to steal his bike and buy a new bike, and the boy would fuck around with him for the bike," Pelligrini said.

Later, at Jaynes's Manchester apartment, he showed something to Sarah Wetterhahn and the witness. "He showed me and Sarah a picture of him with Curley on his lap, in a mall."

Yanetti said, "Did you know who Jeffrey Curley was?"

"I had no idea."

"And it was a mall?"

"Yes. It had photo-booth decor around it—it said WANTED on it."

"Where was Curley?"

"On Jaynes's lap."

"And what expression did they have on their faces?"

"They were smiling."

Defense counsel Kelly stepped up for his turn. "When Charles Jaynes was referring to the fact that he wanted to steal the boy's bike and, to use your words, 'to fuck around with him and fool with him' and lure him into sex, he never mentioned Sal would be involved, did he?"

Pelligrini said, "No."

". . . Did Jaynes indicate he had sex with other young boys?"

"No, he didn't."

"Did he express desires to have sex with young boys?"

"He would make vague comments, but I never took them seriously."

"Were they lewd comments about young boys? What did he say?"

"He would whistle out the [car] window to younger boys he felt were attractive."

On redirect, Yanetti said, "Charles Jaynes made no secret of being a pedophile?"

"Right," Pelligrini said.

Sarah Wetterhahn, from Foxborough, Massachusetts, was a friend of Pelligrini's, through whom she had met Charles Jaynes. She told of the trip that she and Pelligrini had taken to Jaynes's Manchester apartment in his gray Cadillac.

Yanetti said, "Do you recall a conversation about a bike?"

She said, "Yes, Charlie was discussing that he liked a boy with strawberry blond hair, freckles, crooked teeth . . . and that Robert Sicari [the defendant's brother] would hook him up with him, and he said the boy's bike was stolen and that he was going to get him a new bike, and that Curley had said, 'You're going to get me a bike with no strings attached,' and I was disgusted by the conversation and said I didn't want to hear more."

At the New Hampshire apartment, she'd seen the photo described by Pelligrini in previous testimony, the mall photo with Curley sitting on Jaynes's lap, both smiling, with the word "Wanted" underneath.

On cross-examination, Kelly asked her about the

mystery boy who was the object of Jaynes's desire.
"Did he say the boy was from Cambridge?"

Wetterhahn said, "Yes."

"Did he say he had crooked teeth and blue
eyes?"

"Yes."

"What did he say he wanted from him?"

"He said he wanted booty from him."

"What does that mean?"

"That he wanted a sexual relationship with him."
Jaynes showed her the "Wanted" photo, saying this
was the boy. Kelly said, "This was the boy he wanted
'booty' from?"

"Yes."

"Did he mention anything else he wanted to
do?"

"There was another boy, he said—he said he
liked a six-year-old who liked to swallow . . ."

"Swallow what?"

"His cum," Wetterhahn said. "Then I said I was
disgusted and the conversation ended."

Moving on, Kelly said, "Did he say he would steal
Curley's bike?"

"No."

"He just said he would buy a bike for him for
sex?"

"Yes, he said the bike had been stolen and he
was going to buy him a bike."

"And Jaynes had said that Curley said to him,
'You're going to buy a bike for me with no strings
attached'?"

"Yes."

Felix Caesar, a Trinidad-born musician and car
salesman at Honda Village, told of seeing Jeff Cur-

ley at the dealership about a half-dozen times. Yanetti said, "Of those half-dozen times, how often was Charles Jaynes with Curley?"

The witness said that he'd seen Curley with Sicari three times, and with Jaynes three times. Most of those times, Curley was playing around in the showroom, getting into the new cars.

On cross-examination, Kelly said, "You said Curley would play with Jaynes around the cars? And you said the relationship between the two was strange because Jaynes was a grown man?"

"I recall making that statement, but that would not have been all of the statement," Caesar said. "Not just because he was a grown man but also because of him being black."

"But you didn't mention [to detectives] Sal Sicari and his relationship with the boy?"

"Well, I thought Sicari could have been a relative of the boy's."

"But your focus was the relationship between Jaynes and the boy?"

"Yes, because not every day do you see a black man around the age of twenty-five and a nine- or ten-year-old boy playing—if it was two blacks or two whites, it's easier to understand."

Laurie Pistorino, heavyset and thick-featured, with short dyed blond hair, a nose ring, and a sullen demeanor, was Charles Jaynes's fiancée. "In 1995, August, I met him at a BAGLY function [Boston Alliance for Gay, Lesbian, and Transgendered Youth]." She said that they became friends, had a sexual relationship, and that she considered herself engaged to him.

Yanetti asked about an incident on Tuesday, September 16, 1997, when Jaynes planned to take the witness to dinner, picking her up in his gray Cadillac at 9:00 P.M. "What did he say when he picked you up?"

"We were going to pick someone up—Jeffrey Curley," Pistorino said.

"What name did he call him?"

"J.C." She said that they then picked up Curley as he stood alone waiting on a Cambridge "side street," then drove to Boston, to Vinnie Testa's Italian restaurant. They had to wait twenty minutes to be seated. While waiting, Pistorino said, "We talked about my night at work."

Yanetti said, "Who was 'we'?"

"Charlie and I talked about my night at work."

"Was Jeff Curley participating?"

"Just listening."

"Did he say anything in the fifteen to twenty minutes before you were seated?"

"No."

Once seated, they ordered their meal. Yanetti said, "What did everyone order?"

"I ordered chicken picanti and salad, if you must know," Pistorino said sarcastically, "and the boy ordered spaghetti and meatballs, and Charlie ordered the big chicken."

"The little boy was Jeffrey Curley?"

"Yes, J.C." Dinner lasted about forty-five minutes, after which, Jaynes dropped off Curley at home and drove Pistorino to his Manchester apartment.

The witness said she knew Sal Sicari through

Jaynes and Charlene LeTourneau. She told of a time somewhere in the last week in September 1997, when Jaynes had been driving her to a meeting, when he said that he was going to make a last payment on a bike.

Yanetti said, "Did he say who it was for?"

"Yes, for J.C.," Pistorino said. "He said he was buying it because J.C. had his bike stolen in the past and he felt bad, so he bought him a bike."

The questioning moved now to October 1, 1997, to a sudden change in plans made by Jaynes. "I talked to him between five and seven P.M. on the first of October," Pistorino said.

"And what did Jaynes tell you?" said Yanetti.

"He was talking about how he didn't feel well and he wanted me to visit another day instead . . . visit his house with him."

"You mean that apartment in Manchester?"

"Yes."

"What plans did you have for the night of October first?"

"I had plans to go back up there after work."

"That would have been Wednesday," Yanetti said. "Because he wasn't feeling well, he told you another night instead?"

"Yes."

On cross-examination, Kelly established that Pistorino had lived in the Jaynes house on Peterson Street in Brockton, Massachusetts, from 1995 to 1997; that, in fact, she was living there on October 1, 1997. The witness was evasive about where she'd lived when, but Kelly nailed it down. "So, in fact, you were living there [on Peterson, in Brockton] on October 2, 1997?"

"If you say so," Pistorino said.

"No, I am asking you."

"Yes."

"So what you told the jury was not the truth."

"Yes."

"And you still live there?"

"Yes."

"So you never actually did move out?"

"I have stayed with friends."

"Don't you still live there? And on occasion, you live at friends' houses?"

"Yes."

[The reason for the witness's reluctance to be pinned down as to exactly where she lived would become clear the next day, when she was fired from her job at the Boston Public Library for not living in Boston.]

Kelly, moving in, said, "You consider yourself still engaged to Charles Jaynes, to be married, right? He's your fiancé?"

Pistorino said, "Yes."

"And you have been inside his bedroom, right? Did you ever see a Rubbermaid container in that room?"

"Not that I know of."

"Has Jaynes ever shown you any pornographic material that depicts young boys engaged in sex or in the nude?"

"No."

"Did you know or have reason to believe Jaynes was a pedophile?"

"No."

"Did you know he was attracted to young boys?

Did you know he wanted to have sex with young boys?"

"No, I didn't."

"You never knew that?"

"No."

Kelly questioned the witness extensively on her and Jaynes's dinner with Curley at the Italian restaurant in Boston, then asked her about the decor of Jaynes's Manchester apartment, with *The Lion King* posters and TV teen-idol posters. At one point, after the judge reprimanded her to answer the questions, the flustered witness said of defense counsel, "He's badgering me and it's not right."

Kelly said, "You knew he [Jaynes] used the name Anthony Scaccia—do you know why he used that name?"

"Yes," Pistorino said, "because he had written bad checks when he was younger and couldn't use his last name."

"Did you know he had a motor vehicle license in the name of Anthony Scaccia?"

"Yes."

Sharon Snow, an employee of Honda Village, was the receptionist at the front desk where Charles Jaynes had been seen hanging around with Sicari. She also knew Sicari from the time he'd been employed at the dealership.

Yanetti said, "In the summer of 1997 and into September of 1997, how often would you see Sicari and Jaynes together?"

Snow said, "Just a couple of times a week."

"It was clear they were friends?"

"Yes." She identified a photo of Jeff Curley, saying that on September 25 or 26, she'd seen Sicari, Jaynes and Curley together, near her desk. She asked Curley what he was doing out of school, and he said he was getting a bite to eat. Her phone rang, and while she answered it, the trio departed.

Rochelle Cruz had lived in Cambridge during the summer of 1997, when she became a friend of Sal Sicari's. She also knew Jeff Curley as a kid riding his bike around the neighborhood, and knew Charles Jaynes through Sicari. "Charlie was introduced to me as one of Sal's best friends," she said.

She'd seen Sicari in the company of Curley about a dozen times, and had seen Jaynes with Curley once.

Yanetti said, "There was an altercation in July—what happened?"

Cruz said, "Jeff was riding in front of Sal's house on his bike, and Sal grabbed the bike from Jeff and held it in the air—teasing him so he couldn't get the bike, and after Jeff put up a fight to get it, Sal picked him up and body-slammed him on the hood of a car."

"How long did he have the bike up in the air?"

"Forty-five seconds to a minute."

"Was he using one hand or two?"

"One holding the bike in the air."

"And the other hand?"

"He was batting Jeff away as he jumped to get the bike."

"Was Jeff saying anything?"

"Just, 'Give me my bike, give me my bike'—and

Sal was laughing and so was everyone else there," Cruz said.

Sicari put down the bike, then body-slammed Curley onto the hood of a car. Yanetti said, "What portion of Jeff's body hit the car?"

"His back," Cruz said.

"How hard did Sicari do it?"

"Hard enough for a dent to be left on the car afterward."

The prosecutor moved on to an incident that happened about two to three weeks before October 1, 1997, involving Sicari, Jaynes and Curley.

Cruz said, "Little Curley was riding his bike in the neighborhood and pulled over and had a conversation with Sal's younger brother. . . . Sal opened the trunk of Charles Jaynes's car and put Jeff in the trunk and closed it."

Yanetti said, "What type of car?"

"Cadillac."

"Where was Jaynes?"

"He was standing outside near the car, on the driver's side."

"After Sal put Curley in the trunk, what happened?"

"Sal entered the vehicle, put the keys in and started it up, and started revving the car." Curley banged on the inside of the trunk quite a few times, Cruz said. She estimated that he'd been in the trunk for about a minute and a half.

She said, "People in the neighborhood and me told him [Sicari] to let him out of there, and we made a fuss about it and they just said it was a joke, never mind, and we freaked out with *'Get him out*

of there,' and then Sal got out of the car and let
Jeff out."

"How did Jeff look?"

"Kind of red in the face and trying to get out,
and just afterward he just kinda laughed it off, like
it wasn't a big deal to him."

"Where did this take place?"

"Market Street, in front of Sal's house."

Defense counsel Kelly tried to regain some
ground for the defendant after Cruz's potentially
damaging testimony. "Was Jeffrey Curley injured in
either of the two incidents?"

"No," Cruz said.

"Was he laughing when he was slammed to the
car on his back?"

"He seemed upset." But he didn't seem hurt and
wasn't crying, she said.

Kelly said, "And he laughed off the trunk-locking,
too?"

"Yes."

"And Sal is the one who let him out?"

"Yes."

"Nothing further."

Now began the Great Bicycle Chase. Fabio Selvig
had been working as a salesman at International
Bicycle in September 1997. He said that on September 8 and 12, someone named Scaccia had used
a credit card to charge part of the payments on
the purchase price of a boy's bike. At about 4:00
P.M. on Friday, September 26, two men entered the
department, men whom the witness now identified

as Sal Sicari and Charles Jaynes. Jaynes had said, "We want to see some children's bicycles."

At the time, they were looking at a smaller-sized adult bike, which Sicari pointed to and asked if that was the correct size for a child of ten. Selvig said that it was. Jaynes said, "We probably got the wrong bike," and arranged to have the previously made credit payments transferred to a different bike. Selvig applied the deposit to a smaller-sized bicycle.

The receipt for that transaction, made out to Anthony Scaccia, was now entered into evidence, and court recessed for the day.

Day three began with bike salesman Selvig returning to the stand, this time for Arthur Kelly's cross-examination. Kelly showed a monitor-screen image of a bicycle-catalog page depicting the model bike that Jaynes and Sicari had bought. "That bike has training wheels on it, right, sir? You said Sicari said, 'We want a bike for a ten-year-old,' and you showed him this mountain bike?"

Selvig said, "Yes."

"Is it your testimony that that bike is suitable for a ten-year-old child? Sir, that bike is for a three- or four-year-old child, isn't it?"

"It's a little large for three or four—"

"Well, five or six, then?"

Kelly established that the bike bought by Scaccia [i.e., Jaynes] was the smallest bike available in the store, hammering at the point that, with its small size and training wheels, it would have been inappropriate for a veteran bike-rider like Curley.

Kelly next disputed the witness's testimony that Sicari had said he wanted a bike for a "ten-year-old child," suggesting that the prosecutor's question-ings might have prompted Selvig to "remember" it happening that way. He said, "So it wasn't until Mr. Yanetti asked you questions ten days ago that you remembered it?"

Selvig said that when he was first interviewed by police, they hadn't gone into that much detail, but that he'd recalled it later. Kelly went around with him some more, giving him a pretty hard time, until he finally said, "You are under oath, sir, and I ask you one more time—you do not have a memory that Sicari or Jaynes said, 'We're looking for a bike for a ten-year-old child'?"

"To the best of my recollection, sir, he did say it," Selvig said. "It was said."

"Who said it?"

"To the best of my recollection, it was Mr. Sicari."

On redirect, Yanetti asked the price of the first bike that Jaynes/Scaccia had made two payments on. Selvig said, "It was on sale for about three hundred thirty dollars."

"And the bike they put the last payment on?"

"One hundred nineteen dollars."

"And the cheapest bike in the store was what?"

"That was the cheapest bike—we carry nothing below that price range."

Yanetti's point—to be tied up later, in his closing argument—was that since Sicari and Jaynes planned to do away with Curley, all they needed was some kind of bike that they could use for a lure.

When Selvig finally stepped down, the jurors might have been forgiven for thinking they had learned more about bicycles than they wanted to know.

* * *

John Coyle, the owner of a Mobil gas station on Beacon Street, identified a credit card receipt for gasoline that had been issued on October 1, 1997, at 3:34 P.M., charged to the American Express credit card of Edward Jaynes Sr.

Roque Alforo, on October 1, 1997, a cashier at the NHD store in Watertown, told of selling duct tape and a roll of canvas tarp to a customer at about 4:36 P.M. Yanetti said, "How was this customer acting?"

Alforo said, "He was sweating, nervous, and in a hurry."

But on Kelly's cross-examination, the witness was unable to identify Charles Jaynes as the customer.

Dale Bisson, assistant manager at NHD on October 1, 1997, and working on the same shift as Alforo, told of directing a customer to the duct tape and the tarps. She said, "He was extremely anxious, nervous, sweating profusely and he actually made me nervous. . . ."

Yanetti said, "Once you got him the tape, how quick did he ask for the tarp?"

"Immediately—he was extremely nervous. . . . I brought him to the tarps and he made me so nervous that I immediately left him."

A credit card receipt for four rolls of duct tape and one 9' x 12' tarp, dated October 1, 1997, and made out to Edward Jaynes Sr., was entered into evidence. On cross-examination, Kelly had the witness identify Charles Jaynes as the nervous and nervous-making customer.

* * *

James Gavell, a Honda Village employee, knew both Sicari and Jaynes from work, and had seen Jaynes palling around with Jeff Curley at the dealership "a couple of times in the evening, near the candy machines."

On October 1, 1997, at some time between 5:30 and 6:00 P.M., he saw Jaynes and Sicari come into the lounge together. Jaynes made a pay-phone call and then he and Sicari left the building.

The next day, while he was working outside in the back lot, Gavell's attention was attracted by the sight of a couple of people, strangers, coming up the back ramp of the building. The group went around to the front. It was unusual enough to prompt him to go inside to investigate. A police car was parked in front of the building.

"The whole commotion happened after that," he said.

Yanetti said, "What commotion?"

"Yelling and screaming. There were six or so people, and Charlie and Sicari were there, and police officers . . ."

"Who was yelling at whom?"

"Many of them were yelling at Charlie."

"Was Sicari involved?"

"Yes, he was with the group yelling at Charlie—he was yelling at Charlie."

"How many people were yelling at Jaynes?"

"I don't recall—maybe five or six."

"And Sicari was one of them."

"Yes."

* * *

Jason Drew, another Honda Village employee, said that he'd seen Curley with Jaynes a couple of times at the dealership. On October 1, 1997, he got to work at 1:00 P.M., parking next to the dealership on Thorton Street. The problem with parking on Thorton Street, he said, was that police ticketed cars parked in the same place for more than two hours, so every few hours he'd have to go out and move his car to another spot.

When he went out to move his car at around 5:00 P.M., he noticed a car parked next to his. "It was Charlie's."

Yanetti said, "You knew the car?"

"Yes, I knew him to drive a large Cadillac." Drew identified the car from a photo showed to him by the prosecutor.

Yanetti said, "On prior occasions when you saw the car, where was it parked?"

"Downstairs . . . in the cleaning area of Honda Village."

On day four of the trial, Craig Deloreto, senior store detective at Bradlees in Watertown, described the store's video surveillance security system, where sixteen video cameras and seventeen still cameras provided ninety percent coverage of the store at all times. He identified a videotape that was an exact copy of one made at the store on October 1, 1997. Since the store used high-speed seventy-two-hour videotapes, the tape had been slowed down so the court could see what was on it.

The tape from October 1, at 9:04 to 9:05 P.M., was played for the jury, showing first Charles Jaynes at the checkout counter, then Jaynes and Sicari at the counter with the fifty-gallon Rubbermaid container. Sicari carried it out as Jaynes signed the sales slip.

In court, members of the Curley family looked very upset as they looked at the container.

The witness then identified a receipt that was generated at the precise minute a sale was made on October 1, 1997, at 9:04 P.M., made on the American Express charge card of Edward Jaynes Sr.

Michael Silveira, employed by the Home Depot in Somerville, on October 1, 1997, identified a receipt for a fifty-pound bag of concrete and a bag of granule lime bought on October 1 at 10:21 P.M., charged to the American Express card of Edward Jaynes Sr.

Cameras positioned throughout the store were set to record continuously at seventy-two-hour speed. The witness identified a slowed-down copy of a surveillance tape that had recorded that particular transaction. The tape was shown to the jury, depicting two figures buying bags of concrete and lime at the checkout counter of register eighteen. It was Jaynes and Sicari. Sicari took a bag and put it over his shoulder and left the store; then Jaynes took another bag and carried it out.

Newton Police Department sergeant William Byrne told of responding to a call reporting a disturbance at Honda Village on October 2, 1997, where Jaynes was taken into custody, and other participants were requested to come down to the station to sort out the dispute.

Yanetti said, "Who did you also ask to go to the station?"

Byrne said, "The Curley brothers and Mr. Sicari, who I thought was a member of the Curley family—I asked him to proceed back to the station."

"Who went with him?"

"Sicari drove a vehicle with the Curley brothers, all in one car."

Byrne described the inventory search of Charles Jaynes's Cadillac, identifying Jaynes's wallet and its contents, including the driver's license in the name of Anthony Scaccia, with a picture of Jaynes. Also identified were a receipt for a Rubbermaid container from Bradlees, a receipt for bags of concrete and lime from Home Depot, a receipt for a bike from International Bicycle and a receipt from Osco Drug Store for Garcia Vega cigars and No Doz capsules.

Defense counsel Kelly asked, "Was anyone arrested besides Charles Jaynes regarding a disturbance at Honda Village?"

"No."

Before the commonwealth's witness Charlene LeTourneau took the stand, Judge Cowin advised the jury that LeTourneau had been immunized and could never be prosecuted as to "crimes she might have committed as to that of Jeffrey Curley." The prosecution made no guarantee as to the veracity of her testimony, but the jurors were advised to scrutinize it carefully.

LeTourneau was thin-faced and sharp-featured, with long dark hair, not unattractive, in a kind of hard-bitten way. She said that she lived in Brockton and worked at a Superfitness center, and also drove a taxi and had a cleaning job, too. On December 10, 1997, she'd been granted immunity and agreed to tell about phone calls she'd received from Sal Sicari on October 1, 1997.

She'd been the girlfriend of Edward Jaynes Jr., the father of her child, Edward Jaynes III. They did not marry. She also knew Jaynes's younger brother, Charles. She'd been the girlfriend of Sal Sicari from summer 1995 through January 1997.

Yanetti said, "During that time, was there an occasion when you introduced Sicari to Charles Jaynes?"

She said, "Yes, they met at Charlie's sister's house in October of 1996." She and Sicari had moved into the house in September of that year.

Yanetti said, "So, in October, that's when Jaynes and Sicari met?"

"Yes, we all went to Spooky World together—[an amusement park] located in Berlin, Massachusetts."

She and Sicari lived together for two months, and broke up on "good terms," talking on the phone to each other every day.

Yanetti said, "In April of 1997, did you learn something about Charles Jaynes?"

"He was a pedophile," LeTourneau said. "I found things in his room—I was living [on] Peterson in Brockton." She was living there with Edward Jaynes III (her young son), Charles Jaynes's parents, Laurie Pistorino and Charles Jaynes, who had moved back into the house for a while.

Yanetti said, "Where did he stay?"

"In his room."

"Where did you stay?"

"In my room with my son, who was four in 1997," LeTourneau said.

"And you say you found things in Charles Jaynes's room?"

"Yes, little boys' packages of underwear that they had already worn—also magazines and pictures of naked boys."

"And what conversation did you have with Jaynes in regard to these articles?"

"He said that was his life and he was going to do what he was going to do anyway."

"Before you confronted him, what had your relationship with Jaynes been?"

"I referred to him as my brother-in-law."

"And after you saw all this stuff—the magazines and pictures?"

"I hated him," she said.

Yanetti moved on to the matter of the bike. "In the last week of September, did you have a conversation with Sal Sicari?"

"Yes, he said he had a bike for my son," LeTourneau said.

"Did you believe him?"

"No."

On October 1, 1997, LeTourneau, still living on Peterson in Brockton, received a phone call from Charles Jaynes, who wanted to speak to his mother, who was out of the house. This was the first of some eleven phone calls he made that night, about one every forty-five minutes.

Yanetti said, "How often did he ask for her [his mother]?"

"All of those times," the witness said.

"What else did he say when he called that night?"

"Not to let his mother come to his house that night."

"Of the eleven calls he made, how many of them did he say he didn't want his mother to come to his house in New Hampshire?"

"All of them."

At about 6:30 P.M., Sicari paged her and she called him back. It sounded like he was calling from a pay phone. "We argued first about the fact that he said he was working [i.e., employed] and I knew he wasn't, and he said he was buying cement for a basketball hoop and he would call me back later," LeTourneau said.

Twenty minutes later, they talked again, she said. "We continued to argue—I wanted him to go home for me to call him and he said he needed more cement. And I asked, why all the cement? And he said he was tied up in something and would be in trouble if he didn't get it all done tonight."

Yanetti said, "What was your next conversation with Sicari?"

LeTourneau said that she'd asked Sicari about his remark in their previous talk about being in lots of trouble—"I wanted to know what kind of trouble."

But Sicari didn't want to say out loud what kind of trouble he was in, so he used a kind of private code, obliquely reminding her of an incident they'd spoken of the day before, where a car stolen off the lot of the taxicab company where she worked had been involved in an accident and killed someone.

LeTourneau said, "When he first got on the phone, I asked him what kind of trouble, and he said he'd hurt someone real bad and said he couldn't talk about it on the phone, and he referred then to an incident that happened at my work where someone was killed by a car stolen off the lot. . . . He didn't want to speak on the phone, he wanted me to come and meet him.

"I was screaming at him. I said, 'You're on the phone saying you killed someone and you have no remorse,' and he said, 'I could give two fucks—it's like a bowl of cereal. I could eat it or I could walk away from it.' "

The witness began crying on the stand. Yanetti said, "How did he sound?"

"Just like he did every day," she said.

"Any emotion in his voice?"

"No." They talked for an hour, she said.

Yanetti said, "When you hung up the phone with Sicari, did you believe him?"

"No."

The next day, she learned that Charles Jaynes had been arrested for murder and that Sicari had been with him on the day of the crime. She said she hadn't gone to the police because she was afraid she'd get in trouble.

Yanetti said, "Ever speak to him again? That late-night conversation [on October 1, 1997] was the last time you spoke to him?"

"Yes."

* * *

On cross-examination, Kelly quickly established that LeTourneau had seen Sicari around kids many times, her own and his included, and that he was "excellent" with them. "Have you ever seen him mistreat any children he's been in the company of?"

She said, "No."

"Did Sicari ever show interest in young boys to your knowledge?"

"No."

"Ever see Charles Jaynes in the company of children? How did he interact?"

"He would be mean to them, tease them and throw things at them."

Kelly focused on LeTourneau's discovery of Jaynes's pedophiliac tendencies. "In April of 1997, you discovered Charles Jaynes was a pedophile because he showed you certain material?"

LeTourneau said, "Yes, he showed me books with pictures of naked boys."

"That disgusted you? And you say you began to hate him?"

"Yes."

"But you stayed at that address?"

". . . Yes, but he moved out later."

"Did you ever see a large Rubbermaid container with a lock on it? What was in it?"

"Pedophile materials."

"How big was it? Could it fit under a bed?"

"Not under his bed, he had a water bed."

Kelly argued that Sicari's "I hurt someone real bad" was just his trying to impress her with some macho tough-guy talk. "He would say stuff he did, but actually, he didn't do it, right?"

"Yes."

"So when he said that on October 1, 1997, that's why you didn't believe him, right? Because many times in the past he would claim things he did that he didn't do?"

"Right."

"You didn't believe him because he had spoken to you in the past like that before, right?"

"Not that seriously, but he had lied before," Charlene LeTourneau said. "His whole life was a lie."

Next, New Hampshire State Police sergeant Guy Kimball described how he'd been in charge of a team of investigators that entered the premises of Charles Jaynes's Manchester apartment on October 3, 1997, at 5:05 P.M., searching it and collecting evidence.

During that search, they found a silver button from a pair of pants, a clothing label later determined to have come from Curley's dungaree jeans, a long-neck Coors Lite beer bottle, a roll of duct tape and a maroon football jersey.

Referring to the football jersey, Yanetti said, "What did you notice about it when you found and seized it?"

Kimball said, "It had a strong odor of gasoline on it and it was moist to the touch."

Also found were a stirring spoon with fragments of dried concrete on it and a road atlas located in a pile of clothing just inside the entryway of the apartment.

Court would not be in session on the following

day, Friday. Judge Cowin cautioned the jurors not to discuss the case with anyone and to avoid watching the local news, then recessed the court for the weekend.

Monday, November 2, 1998, marked day five of the trial. Direct examination of Sgt. Guy Kimball continued, with the witness stating that the mailbox of Jaynes's Manchester apartment bore the names of Anthony Scaccia and Laurie Pistorino.

Yanetti showed Kimball one of the writings taken from Charles Jaynes's desk drawer on October 3, 1997, and asked him to read it aloud in court. The letter, written by Jaynes, contained the following passage: "Someone made me an extreme offer—I visited friends and while on an excursion that never should have started, I glanced a glimmer of a beautiful boy—beauty, beauty, Lord, why have you forsaken me to carry this burden—he had a lovely tan and crystal blue eyes."

The prosecution now called a parade of witnesses to establish the presence of Jaynes and defendant Sal Sicari in the area of the South Berwick Great Works River body-dump site. David Mahoney, of New Castle, New Hampshire, said that on October 2, 1997, on his way to work, he followed his usual custom of stopping at Bickford's café for a cup of coffee. Arriving at about 4:15 A.M., he noticed a stranger—"a pretty big black man, heavy, overweight"—enter and ask a waitress if he could borrow a coat hanger [when Jaynes and Sicari had locked themselves out of the car].

Now, in court, he identified Charles Jaynes as that man.

William Merrill, a truck driver for Poland Spring water, said that on October 2, 1997, at about 4:45 P.M., he'd stopped at an Exxon gas station in Portsmouth, New Hampshire, where a "big, dark-skinned man" driving a car with out-of-state plates asked him if there were any cheap motels in the area. There was a passenger in the car, but Merrill didn't much notice him.

Merrill told the driver that he didn't know much about the local motels. Yanetti said, "What happened to the passenger while you spoke to the driver?"

Merrill said, "I wasn't paying much attention to him, but he was nervous, looking at the floor, and he kept looking at the driver. . . . He said, 'No, we're tired, we will get a motel.' "

"The passenger said that?"

"Yes, and he looked scruffy, like he hadn't shaved in a while."

Merrill said that later, seeing an article on the crime with Jaynes's picture, he'd recognized him as the driver of the car.

William Smith, an employee of Seabrook nuclear power plant, was driving to work on October 2, 1997, at about 5:00 A.M. or so, when he drove past Cumberland Farms in South Berwick, Maine, about a mile away from the bridge on Route 236 going over the Great Works River. It was still dark, misty—raining.

Yanetti said, "Did you see something unusual?"

The witness said he'd seen a car parked at the side of the road, with Massachusetts plates, facing away from Massachusetts along the roadway. "When I came around the corner, it seemed odd it would be sitting like that on the side of the road."

"How close was it parked in relation to the bridge over the river?"

"Forty to fifty yards down."

On October 7, Smith saw searchers in the same area at Cumberland Farms, so he pulled over and gave a statement to an officer about what he'd seen.

Tracy Carr, a former employee of Doverpoint Variety, a small family-run convenience store, opened up the place for business at about 5:30 A.M. on Thursday, October 2, 1997. Five minutes later, in walked the first customer of the day.

"It wasn't a regular customer—just someone passing through," she testified. "Where we live is jeans and T-shirts on people in their twenties, not dressed up like they went to a club the night before—and this person was dressed like he went to a club the night before."

The stranger bought two coffees, a pack of cigarettes and a Danish pastry. In court, she identified him as Sal Sicari.

Stephen Belanger, a Massachusetts State Police officer assigned to the Middlesex County Detective Unit, was one of the investigators assigned to the murder of Jeffrey Curley. On cross-examination, the defense counsel tried to establish a pattern of police negligence, with Kelly asking the witness, "Did you ever locate or find this WANTED poster with Curley and Jaynes, with Curley on his lap?"

"No," Belanger said.

"Was a search warrant ever applied for that address [on] Peterson Street in Brockton, Jaynes's family's home?"

"No, none was."

"So to this day, you have never gone inside that home?"

"No."

The defense counsel then tried to establish that the defendant had furnished valuable assistance to investigators. "A lot of the information, if not all of it, came from Sicari himself, right?"

"Some from Sicari, and some from witnesses," Belanger said.

"Well, the location of the body?"

"No."

"Description of where the body was dumped?"

"The area was discovered a few days after."

"But in [the] early morning of October third—when Sicari was taken to New Hampshire and Maine to look for the body of Curley—it was Sicari who went alone with Massachusetts State Police who went to aid in the finding of that body, right?"

"Yes."

"Charles Jaynes was in custody on unrelated charges, and he didn't assist or go with troopers to Maine, did he?"

"No, he did not."

"Back to Sicari," Kelly said, "you are familiar with the details of his statement to police, right?"

"Yes."

"And a lot of what he said, if not all of it, was corroborated upon further investigation?"

"Yes," Belanger said.

Tuesday, November 3, day six. Cambridge Police Department detective Lester Sullivan said he had been approached by Sal Sicari at the Curley family residence on the morning of October 2, 1997. Sicari was clutching a fistful of missing-person flyers. Yanetti said, "When you arrived in the neighborhood . . . did you know where Curley was or if he was alive?"

"No," Sullivan said.

"What was Sicari's demeanor?"

"Sicari was talking quickly, very cooperative, eager . . . he said he met Jeffrey Curley on Hampshire Street and Curley was walking his rottweiler and he was attempting to sic the dog on Sicari. At that point, Sicari picked up a brick and told him if he didn't call off the dog, he was going to kill the dog."

"And this was all according to Sicari?"

"Yes."

"And what did he say happened next?"

"That Jeffrey Curley walked toward Bristol Street and went into a green house [his grandmother's]."

"And where did Sicari say he went?"

"That he went to Market Street, where he met up with Charles Jaynes, from Brockton."

"Is that the first time you heard the name 'Charles Jaynes'?"

"Yes."

On cross-examination, Kelly sought to establish

Sicari's cooperativeness with the authorities. "When you asked Sicari as to Curley, you indicated that he was eager, cooperative and spoke quickly, that he wanted to provide you with information?"

Sullivan said, "Yes."

"And the information he gave you was—he wanted to give you that name, 'Charles Jaynes'?"

"Yes."

Taking the stand, Cambridge Police Department homicide investigator Sgt. Patrick Nagle described Sicari's demeanor as "helpful" when Sicari was first brought into the station on October 2, 1997.

At 7:05 P.M., an interview was held in the grand jury room adjacent to the detective bureau. Present were Nagle, FBI Special Agent Nadowsky, a third investigator and Sicari. Nagle explained Sicari's Miranda rights and Sicari signed and dated an agreement form waiving those rights. Nagle asked him if Charles Jaynes did anything weird or unusual. Sicari said that at his Manchester apartment, Jaynes had "little kid posters." Nagle asked why that was weird, and Sicari said that Jaynes didn't have any kids, and those were posters kids would like.

Later, Nagle noticed Sicari had a cut on his hands. Sicari said he'd cut his hands and his knee climbing a barbed wire fence while searching for the missing Curley. Nagle asked if they could take pictures of the cuts and Sicari agreed.

After the pictures were taken, Sicari called his mother and had her find a bike receipt that had Jaynes's alias and Manchester address on it. He passed the information along to detectives.

He said that he'd known the Curley family for

about eight years, that they used to have problems, but for the last couple of years, all had been fine.

Sullivan's interview of Sicari ended at 9:30 P.M. Sicari remained at the station. [Since polygraph evidence was inadmissible in court, the witness was unable to tell of Sicari's lie detector test and its results.]

At 12:30 A.M., Nagle said, Sicari and FBI Special Agents Donlin and Nadowsky went into a room for another interview. Yanetti said, "So now it was twelve-thirty A.M., October 3—what was Sicari's demeanor?"

Nagle said, "He was crying uncontrollably . . . rambling on. At first, he didn't make sense and then I asked him to calm down, and Donlin said, 'Tell him what you told me,' and Sicari says, 'I think something happened to Jeffrey Curley.' "

"What was his tone?"

"Crying loud, gasping for air . . ."

"What manner was he speaking in?"

"Speaking while crying, and he was loud."

"What did you ask him?"

"I asked, 'What do you mean something happened to Jeffrey?' He said, 'I don't know, Charles kept going upstairs when we were at Honda Village working on cars.' I asked if Curley was upstairs and he said, 'I don't know, I just think something happened to Jeffrey. . . .' "

Yanetti said, "Did you confront him when he said Charles must have done something?"

"Yes," Nagle said. "I said, 'I have been with you since twelve noon yesterday,' and asked if he had been straight with me, and I asked him to tell me about the bag of lime purchased at Home Depot."

"How did he react?"

"He put his hands behind his back and said, 'Fuck it, lock me up, I did it.' "

"How soon after you asked him about the bag of lime at Home Depot did the crying stop?"

"Almost immediately."

"And did it wind down, or did it just stop?"

"It stopped."

Defense counsel Kelly was ready to wrangle about Nagle's statement that Sicari had said, "Fuck it, lock me up, I did it." Kelly, visibly irate, said to the witness, "You said he stopped crying immediately and that he said, 'Fuck it, lock me up' . . . and you also say he said the words, 'I did it,' but you didn't put that in the report—why?"

Nagle said, "I didn't recollect it at the time."

"So it wasn't important enough to put it in your report—now those words are very different—the 'I did it'—much different than just 'Fuck it, lock me up'?"

"Yes."

"So you're telling this jury that Sicari admitted that he did it?"

"Yes, that's correct."

"In your report, you say you then asked him, 'What would be the reason for locking you up?' and that Sal then said, 'I fucked up'—not that he said, 'I did it.' "

"He said, 'I did it.' "

"But that doesn't appear in your report, *does it?*" Kelly was yelling.

"No, that's correct," Nagle said.

* * *

Cambridge Police Department detective John Fulkerson told of arriving at the station after midnight on October 3, 1997. At 12:45 A.M., he showed Nagle copies of the actual receipts found by the Newton Police Department in Charles Jaynes's wallet, including the Home Depot receipt for bags of concrete and lime. When Fulkerson later introduced himself to Sicari, the defendant, with an "angry" expression, "began to say, 'I'm guilty, lock me up, get my room ready.'"

This surprised Fulkerson, because as far as he knew, the Curley disappearance was still a missing-person case. Fulkerson read Sicari his Miranda rights on the spot, even knowing that Sicari had previously signed a waiver.

Fulkerson said, "I wanted to know what he meant by 'I'm guilty.' I asked something like 'What do you mean by this, what are you guilty of? Tell us what happened.'"

Yanetti said, "And his response?"

"None at that time—he was standing still, staring and sometimes looking at me and just standing there."

After twenty to thirty minutes of silence, Sicari sat down at the table. "He kind of tucked his face into the sweatshirt, and the sweatshirt was over his nose and mouth and only his eyes were showing," Fulkerson said.

The witness asked Sicari questions for another ten to fifteen minutes without getting an answer. By the end of that time, Sicari's demeanor seemed more "relaxed." Yanetti said, "Did he say something?"

"Yes," Fulkerson said, "he said, 'I'm guilty, but I didn't kill Curley, Charles Jaynes did. . . .' I asked him to start from the beginning and tell us what happened."

"And what did he tell you?"

"He said he started out on October first at three or three-thirty P.M., and he and Jaynes went to Curley's grandmother's house to pick up Curley—when they pulled up, the grandmother was on the stairs and Sal ducked down, Curley walked out of the house and got in the Cadillac."

Sicari said that after going to the Boston Public Library so Jaynes could see Laurie Pistorino, the trio drove to a Mobil gas station where Jaynes used a self-service pump to gas up the car. While doing so, he put $1.50 worth of gas into a rag that he held near the gas tank. Jaynes paid for the gas with his father's American Express card.

They went to the parking lot behind a hardware store, all three getting out to relieve themselves. That's when Charles Jaynes grabbed Curley and shoved him into the backseat of the car.

"Sicari [said he] ran to the car and started shutting all the doors and then jumped in the front seat on the driver's side. . . . He said Jaynes was on top of Curley in the backseat of the Cadillac. . . . He was holding the rag over Jeff's face and Jeff was struggling, and Charlie was just too heavy for Jeff to do anything," Fulkerson said.

"How long did Sicari say he struggled for his life?"

"He said it took a long time for Curley to die—over twenty minutes."

"And did Sicari say Jaynes said anything at the time?"

"He said Jaynes said, 'Don't fight it, kid, don't fight it.'"

After Curley was dead, Sicari said Jaynes said, "He's not going to con a conner and he thought he was going to get a bike and fifty dollars for nothing."

Later, after Jaynes purchased some duct tape and used it to tape the gasoline-soaked rag over Curley's nose and mouth, Sicari said, "The kid is dead—his eyes are still open."

Yanetti said, "Did he describe how Jeffrey Curley's face looked?"

"He said his face looked like he had been beaten badly," Fulkerson said.

The witness went on to detail Sicari's confession of that night, describing the aftermath of the murder, the shopping trips to get what they needed to dispose of the body, the nightmarish scenario of necro-defilement in Jaynes's Manchester apartment, the night drive to Maine with its misadventures on the road, the body-dump in the river, and the return to Cambridge.

Yanetti said, "What did Sicari say happened back in Cambridge?"

"That when he was dropped off at his house, Jaynes told him he should go over and knock on the Curleys' door and ask Barbara Curley where Jeffrey Curley is," Fulkerson said. "Jaynes said, 'We would torture the family—we would get Barbara Curley and keep torturing her.'"

Sicari told the witness he could find the button and tag from Curley's pants and his maroon football jersey at the Manchester apartment. "He said Jaynes said that he wanted the jersey because it smelled like Jeffrey Curley," Fulkerson said.

Kelly started his cross-examination by focusing on what exactly Sicari had said when he threw up his hands and told the officers to lock him up. "Did [Sgt.] Nagle ever tell you Sicari said, 'I did it'?"

Fulkerson said, "No."

"Did you ever hear Sicari in all that time use [the] words 'I did it'—*those words?*"

"No."

"You never heard those words?"

"No."

"What he said to you was, 'I'm guilty, get my room ready,' right?"

"Yes."

"In all the time you were with Sicari, did he ever say he planned to kill Jeffrey Curley?"

"No."

"Did he ever say it was his plan or plan with Charles Jaynes to kidnap Jeffrey Curley?"

"No."

On Wednesday, November 11, 1998, day seven, the origin of Charles Jaynes's alias came out as Newton Police Department detective Edward Aucoin testified about the search of the gray Cadillac at the police station garage, where it had been towed. Officer McCarthy did the actual physical search, while Aucoin wrote down the inventory.

Aucoin said, "He [McCarthy] went to the driver's

side first and inside the rear door pouch he located an envelope that had child pornography in it."

Yanetti said, "Whose name was on it?"

"Anthony Scaccia."

"Did you ever learn who this Anthony Scaccia was?"

"He was a young boy killed on October 3, 1987, struck by a drunken driver."

"And relative to porn material that you found, was there a NAMBLA magazine?"

"Yes."

On Thursday, November 5, day eight, Massachusetts State Police twenty-year veteran Lt. Brian O'Hara, an expert on fingerprint identification, used charts to explain where fingerprints had been found on Charles Jaynes's car. There were nine latent prints on the car: five of Jaynes's and nine of Sicari's. Most potentially damning for the defendant: on the trunk, above the license plate, was one of Sal Sicari's fingerprints—indicating that not Jaynes but rather Sicari himself was the one who'd soaked the rag with gas from the self-serve gas pump.

On cross-examination, Kelly established that no prints belonging to Sicari were recovered from the Manchester apartment. "None on the Rubbermaid label in the apartment, not on the button, not on the spoon, not on the label from the pants, not on the map on the front seat of the Cadillac?"

"No," the witness said.

On October 7, 1997, Dr. Henry Ryan, the Chief Medical Examiner of the state of Maine, but now retired, had performed, in Augusta, Maine, the autopsy of Jeffrey Curley, the body being unsealed from the container and laid out on a slab/dissecting table. Jeff Curley was four feet seven inches and weighed seventy-seven pounds. Disturbing autopsy photos were shown to the jury.

Dr. Ryan said that it was his professional opinion that the lime had been placed in Curley's mouth after he was dead. He'd examined the anus for signs of sexual violation. Yanetti said, "Was there trauma to that area?"

Ryan said, "It appeared there was irritation instead of trauma . . . and other skin irritation, so I couldn't evaluate it, but it didn't appear there was certain trauma to the anus."

"So you didn't find tears of hemorrhages or scars?"

"That's correct."

"Assuming Curley was killed and then after the fact penetrated by a bottle and/or a penis, and by that I mean his anus was penetrated—based on the evidence you saw at the autopsy, do you have an opinion as to if your findings are consistent with this?"

"I can't offer an opinion," Dr. Ryan said.

Yanetti said, "You can't say one way or the other?"

"That's correct—I can't say it did happen, and I can't say it didn't happen."

Friday, day nine, saw the continuation of Yanetti's direct examination of Dr. Ryan, the forensic pathologist, saying, "It's my opinion that Jeffrey Curley died of gasoline poisoning by inhalation."

Yanetti said, "Can you give the jury a step-by-step

account of what happens to a body as a result of inhaling gasoline?"

"First, there's the sensation of the smell of the gasoline—a foreign thing—and whatever sensation occurs as a result of contact with the irritant."

Ryan explained that where the gasoline contacted the flesh, blisters would result. Inhalation of the vapors would cause the blood cells of the lungs to release fluid—not blood but rather the fluid of the cells themselves.

"This is pulmonary edema—the irritant chemical causes the lung to fill with fluid, while the taking in of sufficient oxygen is reduced—it's like internal drowning. . . . The fluid goes where the air is supposed to be.

"Pulmonary edema is simply fluid accumulation in the lungs."

Yanetti said, "What happens to Curley then?"

"He has less opportunity to take in air that has oxygen to allow him to breathe," Ryan said. "As the gasoline vapors become circulated in the bloodstream, they go to the heart, which causes them to circulate throughout the body."

The prosecutor said, "What effect does it have on the heart?"

"It causes arrhythmia . . . an irregular beating of the heart."

"Doctor, when arrhythmia begins, is the person aware of it?"

"Yes. They can feel that something is going wrong."

"When the fluid in the lungs is worsened, what effect does that have on Curley?"

"Further inability to breathe," Ryan said. "Eventually this all works to depriving the brain of adequate oxygen and ultimately brings on death."

"Do you have an opinion as to if Jeffrey Curley died instantly?"

"I do. My opinion is that he did not," Dr. Ryan said.

Lastly, Kathryn Colombo, employed by Cellmark Diagnostics lab, an expert on DNA testing, testified that semen matching that of Sal Sicari was found in the backseat of Jaynes's car, and that samples of semen matching those of Jaynes were found on the kitchen floor of his Manchester apartment. But defense established that there was no way to tell when that deposit had been made.

The prosecution rested its case.

The defense's first witness was Nadine Fallon, an International Bicycle employee. Defense counsel Kelly reiterated his argument that the defendant and Charles Jaynes had bought a bike suitable only for a very young child, one that would have been unsuitable for Curley.

Next, Newton Police Department detective Glen Harris said that on October 9, 1997, he'd gone to International Bicycle to interview Fabio Selvig about "transactions regarding this case." Kelly said, "Did Selvig ever say to you that Sicari had said, 'We're looking for a bike for a ten-year-old child'?"

"No," Harris said.

Rachid Farhat, a Honda Village salesperson, said that Saturday, September 27, 1997, was the last time he'd seen Jeffrey Curley hanging around with Charles Jaynes. "I asked Jaynes to clean a car in

the morning, and they were playing with the hose—
spraying each other with water."

Kelly said, "How long was Curley in the company
of Jaynes?"

The witness thought it had been a full workday,
from nine to five o'clock, because he'd seen Curley
with Jaynes in the afternoon, too. Kelly said, "Had
you ever seen Sal Sicari in the company of Jaynes
or Curley in September or August of 1997?"

"No," Farhat said.

James Rhodey, another Honda Village employee,
told more of the curious relationship between
Jaynes and Curley. "They acted like they were the
best of friends—like they'd known each other for
years."

Shawna Clemens, twenty, from Brockton, knew
Charles Jaynes "through my former friend who was
dating him—Robyn Kneil." In 1996, she said, she'd
been riding with Jaynes in his car, driving through
East Bridgewater. "We were driving down the street
and I hadn't talked to him for about a year and
we saw a group of young boys and he said, 'Ooh,
I'd like to get a piece of that.' He was referring to
one of the young boys."

Kelly said, "How old was the child?"

"Between eleven and thirteen."

"Had you seen him in the company of young
boys?"

"Yes, all the time."

Kelly moved on to another incident. "Were you
with Charles Jaynes alone in Brockton or Newton?"

Clemens said, "Yes."

"What were you talking about?"

"What all of us would do with a body if we killed

someone. He said he would put the body in a container, fill it with cement, and dump it in the river."

"When did he say that?"

"I would probably say 1994, if I had to."

The defense rested its case.

Judge Cowin asked Sal Sicari if he was going to testify. Sicari said, "I don't want to—no."

On Monday, November 9, 1998, day ten, Kelly began his closing argument for the defense. "Jeffrey Curley was killed at four [P.M., October 1, 1997] and he was murdered by one man, Charles Jaynes. Not one witness gave the jury any evidence at all that Sal Sicari was interested in young boys, that he was involved in the plan with Jaynes to lure a young child, with a promise of a bike, into sex. None of the witnesses gave evidence relative to motive or intent to kill."

Charles Jaynes was a pedophile. "We heard from Honda Village people—they saw Curley with Jaynes alone . . . and yes, some people said Sicari was sometimes there, but it was Jaynes who was horsing around with him, had him on his shoulders, etc.

"Charlene LeTourneau says on October first, Sicari calls her—he says, 'I killed someone'—she didn't believe him, he'd lied in the past. What's important is that she says Sicari was excellent around her child and his own children."

Kelly scorned International Bicycle salesclerk Fabio Selvig. "He wanted his fifteen minutes of fame. When interviewed [by police] on October ninth [1997], he said, 'Scaccia [Jaynes] was doing all the talking.' He told you that Sal Sicari said he was looking to buy a bike for a ten-year-old boy . . . but I asked an officer, 'Did he ever say Sicari said he was looking for a bike for a ten-year-old boy?' He hadn't.''

As for Sgt. Nagle, "he writes down that Sicari says, 'I fucked up.' Nagle takes the stand a year later and says he wants us to believe Sicari said, 'I did it.' "

Winding up, Kelly said, "Did we see any evidence whatsoever as to Sicari's motives and intentions to kill? No, it was Charles Jaynes alone who had motive and intent—and Jaynes went alone to pick up Curley; then he picked up Sicari. He killed Curley alone and Sicari did nothing to prevent it."

Jaynes used his father's credit card to pay for the ingredients to dispose of the body; Jaynes's prints were on the cement-mixing spoon; Jaynes's prints were on the road map.

"It was Charles Jaynes who didn't help the police," Kelly said. "Why? Because he has a trail of guilt. It took place months before, starting in summer—the seduction started—by one man, Charles Jaynes."

The Commonwealth of Massachusetts had failed to prove the case beyond a reasonable doubt "in so far as Sal Sicari is not guilty of first-degree murder," Kelly concluded.

But the prosecution called it Murder One, Yanetti arguing in his closing that the case boiled down to a simple fact: "Curley left Cambridge with *two men*—the two men who had spent time with him, seduced him—and he never came home. He never came home because these two men killed him because he wouldn't do what they wanted him to do—that's why we're here.

"Sal Sicari is guilty of murder in the first degree by joint venture and you will know that.

"Though not knowing it, he admits to sharing intent for this crime—in his final statement, he says that when he and Jaynes pulled up to Curley's grandmother's house, he ducked down in the car so no one would see him.

"Why is he doing that? You know why . . . because he knew what was going to happen—he has been involved in the seduction every step of the way, and this was The Day.

"Even putting himself in the best light and shifting the blame, he still says he saw Jaynes put Curley in the backseat and what does he do? Does he do nothing? Was he only a gutless coward?

"No! He closed doors, jumped in the driver's seat, and drove away so Jaynes could finish the job."

Yanetti said that Sicari knew that Jaynes was a pedophile. "In the summer and September of 1997, who spent the most time with Jaynes and with Jaynes and Curley? There's one answer to that question—Sicari.

"Sicari, Jeffrey and Jaynes together—that's the strange relationship between these three. Sicari was the link between Jaynes and Curley. . . . Sicari had gained Curley's trust and Sicari helped Jaynes gain Curley's trust."

Motive?

"I suggest that on October first, that was a big day for Charles Jaynes and his buddy Sal Sicari . . . a big day. . . . The seduction that was orchestrated over the summer and September was about to pay off that day," Yanetti said.

That's why Jaynes and Sicari had gone into the bike shop the day before. They didn't care what kind of bike they bought. It was all window dressing, the bike was *bait*.

Yanetti said, "October first was the big day, but something went wrong. Jeffrey Curley said no—he refused, and that's when these two men made the decision to kill him . . . and then they acted on it—by forcing him to inhale gasoline vapors, and his body couldn't take it anymore, and he died."

Sicari and his cohort Jaynes had killed with "extreme cruelty," Yanetti said. "October first was a big day for Jeff Curley as well . . . because on this day, he got to go with his good friends Charlie and Sal—he trusted them, respected them. . . . He's picked up and he thinks [that] these two guys are going to buy him a bike! Best day of his life . . .

"And that respect turned to horror and distrust and terror when he found why they were really treating him like they were treating him. But by saying no and refusing to do what they wanted him to do, he had to die.

"They had to do that because he struggled, scratched, he clawed . . . all because he was struggling and he did not die quickly.

"The gasoline seeps in and burns his face and mouth—vapors fill his lungs, and that causes difficulty breathing—he panics—'Why are Sal and Charlie doing this to me?' He suffered—Jeffrey Curley suffered, and eventually he died."

Yanetti reminded the jury what Charlene LeTourneau said Sal Sicari had said to her on the phone, talking about murder: "It's like a bowl of cereal. I could eat it or I could walk away from it."

He asked the jury to find Sicari guilty of murder in the first degree, "and nothing less."

During the jury charge, the judge's instructions were ninety minutes long. Jurors later said they found the joint venture theory confusing. The jury was sequestered during deliberations.

The trial had taken nearly three weeks. Starting on Monday, November 9, deliberations lasted twenty-three hours, twenty-four minutes over the course of four days—ending on Thursday, November 12, at 2:29 P.M., when the jury reached a verdict.

The court clerk said, "Charging the defendant, Salvatore Sicari, with murder, what say you? Is the defendant guilty or not guilty?"

The jury foreperson, a woman, said, "Guilty."

"Guilty of what, ma'am?"

"Guilty of murder in the first degree."

"Guilty, so say all members of this panel?"

All: *"Yes!"*

Sicari was also found guilty of kidnapping.

Arthur Kelly later told *Court TV,* "Charlene LeTourneau was a very difficult witness for the defense to combat. . . . She indicated that she had spoken to Mr. Sicari shortly after the murder, and in some respects, he had boasted, or bragged, or showed very little remorse, if any, with regard to the death of Jeffrey Curley."

After victim impact statements by the Curleys, Judge Cowin sentenced Sal Sicari to life imprisonment without parole for the murder (a mandatory sentence) and ten years for the kidnapping, sentences to run concurrently.

No family member or friend of his had ever been seen in the courtroom.

Judge Cowin moved Charles Jaynes's trial for murder and kidnapping to East Brookfield, Massachusetts, one hundred miles away from East Cambridge. The town billed itself as "the youngest town in the commonwealth." Three of the jurors from the Sicari case were curious enough about Jaynes to go to the site to see his trial.

As Sicari's lawyer, Arthur Kelly had tried to put the onus for the crime on Jaynes. Robert Jubinville, Jaynes's lawyer, argued that Sal Sicari was the real author of the crime, intimidating a weak-willed Jaynes into helping carry out the cover-up.

As in Sicari's trial, prosecutor David Yanetti represented the Commonwealth of Massachusetts, presenting much the same evidence as in the previous case: Jeff Curley's maroon jersey, the button and label from his shorts, the concrete-mixing spoon. But Massachusetts state law forbade him from using Sicari's confession in his trial against his joint venturer, Charles Jaynes.

Jurors later said that there was no evidence to show who killed Jeff Curley, where he was killed, or what time he was killed. Jubinville, Jaynes's attorney, argued there was no evidence to show that the boy's body had ever been in the Manchester apartment. "No chemist, no FBI guy, nobody, produced a piece of evidence."

Jubinville contended that Sicari alone killed Curley, then planted the evidence in Jaynes's apartment to frame him. "He set this guy up six ways to Sunday."

Closing for the commonwealth, prosecutor Yanetti painted a dramatic word picture of Jeff Curley's final moments. "He panics. Panics! The vapors fill his lungs. It burns!

"Jeffrey Curley was dead at four-thirty when Mr. Jaynes ran into that NHD store to get that very roll of duct tape that he would later use to wrap that container. Dead in the car. He got that tarp to cover Jeffrey Curley's body in the car—"

Suddenly, Jaynes leaped up from his seat at the defense table, shouting, "I never hurt him! I never hurt J.C.!"

Commotion seized the court, people reacting angrily. Robert Curley shouted something at Jaynes. Jaynes was led out as the court recessed.

Ultimately, his outburst was ignored by the jurors, some of whose members later said that they'd disregarded it as a factor in their deliberations, which lasted nearly ten hours.

On December 11, 1998, they found Jaynes guilty of second-degree murder and kidnapping. At age twenty-three, Charles Jaynes was sentenced to life in prison, but would be eligible for parole in twenty-three years.

For those involved in the case, the nightmares would last a lot longer.

As Massachusetts State Police sergeant Greg Foley told *Court TV*, "It's probably one of the worst cases that I've ever worked on. Just the fact that this could've happened to any boy, anywhere. And if there's any lesson to be learned out there for anybody, for parents and teachers and so on, it is that it could've happened to any child at any time. These were predators that set out to find a young boy; they found this young boy; they set their eyes on him. And they went after him and they got him.

"It's a terrible thing, it's every parent's worst nightmare. And for me, it was possibly the worst case I've ever worked on. Over those twenty-four years, I've investigated over three hundred homicides. And this was a brutal one. It was a brutal ending to the case and the search and everything else, and it's one of the worst cases I've worked on."

Florida v. *Rolling:*
"THE COED
SERIAL KILLER"

In early January 1978, a stranger arrived in the college town of Gainesville, Florida. He liked college towns, they made good hunting grounds. A sexual sadist and serial killer, and now a hunted fugitive, the newcomer was rocketing outward on the final wild trajectory of a raging lust for destruction. Late one Saturday night in mid-January, he exploded in a nightmarish outburst of savage brutality, leaving two young lives snuffed out and three more critically wounded. After an intensive manhunt, the killer was caught, tried, sentenced to death and, after wending his way through a long delaying maze of legal appeals and ploys, finally executed.

He was Ted Bundy, one of the most notorious serial killers of modern times. His Saturday-night massacre at the Chi Omega house on Sorority Row threw Gainesville into a panic, terrorizing it in ways that would take years in which to recover.

In the third week of August 1990, eighteen

months after Ted Bundy was put to death, a lone drifter blew into town. . . .

THE CRIME

Located in north central Florida, south of Jacksonville and Tallahassee and north of Tampa, Gainesville is the site of the University of Florida and a cluster of colleges. In late August, the town's summertime population of about 15,000 swells to 35,000 as students return for the fall semester. This is the time when next-door neighbors are still strangers to each other. With a large transient population and the easygoing tolerance often associated with the college lifestyle come anonymity and freedom from suspicion. In the words of Wayland Clifton, former Gainesville Chief of Police, "It is a particularly vulnerable time."

On Sunday, August 26, 1990, the parents of Christine Powell, seventeen, a freshman at the University of Florida, were deeply concerned by their inability to contact their daughter for the last three days. Leaving their Jacksonville home, they arrived at the Williamsburg apartment complex at Southwest Fifteenth Avenue in Gainesville, where Christine lived with her roommate, Sonja Larson, eighteen, also a freshman at the university.

At the apartment in Building 11, a day or two's worth of notes from friends seeking to contact either Powell or Larson was attached to their door. Powell's worried parents spoke to the handyman, who, reluctant to enter a tenant's apartment without the authorities present, called the police.

Officer Ray Barber of the Gainesville Police Department (GPD) responded to the call. Arriving at the Williamsburg Apartments, he told Powell's parents to wait outside while he checked to make sure everything was okay.

The maintenance man couldn't find a key, so he and Barber ended up breaking down the door. Barber went in, coming face-to-face with murder.

The bloody body of Christine Powell, who'd wanted to study architecture so she could design housing for the poor, now lay posed on the living room couch—posed by her killer. It would be learned later that her hands had been tied behind her back with duct tape and that she'd been gagged with a double strip of duct tape. The killer had taken the duct tape with him.

Powell had been raped, then stabbed five times in the back. Her nipples had been cut off and taken away, and her legs were posed spread in a sexual position. The killer had cleaned the body with dish-washing liquid.

Upstairs, Sonja Larson, an active churchgoer who'd wanted to be a teacher, lay naked and dead in her bed in a mass of blood. She'd been gagged with duct tape, stabbed to death and sexually posed.

Going back outside, a shaken Officer Barber told Powell that he and his wife should continue waiting outside and not go in. Barber said, "There's something very wrong here."

Wayland Clifton, then-Gainesville Chief of Police, was off-duty at home that Sunday, watching a preseason football game when he got the news. A phone call from his deputy chief informed him that there'd been a double homicide and that Clifton was needed on the scene. On a weekend, that meant it must be something highly unusual.

Clifton went to the site, noting that the Williamsburg complex was bordered in places by patches of wood, with thick semitropical undergrowth that could screen an individual only a step or two inside the foliage.

Clifton later told *Court TV*, "I realized on the first view of the scene that this was not what you would call a routine homicide, a domestic dispute or anything like that. That we had a real serious situation."

This was urgent. The killer would kill again. "We are a university city and I realized here we had forty thousand potential victims on our hands and somebody that would not be satiated with this first murder. I knew that he would strike again," said Clifton, whose own son was at that time a recent University of Florida graduate.

"The victims were posed," Clifton said. "Not only murdered but posed, kind of baiting the police, letting us know that this was something that would be a signature type of crime, and it was. . . .

"There were two victims, there was mutilation, body parts taken from the scene. This was something that, as a police officer for twenty-five years, I had seen before. But when I had seen it before, I knew that I was working with a serial murderer. There is a kind of savagery about these scenes, and the specific scene as far as the two victims at Williamsburg just kind of shouted out, 'This is not the last' . . . and that is exactly the way it turned out to be."

Clifton moved immediately to call on as much outside help as he could get, to marshal resources to thwart a killer. He spent most of Sunday night into Monday morning calling on various law enforcement contacts, seeking "federal assistance, state assistance, military assistance."

The chief managed to snatch about two hours of sleep before being awakened early Monday morning, August 27. The Alachua County Sheriff's Office (ASO) called, notifying him that they'd found a second case, similar to the first, but with even more mutilation. This time, the victim had been beheaded. The body had been discovered about eight to nine hours after the Williamsburg crime scene.

Clifton went to a duplex on Southwest Twenty-fourth Street, the residence of Christa Hoyt, eighteen, from Archer, Florida. She attended Santa Fe Community College and worked as a records clerk at the local sheriff's office.

Officer Keith O'Hara was a colleague of Christa Hoyt's at the Alachua County Sheriff's Office. After Hoyt failed to report to work on the midnight shift, he was dispatched to go to her apartment to see if there was a problem. He knocked on her front door to try to wake her up. After that failed, he located resident manager Elbert Hoover, telling him that Hoyt had not shown up for work recently and asking him to open her apartment.

As they went to the rear of the apartment, Hoover noticed that the gate accessing Hoyt's area was unlatched. This worried him, as earlier on Saturday, August 25, he'd also noticed it was unlatched and had spoken to Hoyt about it. She'd said that she thought it had been unlatched by a telephone line repairman who'd been working in the area. The gate had then been relatched.

Now the gate was once again unlatched, and a chain-link security fence leading into the property had been pulled or pushed down, further alarming the landlord.

By crouching down on the rear patio, O'Hara was able to peek into Hoyt's bedroom through a sliding glass door. Her body was in a sitting position on the bed, nude but for tennis shoes and socks. He could see that she was dead. Of that there could be no doubt—her body was missing a head.

Hoover opened the door and the lawman went inside. Hoover asked him if Hoyt was okay. O'Hara said that Hoyt was not okay.

Sheriff's deputy John Nobles, responding to the call, became concerned shortly after his arrival at the scene outside, when someone canceled the ambulance. Finally he was told, "John, she doesn't need an ambulance."

Inside, investigators discovered a blood-orgy of destruction, carefully staged for maximum outrage. The killer had moved a bookshelf into the victim's bedroom. On it, he placed Hoyt's severed head, the mouth sealed shut with a double strip of duct tape. It was surrounded by mirrors, perhaps to multiply the horror or to reflect back the finder's shocked expression at the sight of the grisly tableau.

The killer had not stopped there. The victim's body was gutted, carved open from pelvic bone to breastbone. The breasts had been viciously slashed and mutilated. Chief Clifton, of the Gainesville Police Department, told *Court TV*, "In twenty-five-plus years I had not seen a scene like that, and I was an embalmer in a funeral home even before I became a police officer. So that was by far the worst, the most brutal crime scene that I had seen. It immediately verified exactly what I'd said just a few hours [before] on the previous evening, that we had a serial murderer, we had forty thousand potential victims. He was loose in Gainesville and he was bent on killing."

News of Sunday's double-homicide discovery was public knowledge on Monday, widely circulated in the early edition newspapers and on early morning radio and TV news. Finding the third victim at dawn sparked a panic. The Gainesville Police Department was swamped with thousands of calls requesting that officers check out backyards and "suspicious" neighbors.

Chief Clifton contacted Florida senator Bob Graham, in Washington, D.C. Clifton had been a member of Graham's staff back in the early 1980s, when Graham had been governor of Florida. Now, Senator Graham paved the way for the participation of local Navy, Air Force and other military units.

Clifton noted, "He came through because an investigation like this would cost . . . I think the initial cost was four million dollars and they'd gone to six million. If you put in the prosecution part of the case, probably seven or eight million. That would have completely bankrupted the police department . . . that was all paid by the federal government." But that came later.

After the discovery of Christa Hoyt, a joint meeting of investigators from the Gainesville Police Department, the Alachua County Sheriff's Office and the statewide Florida Department of Law Enforcement (FDLE) was held, to discuss working the cases together. Six FDLE agents were assigned to the case. The governor swiftly sent eighty-five state troopers and one hundred more FDLE investigators to Gainesville.

By late Monday afternoon, August 27, a Homicide Task Force had already been established. Investigators were formed into teams, canvassing and searching neighborhoods, interviewing residents in the vicinity of the victims' apartments. Police maintained high visibility, providing reassurance and deterrence. They put out the word to the students and the rest of the community at large: Be careful, lock your doors, stay inside, don't go out at night. A killer was loose.

Chief Clifton grabbed a few hours' sleep on Tuesday, August 28, from 3:00 to 7:00 A.M., when he was once again awakened by a call from the Sheriff's Office, informing him that they'd found two more victims in Gatorwood, "again right off of Archer Road."

The site was Gatorwood Apartments on Southwest Archer Road. Sharing an apartment were roommates Tracy Paules, twenty-three, and Manuel Taboada, twenty-three. Paules, an honor student and a political science major at the University of Florida, was a former class president at American High School, in Miami. Taboada, her longtime friend from high school and current, nonromantic roommate, attended Santa Fe Junior College, and wanted to be an architect.

Mutual friends of Paules and Taboada became worried when they were unable to contact them on Monday, August 27. On Tuesday morning, Paules's boyfriend, Tom Carrol, was worried because she hadn't returned his phone call from the night before, so he went to the Gatorwood apartment. Paules's car was parked outside, as was Taboada's, but there was no reply when Carrol knocked on the front door.

At about 7:45 A.M., Carrol called the emergency contact number at the leasing office. The maintenance man came and went with Carrol to check. They went to the apartment. The maintenance man knocked on the door twice. He opened the door. He and Carrol went in—about four or five feet— then stopped in their tracks as they discovered Paules's body. She'd been raped, stabbed to death, then posed, propped up in the hallway.

They called the police. Responding to the Gatorwood call, Deputy Dan Alexander went to the scene. Upon entering the apartment, he found a female lying in the hallway between the two bedrooms—Tracy Paules. Her mouth had been taped shut and her hands tied behind her back with duct tape. Her nipples had been cut off and taken away.

Stepping over her, the deputy proceeded to search the apartment. A male was dead in a room to the left of the hall. He could tell the man was dead and didn't need first aid.

Alexander exited the apartment. He and another deputy kept the scene sealed until investigators arrived. ASO investigator Greg Weeks noted that the apartment's front door had been damaged, as if it had been forced open.

Steve Leary, an FDLE crime lab analyst, arrived at Gatorwood at 10:30 A.M. and searched the scene. There was a towel between Paules's legs. He collected adhesive residue from her wrists, where they'd been bound with duct tape that the killer had taken away. It appeared she'd been dragged from the bedroom to the hallway. Her bedroom window curtains had been duct-taped shut by the killer, presumably so no one could see inside while he was having his fun. Leary found blood in the kitchen, cleaning fluids, bloody towels and bloody paper towels.

A high school football star, Manny Taboada was strong, athletic, powerfully built—and the only male victim of the rampage. He'd been killed in a waterbed, knifed to death, stabbed over thirty times. Savage defensive wounds on his arms and upper body bore evidence of a desperate struggle for life. One knife thrust to the solar plexus had gone so deep into the chest that it damaged his spine.

The first two killings were in Gainesville, falling under GPD jurisdiction, but the other three fell under the jurisdiction of the Alachua County Sheriff's Office. By Tuesday, August 28, they'd been augmented by the State Police, FDLE investigators, military personnel, and the FBI, including profiler John "Mind-hunter" Douglas of the forensic team.

The Homicide Task Force had about 260 GPD police officers, 200 from the Sheriff's office, plus backup from the University Police Department. State troopers and military Special Forces operators fanned out into the woods, searching night and day.

There was panic on Monday, but the terror in Gainesville peaked on Tuesday, after the finding of Paules and Taboada. All days off were canceled as local law enforcement agencies put their members on twelve-hour shifts. Woods were searched; ponds were drained for clues.

As Chief Clifton recalled, "By that [Tuesday] evening, Gainesville was literally a police state. If you were on Archer Road, you couldn't go ten feet without seeing one or two or three or four police officers." There were six or seven helicopters in the air: "customs, FDLE's helicopters, helicopters from the county surrounding Gainesville. The FBI brought what they call the Night Stalker [aircraft], ten thousand feet up, infrared (IR), can see anything that's one foot square and gives off heat." But it didn't see the killer.

The city of Gainesville was in a panic, an armed camp. Parents were taking their children home from the university. Female students slept twenty to a dorm room. Business fell off by sixty-five percent.

But neither the University of Florida nor Santa Fe Community College canceled classes. University of Florida president John Lombardi stood beside Chief Clifton, urging students to keep calm at a session attended by a horde of media representatives and cameras, as well as students. The chief held daily briefings for the media. Rumor control kept in check unconfirmed stories, such as the rumor the killer was dressing and posing as a police officer.

Commissioner Moore, of the Florida Department of Law Enforcement, made the case a priority, as more than thirty additional agents and crime scene analysts were sent to Gainesville. By Friday, August 31, more than 160 FDLE investigators were on the scene, as well as five FDLE aircraft and three other state aircraft.

Helicopters with IR body-heat detectors overflew Gainesville nightly. People complained until they found out what it was all about, then later complained when the night flights were curtailed.

Chief Clifton described the profile of the killer as worked up by analysts. "A white male, a young person, somebody under forty, probably somebody under thirty-five or within that range." It was not much to go on, but it was a start.

Hundreds of leads poured in, not just from the immediate area but from all over the United States. The FBI provided computer equipment to handle the masses of data. The computer system eventually had approximately 40,000 names in it that were associated with the investigation—more individuals than the population of Gainesville. During the investigation, 6,925 leads were received and investigated, generating more than 4,580 investigative reports.

Leads were categorized according to priorities, with the hottest leads getting top priority. They would then be divided up among FDLE, GPD, UPD and the Sheriff's Office investigators.

After about three weeks, a special subunit was formed: "The head shot, a group of officers and investigators that took the leads that the officers couldn't see any connection with to the crime scenes and actually kind of reviewed each one of those leads to see if they had any connection to the crime scene," Clifton said.

An early prime suspect was University of Florida freshman Edward Lewis Humphrey, eighteen, who lived near the Gatorwood Apartments where Taboada and Paules were killed. Once a handsome and popular high school student, his parents' divorce had plunged him into depression and a downward spiral, culminating in a serious car wreck that had left him with a faceful of scars. He was on lithium for manic-depression, but he wasn't taking it. He was big, confused, violent and potentially dangerous. He liked to wear military-style fatigue pants, carried a hunting knife, and prowled around in the woods after dark.

Word of Humphrey's erratic behavior reached police, who began surveilling him. Chief Clifton said, "He made an extremely good subject." FDLE Special Agent Ed Dix told *Court TV* that students had told him about Humphrey's "liking of knives, that he would go out late at night or early in the morning carrying a large knife. He'd be dressed in camouflage. Many times, he'd put a bandana on and tell them he was going out on recon."

Humphrey had been seen peeking into windows at women, and made frequent reference to his invisible Rambo-style companion, John. More damningly, two days after the bodies of Taboada and Paules were discovered, Ed Humphrey was arrested by Brevard County, Florida, authorities and charged with battering his seventy-nine-year-old grandmother. That kept him safely in custody, while the investigation continued.

Perhaps it was the resilience of youth, but by the end of the week, the panic died down. Students began going out jogging again, and life returned to its natural rhythms, so much so that the Gainesville Police Department felt obliged to issue continual warnings that the killer was still loose and that the public should still maintain precautions.

The first few weeks after the killings were spent surveilling Gainesville and its environs: "The strongest surveillance, the most intense surveillance you could possibly have in any crime scene," Chief Clifton said.

Early on in the investigation, the Homicide Task Force received a call from a detective from Shreveport, Louisiana, where they had an unsolved triple homicide whose modus operandi (the way the crime was committed) was similar to the Gainesville student murders.

In November 1989, Julie Grissom, twenty-four, her father, Thomas Grissom, fifty-eight, and her son, Sean, eight, were all slain in Thomas Grissom's house. Police theorized that Julie Grissom, a nursing student, had been the primary object of the attack. She'd been raped and stabbed in the chest and back. She'd been bound with duct tape, which the killer had taken with him. Her body had been cleaned, swabbed with vinegar, presumably in an attempt to destroy evidence. She, too, had been posed, her nude body found arranged on the bed with her long black hair fanning out.

The boy and his grandfather had been killed by being stabbed in the back with a military-style knife. Investigators believed that they'd come home and surprised the rapist-killer in the act—Thomas Grissom had been killed while trying to escape.

Two days after the Shreveport detective's call, the Grissom murders were again brought to the Task Force's attention, this time by the FBI's computerized Violent Criminal Apprehension Program, (VICAP), whose database on violent crimes lists unsolved crimes with their modus operandi.

Task Force investigators could place prime suspect Ed Humphrey in Gainesville at the time of the first crime, but they couldn't place him at the second or even the third crime scene. Chief Clifton said, "We knew he could not be involved in the third crime scene because we had telephone tolls. He was down on the Florida turnpike calling his grandmother back in Melbourne, the same one he battered later and we put him in jail for."

The Gainesville killer had gone to some lengths to clean the bodies of the rape-murder victims to destroy evidence, yet he'd left semen at all three crime scenes. Chief Clifton noted, "The murderer was not leaving information except that he was leaving body fluids there, which he didn't know he was leaving."

Analysts classified the killer's blood as Type B. Ed Humphrey's blood was Type A. More than anything else, that lack of a matching blood type helped get him off the hook as the prime suspect in the Gainesville slayings.

Between 1,200 and 1,500 blood samples were taken from various subjects. Clifton said, "If Gainesville had not had the resources of the state and the federal government, we could never have gotten through this. This would maybe have taken months and months and months and maybe never [have] been solved."

In November 1990, the Shreveport Police Department called the Task Force again, passing along a tip. They'd received a call from a woman, living on the Texas/Louisiana border, who'd seen a news report about the arrest of a man in Ocala, Florida, for armed robbery. The suspect was from Shreveport, and had been in town at the time of the Grissom murders, whose modus operandi was similar to the Gainesville murders. The Shreveport police also requested that the FBI check the suspect's military records for blood type.

Chief Clifton said, "We found in Marion County Jail, in the county to the south of Gainesville, thirty miles away in Ocala, we found an individual in jail there that was from Shreveport, Louisiana. His name was Danny Rolling and he voluntarily gave us blood and pubic hair [samples]."

On September 7, 1990, thirty-six-year-old Louisiana drifter and career criminal Danny Rolling was arrested for armed robbery in Ocala, Florida. After robbing a Winn-Dixie supermarket, Rolling had led police on a high-speed chase that ended when he crashed his 1983 Mustang into a police car.

The Mustang had been stolen earlier in Tampa by a thief who broke into an apartment at night while the owners were asleep in bed. Jimmying open a sliding glass door, the burglar stole the car keys and two watches, pausing during the burglary to take a banana from the fridge and eat it, leaving the peel draped over the back of a chair.

While in Tampa, Rolling had also robbed a Save-n'-Pack grocery store, narrowly escaping capture in a wild car chase. A second car, which he'd abandoned in Tampa, turned out to have been stolen in Gainesville, a fact that the Ocala Police Department passed along to the Gainesville Police Department. Rolling was being held in the Marion County Jail.

Who was Danny Rolling? Born on May 26, 1954 to James and Claudia Rolling, he was a cop's son. Lt. James Harold Rolling, his father, was a twenty-year veteran of the Shreveport, Louisiana, Police Department. The Follings had another son, too, younger Kevin.

After the tenth grade, Danny Rolling dropped out of high school. A brief stint in the Air Force led to a general discharge. He went back to his parents' home in Shreveport, where he joined the United Pentecostal Church, saying he'd found God. When he was nineteen, he prayed for a wife, soon meeting O'Mather Halko, a petite brunette, whom he wed in 1974 after about a six-month courtship. In 1976, a daughter was born, and in 1977, his wife divorced him, getting custody of the child.

In 1979, at age twenty-five, Rolling's crime career began in earnest. On May 25, 1979, he robbed a Winn-Dixie supermarket in Montgomery, Alabama. On May 31, in Columbus, Georgia, he knocked over a second Winn-Dixie. These first armed robberies were committed with his father's service revolver.

He was arrested, and in July 1979, he was convicted of two counts of armed robbery and sentenced to serve six years in Georgia State Prison.

In October of that year, he escaped briefly, being recaptured a few hours after his breakout.

In February 1980, while still in prison in Georgia, he pleaded guilty to robbing the Winn-Dixie in Montgomery, Alabama. He was convicted of one count of robbery and sentenced to ten years, two of which he eventually wound up serving. On June 7, 1982, Rolling was finished serving his sentence in Georgia and was released to Alabama State Prison, to serve his sentence for the Alabama heist. A month later, he escaped but was recaptured two days later.

He served out the rest of his term without incident, and on June 7, 1984, two years to the day from the time when he'd gone inside Alabama prison gates, he was released. Wasting little time, Rolling soon returned to pulling down scores. On July 22, 1985, he held up a Kroger food store in Clinton, Mississippi, and was soon arrested.

His postarrest behavior could be described as eccentric. Awaiting sentencing in Mississippi in 1985 for robbery, he'd asked his lawyer if the judge would agree to cutting off his hands. He also shaved his head and eyebrows. Convicted on one count of robbery, he was sentenced to a term of fifteen years (twelve suspended, three probation).

Rolling was incarcerated in the state prison at Parchman, Mississippi, a tough—some might say harsh—penal institute. He would later complain about having had to eat his meals in a cell whose floor was covered with three inches of "raw sewage," and for years after maintained that he was still enraged by the "inhuman" conditions he claimed he'd been forced to endure while imprisoned there.

He served three years in Parchman, from July 1985 through July 1988. His stay was interrupted from April 15 to April 22, 1986, during a brief escape attempt that got him as far as El Paso, Texas, before being recaptured. On July 29, 1988, he was released on five years' probation, until July 1993.

After each prison term, Danny Rolling would always return home, and this time was no exception. Paroled from the state of Mississippi, he went back to his parents' Shreveport, Louisiana, home. Neighbors from that period recall him as an oddball, jogging around in camouflage clothes with a heavy log draped across his shoulders. They also remembered him as being physically strong—very strong. He used to practice martial arts on trees, kicking and punching them.

On May 19, 1990, Danny Rolling got into an argument with his father, James Rolling, who was already sore because his son hadn't rolled up the car windows when it was raining. There were harsh words, with the senior Rolling brandishing his handgun. Danny Rolling ran into a shed and grabbed two guns. James Rolling had gone inside the house. Danny kicked open the door, saying, "You want a shoot-out, we'll have a shoot-out." He shot his father in the face and stomach, then ran. James Rolling survived, though blinded in one eye.

Danny Rolling was again on the lam. In addition to the shooting, he was now a parole-breaker.

* * *

"As a matter of fact, Danny Rolling came in as a priority three. He was one of our lower priorities," Chief Clifton recalled. "When I first had an opportunity to view Danny Rolling, that was probably one of the strangest moments in the whole investigation for me at least, because here was this individual that was bright, not educated, uneducated but bright. He looked rather pitiful. He had a look about him that almost made you feel sympathy—if you had not seen these crime scenes. Seeing those crime scenes, I had absolutely no sympathy for him at all.

"But he simply did not meet the physical criteria that I was looking for in a serial murderer. As I say, he looked rather pitiful. His facial expressions looked rather meek and mild to say the least. Kind of evoked a sense that you know this person. So that was one of the most strange moments.

"Of all the suspects . . . almost every one of them physically looked more like what you would conjure up in your mind as a serial killer than Danny Rolling."

On January 1, 1991, Rolling started off the New Year by throwing a toilet against a dayroom window several times in an apparent escape attempt from Marion County Jail. The window remained unbroken, the toilet bouncing off and landing on Rolling's foot. His hands were severely cut from pulling the toilet off its mounting. He was already missing the tips of two fingers from a prison bakery accident.

On January 2, FBI records indicated that Rolling

had the same Type B blood group as the suspect in the Gainesville homicides. The next day, Rolling consented to the taking of a blood sample. On January 11, lab analysis indicated that Danny Rolling had the same enzymes in his blood as the Gainesville suspect. This was a significant step toward narrowing the focus to a high-probability lead. Also that day, a Gainesville Homicide Task Force member contacted Marion County Jail, requesting that they be notified if Rolling was ever released.

On January 19, the DNA results of Rolling's blood indicated a match with the Gainesville suspect's semen. That sent Danny Rolling bulleting to the top of the prime suspects list.

On January 22, in jail, Rolling had a tooth extracted by a dentist. After the tooth had been wrapped in gauze and thrown away, a prison guard retrieved it, turning it over to the authorities. The following day, Homicide Task Force investigators arrived in Shreveport and began probing Danny Rolling's background.

What had Rolling done after shooting his father and fleeing in May 1990 and the time of the Gainesville slayings, three months later?

Investigators learned that Rolling had first gone to Kansas City, Kansas, staying at various motels. In June, he burglarized the home of the parents of Michael Kennedy, a deceased Vietnam veteran whose ID and identity were appropriated by Rolling as an alias.

Leaving Kansas City on July 10, Rolling headed southwest, surfacing in Tallahassee, Florida, where he stayed at a motel from July 17 to July 22, registered under the name "Mike Kennedy." From July

22 through August 18, Rolling was in Sarasota, Florida, where he stayed at two motels. He carried $15,000 in cash, indulging in showy spending sprees and dating two different women.

On August 18, Rolling checked into Gainesville's University Inn, a few blocks away from the University of Florida campus. On August 23, he checked out of the hotel and bought a tent and a foam mattress at a nearby Wal-Mart. While there, he shoplifted duct tape, athletic gloves and a screwdriver.

On August 28, the day after the First National Union Bank on Archer Road was robbed, police discovered Rolling's campsite in a wooded area owned by the University of Florida. Eluding police, Rolling burglarized an apartment and stole a car, heading south to Tampa, where he robbed a grocery store, burglarized three apartments, and stole another car, driving to Ocala and the Winn-Dixie heist resulting in his capture.

Chief Clifton recalled, "It turned out that Danny Rolling was a career criminal, which usually would indicate then that that person will not be your serial murderer if you're a career criminal. He's probably the best cat burglar, a person that breaks into homes, residences and cars to steal, that I've seen. . . .

"So that would generally give you an indication that that kind of career criminal is not a murderer."

In June 1991, during a hearing, Rolling's public defender questioned Rolling's competency. When the judge asked him, "Have you ever had any mental problems?" Rolling said, "Mental problems? I guess we all have a certain amount, huh?"

In July 1991, three Tampa mental health experts found that Rolling was competent to stand trial.

On September 18, 1991, Marion County Circuit judge Thomas D. Sawaya presided over Danny Rolling's trial for the previous year's armed robbery of an Ocala Winn-Dixie. Rolling was convicted for robbery with a firearm, aggravated assault, burglary, grand theft and grand theft auto.

Judge Sawaya asked Rolling if he had anything to say before his sentence was passed. Rolling said, "God bless the people of Florida and the Lord help me."

Sawaya gave him three life sentences plus a total of 130 years. The sentence was overturned on appeal and a new sentencing hearing scheduled.

On that same day, former prime suspect Ed Humphrey was released from prison, where he'd served ten months of a twenty-two-month sentence for beating his grandmother. Humphrey subsequently had plastic surgery on his face, lost fifty pounds and got his life back on track, ultimately graduating from college with honors.

On Friday, November 15, 1991, a grand jury indicted Danny Rolling on eleven charges relating to the Gainesville slayings, including five counts of murder, three counts of rape and three counts of armed robbery. The DNA testimony linking Rolling to the three murder scenes seemed to carry weight with the grand jurors.

On May 21, 1992, in Gainesville, in federal court, U.S. District judge Maurice Paul presided over the trial of Danny Rolling for armed bank robbery of the Gainesville bank. Before the sentencing, Rolling said, "This is a little unusual, Judge," and then said that he wanted to make a statement. Courtroom spectators wondered if he was going to confess to the Gainesville student murders. Instead, Rolling began singing a three-minute song about his love for Jesus.

When he was done, he was sentenced to twenty-five years for robbing the First Union National Bank, on Archer Road in Gainesville, with five years for being a convicted felon using a firearm and life in jail as a violent career criminal. He was then imprisoned at Florida State Prison.

On June 1, 1992, Rolling was put under suicide watch after having draped a sheet around his neck in what could have been an attempt to take his own life. Inmate Russell "Rusty" Binstead would later testify that Rolling had faked the suicide attempt to keep from being transferred out of the psych ward.

On Tuesday, June 9, 1992, Rolling, in his state prison cell, was formally charged and arrested for the Gainesville slayings. He pleaded not guilty. In mid-July 1992, authorities held their first meeting with convict Rusty Binstead concerning statements about the Gainesville slayings that Binstead claimed Rolling had made to him.

Rodney "Rod" Smith, a native Floridian, was elected State Attorney of the Eighth Judicial Circuit (five counties, including Alachua) in November 1992, taking office in January 1993. He was an avid outdoorsman and golfer, with three children.

Elected midterm as a state's attorney, Smith was

flung headfirst into the vortex of the Gainesville student murders investigation. His first act upon taking command of the Homicide Task Force was to tighten security against leaks. He felt that there was already too much confidential material about the investigation floating around out there in the media-sphere. Vital points of evidence withheld from the public could be crucial in separating out genuine suspects from a mass of false leads and blind alleys.

Tightening up the dissemination of vital information, Smith brought together lead investigators from the three main law enforcement agencies comprising the Task Force: the Alachua County Sheriff's Office, the Florida Department of Law Enforcement and the Gainesville Police Department. They were housed in a room that used to be a bank vault.

It was checked for bugs. This was the hottest story in Florida, with intensive national and worldwide media attention, and there was no telling what some enterprising types might do to get any first breaking news in the case. The Task Force was sealed in with lawyers, secretaries and administrative assistants, with access restricted to authorized personnel only. All evidence was housed in this one secure area.

Smith recalled, "If I had to look back on it in terms of things I think that turned around the direction of the case, I felt that move did, because I believe we were then allowed to have people who focused."

* * *

In the meantime, in true only-in-America celebrity serial-killer style, love had found Danny Rolling, and vice versa. Romance entered in the form of Sondra London, forty-five, a hefty but not unattractive brunette with a professional and personal penchant for men who kill people.

A technical writer by trade, London had an epiphany after reading true crime writer Anne Rule's 1987 book, *The Stranger Beside Me,* a nonfiction account of Rule's friendship with killer Ted Bundy, who'd worked beside her at a crisis intervention phone line, with Rule unaware that the pleasant-seeming fellow working next to her was one of the nation's most dangerous serial killers.

This appealed to London. She, too, was not without credentials in the celebrity serial-killer field. In high school, she'd dated John Gerard Schaefer, known to tabloid headline writers as the "Sex Beast." In fact, she claimed to have lost her virginity to him. Schaefer, a former Martin County, Florida, deputy sheriff, was convicted in 1973 of the murders of two teenage girls, whose bodies had been mutilated and decapitated. Police also found two gold teeth of a missing twenty-two-year-old woman and the locket of a missing twenty-five-year-old woman in his house, though he was not charged with these crimes. He was suspected but ultimately cleared in the deaths of two girls, eight and nine, a charge he indignantly denied as being "beyond the pale." He never murdered any girls under the age of sixteen, he said.

Two months after his murder conviction, Schaefer's wife divorced him, marrying his defense attorney a few days later. However the attorney explained it to Schaefer, it must have been convincing, since he had the lawyer handle his appeal, which was denied. London contacted Schaefer while he was serving a life sentence in Florida State Prison at Starke. They struck it off once more, and an intense correspondence followed, inspiring Schaefer to pen *Killer Fiction: Tales of an Accused Serial Killer,* a collection of stories predominantly featuring the mutilation and murder of prostitutes.

"These stories are designed to make you throw up and leave you looking over your shoulder for a long time," the proud author boasted. He also said that while they were in Florida State Prison together, Ted Bundy had told him that he, Schaefer, had been Bundy's inspiration.

Killer Fiction was available from London's mail-order publishing house, Media Queen News and Information Service, in Atlanta. Florida's version of the Son of Sam law prohibited criminals from profiting from their crimes. London owned the stories; Schaefer didn't get any money from them.

Schaefer's next work, *Beyond Killer Fiction: More Stories of Madness and Mayhem,* was followed up by *Jesse in Flames,* a sympathetic account of the botched electrocution death of Florida condemned killer Jesse Tafero as he burned in the electric chair. The woman-killing and female-mutilating author tsk-tsked over what he said was the prison guards' open satisfaction in watching Tafero burn.

Sondra London worked as a consultant for the tabloid TV show *A Current Affair,* and collaborated on a screenplay entitled *Red Bone* with Bobby Lewis, the only convict to escape Florida's death row and live (after being recaptured, his sentence was commuted to life imprisonment). Lewis gave Rolling the screenplay, and after reading it, Danny Rolling enthusiastically wrote London on June 23, 1992, beginning an intense and extensive correspondence between the two.

As a celebrity serial killer, Rolling got lots of mail in prison, including many fan letters from "lovestruck" would-be groupies, soulmates and confidantes, but this was different. Rolling seemed smitten.

London said Rolling offered her exclusive rights to his story in his first letter. By September, it had become more personal. "By Christmas, we began to be using the word 'love' between us," she told *Court TV.*

On Friday, February 5, 1993, Rolling and London met for their first (and last) face-to-face meeting at the prison. Following it, London described Danny Rolling as "one gorgeous hunk of man."

An article in the *Miami Herald* quoted Lillian Mills, of Shreveport, a former Rolling girlfriend in 1988 and 1989, as saying, "We're all freaked out he trusted a total stranger."

The *Gainesville Sun* was told by Rolling's mother, Claudia Rolling, "She's [Sondra London] just like everybody else—she's trying to make money off of Danny." London went on-line with a Danny Rolling Web site and began marketing his writings, drawings and songs.

Inmate and convicted murderer Robert "Bobby" Lewis, forty-five, befriended Danny Rolling shortly after he arrived at Florida State Prison to await trial for the Gainesville homicides. Lewis, five feet seven inches, 160 pounds, from Jacksonville, Florida, was a career criminal, drug dealer, pimp and killer since age sixteen. He was now a trusty inmate in the maximum-security prison's W-wing, where Rolling was being held, a high-security area with ninety-six other inmates, all housed in individual cells but able to socialize in several areas of the prison.

Now, Lewis was talking to prison officials and law enforcement authorities—on behalf of Danny Rolling, he said. Lewis said that Rolling was "scared" of being harassed by other prisoners. Within a few weeks after arriving, Rolling spoke several times of his involvement in the Gainesville crimes. Figuring that he could either sell the information to Sondra London or use it to deal with the prosecution, Lewis had his lawyer contact State Attorney Smith, who replied that the state would not enter into any kind of agreement with Lewis for information he might have regarding Danny Rolling or the murders.

From July through December 1992, Rolling was held in the mental health facility at Chattahoochie, then returned to Florida State Prison, where Lewis resumed cultivating his acquaintance. Both Lewis and Rolling had individually requested that they be moved to the "protective management" program at the prison because of safety concerns.

Now, Rolling decided that he wanted to help out Lewis in his plan to broker what Rolling had told him about the murders to strike some kind of deal with the state. To maximize Lewis's leverage, Rolling made him his "confessor"—instructing Lewis to write out in his own handwriting each of Rolling's written statements about the homicides and then return the originals to be destroyed.

On January 17, 1993, Lewis advised prison officials that Rolling desired to talk with Task Force investigators regarding the Gainesville murders. The next day, investigators met with Rolling at the prison, informing him that his conditions were unacceptable and that his lawyer "would not be happy" if he spoke with them.

In the month of January, Lewis met with prison officials and state law enforcement officials at least twelve times to try to make something happen. Rolling himself advised the authorities that he wished to talk to Task Force members about the student murders.

Rod Smith recalled, "I was a newly elected state attorney, I had never prosecuted a case in my life, and here's a man represented by a team of lawyers, and we want to take his statement, we don't want his lawyers to know we're taking his statement, and we want that statement to be usable in court and be upheld on appeal."

His strategy: "[We'd] go out and tell Danny that we're not going to talk to you. We don't want to talk to you. You need to get your lawyers—and then [we'd] leave, and hope that he—but if you call us back, we can come back, but it's got be you, and you ought to call your lawyer."

He gambled that Danny Rolling wanted, needed to talk, and that he'd play ball. "You have to understand the mind-set of Danny. The history of Danny Rolling is that he confesses, that he talks. . . . As I got to know him through the files and through his history, I thought Danny would talk because it was consistent with the way he was in the past and it's consistent with his makeup and his religious view. I think Danny has to confess. He's got to write a book, he's got to talk about it, he's got be a central character in his own worldview, in his poetry. His poetry is about Danny, his songs are about Danny."

The gamble worked. On January 31, 1993, Task Force members met with Rolling, setting up the terms for the interview. They were unhappy about the "mouthpiece" format, wherein they would ask questions and Lewis would answer them, based on what Danny Rolling had previously told him about the Gainesville crimes. They were unsure if this format would hold up later in court as a real confession. They fought to change the format, but Rolling was adamant, and finally it was agreed that Lewis could serve as Rolling's "mouthpiece" during the interview, with Rolling verifying the accuracy of each of Lewis's statements.

Smith noted, "Danny did cling for friendship with Bobby, and Bobby played that to the hilt. Danny does need admiration, but it was also a little bit of a power play to him. . . . This was all kind of a power play of Danny, kind of playing us, I think, that's the way I always looked at it. Just kind of a little tease by Danny, and also kind of building up his own importance, because Danny is the central character in everything that Danny does or sees about the world."

The visitors once again stressed that they could promise no benefits for any information relayed by Rolling through Lewis. Rolling and Lewis agreed to the terms for the interview, with Rolling confirming that he wanted to waive his right to counsel and talk to investigators without his attorney.

Present for this first, audiotaped session were Alachua County Sheriff's Office investigator LeGran Hewitt, FDLE Agent Ed Dix and Gainesville Police Department's Steve Kramig, and inmates Bobby Lewis and Danny Rolling. It took place in a small room with a table and chairs. The agreed-on format was that investigators would ask the questions and Lewis would answer them, with Danny Rolling whispering in the other's ear to prompt him, should Lewis be unable to answer the query.

Rolling told them the murder weapon and a pair of gloves were buried in an old stable near his Gainesville campsite. (Although the police spent ten days moving tons of earth at the dig—some abandoned University of Florida deer pens off Archer road—the knife was never found.)

Probers found a way to break free of the mouthpiece straitjacket and have Danny Rolling acknowledge his complicity in the crimes. During the interview, Dix began asking the questions and Lewis would answer, with Danny Rolling telling him what happened. Out of the blue, Hewitt said, "Is that right, Danny?"

The worry that the interview might have been blown was dispelled when Rolling said, "Yeah, that's right."

As the interview progressed, the elaborate charade erected by Rolling collapsed, because every few minutes, Hewitt would say, "Is he getting it right, Danny?" And Rolling would say, "Yeah, he's getting it right."

Rolling told them how he selected the victims,

recalled the layouts of each slaying scene, and described how the five students were killed, including how the wounds were inflicted. The statement was audiotaped. On February 4, he made a second statement, which was videotaped. Lewis again served as Rolling's "mouthpiece" and Rolling confirmed the accuracy of Lewis's statements during these interviews.

On February 19, Bobby Lewis told a reporter that Danny Rolling said he wanted to confess so he could get right with God. Lewis was his "confessor."

On February 14, 1993, Danny Rolling sent Sondra London a handmade Valentine's Day card, depicting cartoon skunk Pepé Le Pew embracing an unwilling female "skunk," with the legend "You can run—but you can't hide."

In a February 20, 1993, letter, Danny Rolling proposed to London, writing that he loved her and wanted to marry her. London told reporters that this was no "joke," this was the real thing. She said that by coincidence, she'd written him the same day, asking him to marry her. He would be her fourth husband. She also announced that she'd obtained exclusive rights to his writings and drawings.

However, there was an obstacle in love's path. The Florida Department of Corrections refused to allow her to see Rolling at Florida State Prison. Prison officials said she'd misrepresented herself as Rolling's girlfriend, not a writer, during her first and only visit. The Department of Corrections denied London's request for a permit to marry Rolling.

About this time, the state started investigating

London for possible violations of Florida's version of New York's Son of Sam law. In late April 1993, State Attorney Smith asked a judge to issue a temporary injunction against proceeds arising from London's collaborations with Rolling, citing a statute barring felons from profiting from their crimes. Smith said London was an agent for Rolling. London's lawyers declared the law unconstitutional, a violation against her First Amendment free speech rights. In fact, the U.S. Supreme Court had found New York's original Son of Sam law unconstitutional and had thrown it out.

In mid-May, the court ordered the proceeds from the London/Rolling collaboration to be held pending a ruling as to how Florida's victims' restitution law would affect the case. This was the first such use of the law, which Smith hailed as a victory for victims' rights.

This first filing would be overturned in January 1994 by the Florida First District Court of Appeal, which found that Rolling hadn't yet been convicted of the Gainesville murders at the time the state sought to apply the law.

On September 27, 1993, Danny Rolling was back in Marion County, Florida, in Judge Thomas Sawaya's court, for a hearing on the Winn-Dixie armed robbery charge, whose life sentence from Sawaya two years earlier had been overturned on legal-technical grounds.

Plenty of media were present, including Rolling's fiancée, crime writer Sondra London. She said that she was "excited" to be in his presence, only her second time since that previous prison visit.

Most of the forty-five-minute hearing related to

Rolling's mental competency to understand the resentencing. He'd sung a gospel song at his federal resentencing hearing. Now he asked Judge Sawaya if he could address the court. The judge agreed. Rolling then turned to Sondra London, sitting in the back of the court, and began serenading her with a mournful tune, which included the lyrics "Tell me, baby, what were the words, all my tears run together."

He was then resentenced to life in prison plus sixteen years (for robbery with a firearm, fleeing and attempting to flee).

By November 1993, London's former high school sweetheart and partner in literary taboo-breaking, convicted "Sex Beast" John Gerard Schaefer, perhaps envious of the attention Danny Rolling was getting, soured on London, trying to file suit against her for "literary piracy." The litigious jail-house lawyer and convicted killer also said it was "baloney" that London had lost her virginity to him.

The party got rough, with London complaining to federal and state authorities that Schaefer was sending her death threats through the mail. She said publicly that she'd like to see him confined to "the hole" at Florida State Prison, a disciplinary lockup.

Schaefer replied that while he could say he wanted her killed, he planned to do his talking in court. "If she didn't like it, tough titty," he said.

An important ruling was made at the end of December 1993, when Circuit Judge Stan Morris moved to allow all statements made by Danny Rolling at Florida State Prison to be used at trial, including statements made to Bobby Lewis as well as to investigators during his confessional sessions in late January and February 1993. Judge Morris found that the evidence was admissible because Rolling himself sought out the contacts with law enforcement officials, and had been repeatedly advised of his constitutional rights against self-incrimination.

THE TRIAL

For the state of Florida, the lead prosecuting attorney Rod Smith was seconded by James "Jim" Nilon, a tall, clean-shaven assistant state attorney with both civil and criminal trial experience. Nilon's colleagues described him as "meticulous" and "thorough"—not surprising for one who'd also received an M.B.A. enabling him to work for banks and the SEC, which he'd done for a few years before returning to the State Attorney's Office. Assistant State Attorney Donald Royston, forty-four, brought his formidable computer talents to the team.

Handling the defense was C. Richard "Rick" Parker. Of medium height and bearded, the ten-year veteran public defender for the Eighth Judicial Circuit was described as detail-oriented. Co-counsel Johnny Kearns, with a salt-and-pepper beard, was officially recognized by his peers as one of the state's outstanding public defenders. He was in charge of death penalty cases in this district.

Also on board were Barbara Blount-Powell, whose role in court was to challenge statements made against Rolling and those who made them, and

John Fischer, specializing in combating the state's scientific DNA and blood evidence.

The judge was the Honorable Stan Morris, forty-six, a onetime Gainesville prosecutor in the 1970s who'd also served in private practice as a criminal defense lawyer, who was now an experienced county and circuit judge. He was not unaware of the tremendous cost of the trial to the taxpayer, and the necessity of making sure there were no errors that could be used to retry the case.

Nobody wanted to try this case more than once—not on the prosecution's side. Rod Smith recalled, "There's an odd moment in the pretrial at which one of the lawyers walked up to me and said something like 'Boy, Danny's acting kind of strange today; he said to me, "Why do you think Rod Smith doesn't like me?" ' The bottom line is, you kill X number of people viciously, the law says you should be executed, and that's my job to carry out the law, but Danny saw the focus of this as not what's going on or what he had done, but Rod Smith disliked him, and that's the kind of character we're dealing with."

A jury of nine women and three men was selected. Before the trial could get under way, in a surprise move on February 15, 1994, Danny Rolling pleaded guilty to all charges: five charges of first-degree murder, three charges of sexual battery and three charges of armed burglary. When he pleaded guilty, he told Judge Stan Morris, "Your Honor, I've been running from first one problem and then another all my life . . . but there are some things you just can't run from. And this is one of those."

Defense attorney Rick Parker said Rolling

pleaded guilty because "he wanted to do the right thing," and praised his client's "admission of personal responsibility."

Rod Smith told *Court TV*, "Danny talked because he wanted to, because he needs to. Danny writes the books and writes the stories and does the interviews because he has to. It's Danny seeing himself in the best light. The reason he pleaded guilty was because he was about to face some facts that he could not face, that were very revealing about the kind of vicious person he was and the horrible things that he'd done, and Danny didn't want to face that side of him."

On Wednesday, February 23, 1994, the state attorney, Rod Smith, moved to prevent Danny Rolling and associates from profiting on the sale of Rolling's account of the crime. Smith filed a motion in circuit court, at Starke in Bradford County (where Rolling resided, in Florida State Prison), seeking to prevent Danny Rolling, his brother, Kevin, Sondra London and the editor of a true crime magazine from making any proceeds from the sale of Danny Rolling's story. The state sought to disburse the proceeds to the victims' families, according to the state's victim restitution act.

The guilt phase of Danny Rolling's trial having been settled when he pleaded guilty to all five murders, the proceedings now moved into the latter half, the penalty phase. The prosecution was asking for the death penalty. The state attorney told *USA Today*, "He pleaded because he did it. . . . And with all due respect, we were going to prove that he did it."

The jury would recommend a sentence to the judge of either death by the electric chair or life imprisonment. Of all states that employ juries in capital sentencing, only Florida allows a death penalty recommendation by a bare majority—here, seven out of twelve jurors. The judge would not be bound by the jury's recommendation, but it would carry a lot of weight.

Now prosecutors didn't have to prove Danny Rolling committed the murders, but they would have to explain the murders to the jury and enter testimony into evidence, including DNA recovered from semen at the crime scenes that matched Rolling's, and Rolling's statements to cell mates and investigators.

Of eleven possible aggravating factors in the death penalty case, five seemed to apply. The gist of the argument was that the defendant had prior convictions and committed a particularly heinous act.

The defense would claim Rolling was mentally ill, with a history of abuse and mental problems. It would introduce evidence seeking to mitigate the defendant's actions. The mitigator most applicable to the case was number two: "The capital felony was committed while the defendant was under the influence of extreme mental or emotional disturbance."

The trial began on March 7, 1994, at Gainesville's Alachua County Courthouse, on the fourth floor in courtroom 4A. Danny Rolling was brought to court wearing a bullet-proof vest. Wearing dark glasses and bearing press credentials from the *National Enquirer*, Sondra London was present at the session, sitting by herself.

Judge Morris had ruled outside the jury's hearing that evidence of postmortem mutilation was irrelevant to the question of whether Danny Rolling should be executed, because it wasn't one of the statutory aggravating issues. It couldn't enter in unless the defense brought it up as some sort of mitigator, which was unlikely. No evidence of the decapitation or mutilations could be entered by the prosecution.

Rod Smith opened for the state. "On July 18, 1990, Danny Harold Rolling walked into an Army-Navy store near the bus station in Tallahassee, Florida." He was referring to the $34 purchase of a Marine Corps Ka-bar knife that Rolling had made.

Smith said, "The state will prove to you that the reason he selected this particular knife is that Danny Rolling considered it the 'best knife for killing.' It would slash through flesh and bone. In a very real sense, that purchase began an episode that will forever be remembered as the Gainesville Student Murders. A rampage by one man that resulted in five brutal deaths: Sonja Larson, Christine Powell, Christa Hoyt, Manuel Taboada and Tracy Paules."

He said that the victims' families, the community, the jury, all had awaited the day when the state would prove the guilt of some person standing accused of those heinous crimes. But that day would never come to pass.

"Danny Harold Rolling, on the very day he was to finally face the mountains of evidence compiled against him, removed all doubt by entering his plea of guilty to each of the crimes charged in the indictment," Smith said.

The defendant pleaded guilty to five counts of first-degree murder, plus armed burglary and rape. Therefore, the jury had only to recommend the punishment that Danny Rolling had earned for the crimes of August 1990, and the state only had to show how the crimes occurred, in order to show the aggravators.

Smith then presented a graphic and emotional retelling of the crimes. After buying the knife, Danny Rolling left Tallahassee for Sarasota, Florida, where he bought a .9mm automatic pistol. On August 18, 1990, he arrived in Gainesville, armed with knife and gun. He checked into the University Inn, using the alias "Mike Kennedy."

On August 23, he moved out of the Inn and into a campsite in southwest Gainesville. That same day, he went into a Wal-Mart, where he bought a tent and a sleeping mattress.

"The state will prove that it was during that same trip that Danny Rolling stole a few items very important to his plan. The items that he stole were a screwdriver, some duct tape and two pairs of tight-fitting athletic gloves," Smith said. These items were ultimately used to carry out the three break-ins, during which Rolling committed the crimes he'd now pleaded guilty to.

On the evening of August 23, Danny Rolling sat in the woods, turning on his tape recorder to complete a tape he'd begun in Sarasota. Smith said,

"He concluded that tape by a statement that will always be recalled as surely among the most ominous phrases ever uttered in Gainesville.

"When Danny Rolling finished the tape, he signed off to his brother to whom he had just explained the art of killing a deer by a lung shot. He bids a farewell to his father and his mother, then ends the tape saying, 'I'm gonna sign off for a little bit. I've got something I've got to do.'

"The state will prove that what Danny Rolling had to go do was nothing less than cold, calculated and premeditated murder. We will show that Danny Rolling roamed the southwest area of Gainesville preparing to commit rape and murder."

Danny Rolling first peeked at a single woman. He prepared to take her but was seen by a passerby and fled. He went to another complex, where he peeked at two women. But before he could make his move, he was spotted by a security guard and again fled.

At 3:00 A.M. on August 24, Rolling approached the rear of an apartment in Building 11 of the Williamsburg Apartments. Smith said, "He was wearing a black ninja outfit—clothes of the killer. Dark clothing for the dark night and the dark purpose. He was wearing a ski mask. He didn't want to be identified."

Rolling popped open the apartment door, entering. Christine Powell lay sleeping on the couch. He crept upstairs, finding a sleeping Sonja Larson. He decided to kill one woman so he would be free to concentrate on what he was going to do to the other. He decided to kill Sonja Larson.

He was armed with a gun and a knife. But the

knife was quieter. He wanted the silence. He stabbed Sonja Larson in the upper chest. She awoke, struggling for her life.

"It was too late," Smith said. "She could not scream in pain. She could not scream a warning. Danny Rolling had thought of everything. . . . Just at the moment he plunged the knife into her upper chest, he placed a double strip of duct tape over Sonja's mouth. It muffled her cries. As she struggled, he stabbed her several more times. He watched her as she died."

Then it was Christine Powell's turn. "Seventeen-year-old Christine was still asleep. He was upon her before she could wake or resist. He taped her hands behind her back," Smith said, pointing out that according to Rolling's own statements she was "thoroughly terrified."

"She could see the blood all over Danny Rolling. Danny Rolling began to sexually toy with her. He had her commit oral sex upon him. He cut off her blouse with a knife. He cut her bra with the knife while her hands were strapped behind her back. She didn't make much noise. He took off her panties. He raped her. She indicated she was in pain. Danny must have liked that because the state will prove that he said, 'Take the pain, bitch—take the pain.'

"Danny Rolling, after he raped her, after he told her what he was going to do with her, killed her by stabbing her in her back," Smith said.

After killing Christine Powell, or before it, while she was lying on the floor, depending on which of Rolling's versions the jury cared to believe, Danny

Rolling helped himself to some fruit from her refrigerator—a banana and an apple—and ate it.

Then he went to pose the bodies. "He posed the body of Sonja Larson," Smith said. "He came back downstairs. The state will prove that Danny Rolling cleaned and douched Christine Powell with dishwashing liquid. He wasn't going to leave evidence when he left the apartment."

The killer was far from satiated. The next murder was already in the planning, the victim had already been selected. Earlier in the week that the killings began, Rolling had made his way to the rear of a duplex apartment in southwest Gainesville. At night, in the dark, he peeked through a window and saw a young woman emerging from the shower. She was Christa Hoyt. He left—then.

On August 25, 1990, at 10:00 P.M., he returned, using a screwdriver to pry open the sliding glass door at the rear of her apartment. Again, he wore his black ninja-style clothes. Inside, he noticed a lightweight bookshelf filling an alcove next to the front door. He moved the bookshelf to the rear bedroom. He returned to the alcove, where he could stand by the door while looking out the front window, waiting for Christa Hoyt to return.

Sometime after 10:00 P.M. she arrived, coming from playing racquetball with friend Paul Schwartz. Entering the apartment, she sensed something was wrong, but it was too late.

"Danny Rolling was upon her from behind," Smith said. "They struggled. He took her to the ground. He taped her mouth. He taped her hands. He held her in a chokehold until her resistance subsided. He marched her into the bedroom. He cut off her blouse and her bra with the knife. Since he cut them off from the front, she saw the knife.

"He removed her shorts and cut off her panties. He laid her on the bed and he began to play with her. He played with her for what will be described as a pretty long time. He discovered she was on her period. He pulled out her tampon and threw it in a corner. He talked to her through his mask but she could only respond in muffled tones through a double strip of duct tape.

"After a while, Danny Rolling raped her. He turned her over after he raped her. He stabbed her in the back with the same knife. She died quickly."

Smith's delivery continued, slow, steady, measured. "He posed her body and left. He returned to the campsite. Then he realized something was wrong. He had either lost or misplaced his wallet."

Rolling thought he might have left his wallet at Hoyt's apartment. He returned to the apartment, looking for it, not finding it. "He then re-posed Christa's body in a fashion that only rigor mortis would allow," Smith said.

Due to the judge's ruling that evidence about the mutilations was inadmissible, Smith couldn't tell the jury that Danny Rolling had decapitated and gutted Christa Hoyt's corpse. "The state will show that Danny Rolling wanted to send a message to all of Gainesville," Smith said.

After leaving the apartment, Rolling called the Gainesville Police Department. Giving his name as Mike Kennedy, he said that he wanted to report that his wallet had been stolen. Then he returned to the campsite.

On August 27, 1990, at 3:00 A.M., Rolling was

peeking into one of the Gatorwood Apartments, where he saw Tracy Paules. Waiting in the dark to make his move, he used a screwdriver to bend the pin on the sliding glass door at the side of the apartment. He entered, again prowling the site as he'd done at the Williamsburg Powell/Larson apartment. Here he found the sleeping Manuel Taboada. Rolling stabbed Taboada with a massive forceful blow to the solar plexus.

"But Manny surprised Danny Rolling," Smith said. "Manny awakened and fought for his life. He cursed Danny Rolling. He struggled with him. . . . We'll have medical evidence that even after having been stabbed with that first forceful blow it took many blows to kill the struggling, fighting, cursing Manny Taboada.

"Just as Manny Taboada died, Tracy Paules came out of her room with a curling iron in her hand. We'll have a witness to say that Danny thought for a moment she was armed. He chased her down. She got through her bedroom door. He knocked it open. Her door would later prove to be stained with Manny's blood.

"She stopped. She saw the man in black. She saw the ski mask. She saw the blood. The state will prove to you that Tracy Paules had just a few hours earlier called a friend and complained about being scared about staying in her apartment because she had heard that the bodies of murder victims had been found.

"The state will show you that at that moment Tracy put it all together, because we will show you that she said to Danny Rolling, 'You're the one, aren't you?' To which, he replied, 'Yes, I'm the one.'

"He then taped her hands, taped her mouth; he cut off her T-shirt; he played with her sexually for what will be termed a fairly long time. To facilitate his horrible playtime, he used a strip of tape to close the drape over Tracy's window.

"He then raped Tracy Paules by committing anal sodomy on her. After some time, he turned Tracy Paules over and he stabbed her to death. He dragged her off the bed. He cleaned her off with dish-washing detergent. He posed her body."

Danny Rolling then exited, disposing of the knife and bloody gloves by burying them in an old, dilapidated building.

Smith said the aggravation in each murder was massive, and that the state would prove four or five aggravating factors for each of the five murders. He went over Rolling's lengthy criminal history—"an incredible history of prior violent crimes"—which included a dozen convictions over fifteen years in five states. He said that the state would establish the heinous nature of the offense; the cold, calculating and premeditated manner of death, and the fact that Danny Rolling committed murder while also committing burglary and rape—aggravators all.

Investigators had unearthed damning evidence about the murder weapon, Smith said. "The state will prove through testimony that Danny Rolling even later stated with precision how the knife was built and the fact that it was so good for slashing through both flesh and bone because of the bloodline along the edge of the knife."

A fellow prison inmate would testify that Rolling said he'd bought the Ka-bar knife for the specific purpose of committing murders. "Nearly a month before he ever arrived in Gainesville, Danny Rolling was already preparing, planning and calculating for the slaughter he would ultimately commit," Smith said.

Jurors would be shown evidence, photos, charts and computer-enhanced graphics to show, in part, how Danny Rolling killed. "You will be shown pictures, some cropped by order of the court [because of the ban on mutilation evidence] that depict how Danny Rolling inflicted death upon these innocent young victims. You will see how he posed his victims, you will see in part what he did to them, you will be shown the tape marks on their arms and faces.

"You will be shown in the cases of Manny Taboada and Sonja Larson wounds not only to the trunk of their bodies but also on their hands, arms and legs, proving how they struggled to continue their young lives."

The jury would see evidence of what Smith called "the handiwork of this murderous artisan"—the way he moved around the furniture in Christa Hoyt's bedroom to showcase his display, the blood spattering the walls of the room where Manny Taboada struggled for his life, the fruit in the refrigerator at Williamsburg that Danny Rolling snacked on after the rape and murders, the "sheen on the body of Tracy Paules to establish how calculatedly Danny went about cleaning away the evidence of his murder."

Jurors would see the evidence from the campsite, too: "the screwdriver, the ski mask, the tape, the gloves, the pants and the .9mm pistol." They'd see and hear the defendant's audiotape from the campsite, and the audiotaped and videotaped confessions he'd made while in prison.

Smith said he'd present testimony from two inmates whom Danny Rolling had taken into his confidence [Bobby Lewis and Rusty Binstead]. They'd received nothing for their testimony—"no deals, no sentence reduction, no promise of parole." They'd tell what Rolling had told them about the crimes, how he'd planned and carried them out, and how he'd mistreated his victims.

He cautioned jurors that the defense would seek to present evidence about Danny Rolling's home and family life as potential mitigators, and asked them to keep an open mind throughout, until the whole picture was finally put before them.

After seeing all the evidence and following the instructions of the law, the jury would do their duty by recommending to the court that Danny Rolling receive the death penalty for each of the five murders he'd committed.

"It is an ominous responsibility upon you, but the state has every confidence you will perform your duty," Smith said.

Defense attorney Johnny Kearns opened with a low-key approach as he asked the jury to ensure that Rolling would be in prison for the rest of his life. He said he was asking for the Almighty and not the state of Florida to determine when Rolling would die. In this type of trial, he said, the issue is not who did it, but why they did it.

There was a cause-and-effect relationship between Rolling's childhood and his acts as an adult, Kearns said. People like Danny Rolling suffer from poor self-esteem, a lack of empathy and the inability to express emotion. The defense counsel said he was concerned about the jury having an emotional reaction to the state's case, and encouraged them to want to know not only what but why.

He said he'd call two groups of witnesses: a group of friends and family who'd testify about Rolling's youth, and a group of mental health experts who'd testify about what that childhood had done to Rolling. They would concentrate on the physical and emotional abuse and Rolling's emotional instability.

Kearns detailed Rolling's life [as the defense saw it]: he was born in Louisiana in 1954 to a father who beat him and hated him. When the father first saw him, he said, "That's not my fault."

The defense attorney detailed a terrible childhood of no praise, failed third grade, physical abuse, a suicide attempt (he scrawled on a mirror in lipstick: "I tried, but I just can't make it"), dropped out of high school, failed in the military, etc.

He ended up in Gainesville "to fulfill the expectations set forth by his father." Rolling also believed he was possessed by demons, Kearns said.

Before calling any witnesses, the prosecutor read into the record Rolling's guilty pleas in this case and his lengthy criminal history.

The first witness was Alachua County Sheriff's Office investigator and Task Force member LeGran Hewitt, who testified that Rolling had arrived in Gainesville on August 18, 1990, had stayed for a time at the University Inn, and that he left town on August 30. FDLE Agent Cindy Barnard, another Task Force member, identified a gun related to a bank robbery as being registered to Michael Kennedy, a Danny Rolling alias.

FDLE Agent Frank Troy, a veteran officer, traced Rolling's movements in Tallahassee, Florida, from July 17 through July 22, 1990, a month before he arrived in Gainesville. Hotel receipts from that time show that Michael Kennedy (Rolling's alias) stayed at the Travel Lodge in Tallahassee.

When Rolling confessed in prison about the Gainesville student murders, Agent Troy went to the Army-Navy store in Tallahassee where Rolling had bought his Ka-bar knife. Store records showed a receipt for the purchase of such a knife during the time Rolling was in Tallahassee. It was the only one of that type sold during that time period. Troy bought a duplicate of the knife, which he showed in court.

A female employee of the store testified that the knife that Troy had bought was a replica of the one bought by Rolling.

On Tuesday, March 8, 1994, day two of the trial, the state highlighted the testimony of crime scene witnesses of the first two crimes. Prosecutors were careful not to mention the decapitation when questioning the witnesses at the Hoyt crime scene.

Scott Henratty took the stand, telling of how he'd gone to Sonja Larson's apartment twice on the day she was killed, unable to contact her. A friend of Sonja Larson's since middle school, he'd met up with her in Gainesville two days before her death. He and Larson went out to eat with two other friends. After they ate, Henratty and his friend left.

On Saturday, August 25, 1990, Henratty stopped by Larson's place at about 11:30 A.M. He knocked on the door, but there was no answer. He saw her car out front. At about 10:30 P.M., he and some friends stopped by her place again. He left a note on her door, saying he'd stopped by.

The next day, Sunday, he stopped by Larson's place once again. Police were there, and Henratty found out that Sonja Larson had been murdered.

Gainesville Police Department officer Ray Barber said he'd entered the apartment on August 26, 1990, finding the bodies of Powell and Larson. Brad West, a former Gainesville cop who'd worked the Powell and Larson crime scene, showed jurors parts of the doors in the apartment, to show that the locks had still been locked when police first entered the room. Rolling had broken in through the back door, using a screwdriver.

Landlord Elbert Hoover told of a conversation he'd had with tenant Christa Hoyt on August 25, 1990, at about 5:00 P.M. Hoover had noticed that a gate accessing the rear of her apartment was un-latched, which he thought unusual. He asked Hoyt if she had unlatched the gate. She said that she thought it was the telephone repair man who must have unlatched it, which eased Hoover's concern.

The witness wept as he told of going with Officer Keith O'Hara to check on Christa Hoyt.

Paul Schwartz, a friend of Christa Hoyt's since childhood, said that on Saturday, August 25, 1990, he'd played racquetball with her from 7:30 to 9:00

P.M. They'd gone to Schwartz's house and talked until about 9:30 or 10:00 P.M., when she'd left. He never saw her again.

Deputy Keith O'Hara, of the Alachua County Sheriff's Office, said that early in the morning of Monday, August 27, 1990, Christa Hoyt was due to work the late shift at the ASO. She was late, and her coworker from the previous shift was waiting for her to take over. Christa Hoyt was punctual and not one to arrive late for work with no reason. A dispatcher called Hoyt at home; the phone went unanswered.

O'Hara went to Hoyt's place to investigate, finding her body. His testimony about the crime scene was constrained, since he was not allowed to testify that the victim's head had been removed from her body.

The jury saw graphic photos of three of the five victims. Evidence of postmortem mutilation was cropped out or masked, so the jury didn't see the decapitation or the women's mutilated breasts. Jurors were presented with one picture of Christa Hoyt from the side, so they could see her head was gone. The defense objected to the photos and did not cross-examine any of the witnesses. Parker said there was no need to, because he didn't dispute that Rolling committed the murders.

Parker said Danny Rolling was upset when the photos were introduced into evidence this day, and that Rolling had asked that the pictures not be passed by him so he wouldn't have to look at them.

The prosecution said that it was very hard on the victims' families to sit in court while the photos were introduced.

Later, in an exclusive *Court TV* interview, Danny Rolling offered his explanation of why he couldn't look at the crime scene photos. "I don't want to see them. I've been offered the chance to see them and I don't want to see them. Because, no, I don't want to see that."

"Why?"

"Because when I look at it, then I got to realize that I did that."

"What was going through your mind when you did that?"

"It was like going to a movie. Like a horror movie. Like you're sitting in the front row, and you can see everything planned out before you. I could see my hand doing what it was doing, but it wasn't really like it was my hand."

"Did you feel any exhilaration when killing these people?"

"Well, that's a very hard question because, you know, we are talking about dealing with a moment when somebody dies here, you know. Only thing I could answer in retrospect to that would be, well, an overdose of adrenaline. You get so much of it, so much adrenaline can blind you. It makes your vision not so good, you know. And, I don't know how else to describe it. It's not a good thing."

Did he pick his victims according to their looks?

"No, Gemini picked them," Rolling said. "That demon led me to those people. He told me before when I passed through Gainesville, Gemini whispered in my ear, 'It will happen here.' I knew what he meant, but I didn't think it would happen on a scale like that."

Prosecutor Rod Smith told *Court TV*, "We all had

some nights—if you spent a day going through the photographs, which of these scenes are we gonna use, there were nights when you would wake up in bed saying, 'Oh, Lord,' kind of catch your breath and realize everything was okay."

Wednesday, March 9, day three, focused on evidence from the second and third crime scenes and the campsite where Rolling stayed at the time of the murders. Homicide Task Force investigator Le-Gran Hewitt returned to the stand, telling of the last hours of Christa Hoyt's life. He estimated that she arrived home at about 10:00 P.M. Danny Rolling told police he entered the apartment by breaking in with a screwdriver, then hid by a bookshelf.

Next came the matter of Hoyt's gate, which had been unlatched sometime on the day before her death. Danny Rolling had been on the east side of the property, where the gate was ajar. The witness said, "During the interview with Danny, he told us he'd been in that area, going back to Christa's back door to peek on her."

Tracy Paules's friend Lisa Marie Buyer had known both Paules and Taboada since high school. She testified that she called Paules on Sunday night at about midnight. Paules had been out of town and hadn't heard about the Powell and Larson murders. Buyer told her about them during an hour-long conversation.

The prosecutor said, "When did you next hear back from her?"

"I didn't," Buyer said.

Buyer called Paules back in the next couple of

days—no response, no reply. She called a mutual friend, Tom Carrol. Originally from Jacksonville, he'd grown up with Paules and Taboada and had known them for many years.

Carrol testified that he'd last talked to Tracy Paules at about 6:00 P.M. on Friday as she was packing her car to go out of town. He called her several times on Monday, leaving messages, when Buyer called to tell him she was concerned that she couldn't find Tracy Paules.

He wasn't alarmed, at first. He called Bennigan's—employee Manny Taboada wasn't there, but no one told Carrol that Taboada hadn't come into work as he was supposed to do. He and Buyer did nothing further that night because they didn't know Taboada was scheduled to go to work and hadn't shown up.

They left messages telling Taboada and Paules to please call no matter what time it was.

Early the next day, Buyer called Tom Carrol at 6:30 A.M. and asked him to go check on Paules and Taboada. She said that if he wouldn't go over and check on Tracy Paules, she would drive up from south Florida. He went over.

Tracy Paules's car was there. He didn't recognize Manny Taboada's car, even though it was there, too. He knocked on the door, no answer. He located a maintenance man who unlocked the apartment.

Deputy Dan Alexander took the stand, testifying about entering the Gatorwood apartment and finding the bodies. Crime scene investigator Steve Leary told of collecting evidence at the scene, including adhesive on Paules's wrists, as well as bloody towels and cleaning fluids. All the evidence collected was placed in brown paper bags, taken to a regional crime lab, and submitted to evidence distribution.

The witness had attended Manuel Taboada's autopsy, and now identified photos taken there. One showed wounds to the victim's hands, another to the hand and lower portion of his arms. Later that day, after the jury got stuck in an elevator, court ended early.

Thursday, March 10, 1994, day four. First up was state's witness Paul McCaffrey, a forensic serologist formerly employed at the FDLE Laboratory. He tested blood from the crime scenes. He identified a T-shirt belonging to Tracy Paules, which he'd examined and analyzed. He said that some of the blood found on the shirt was Manuel Taboada's. The point being that Taboada had already been killed by the time Danny Rolling attacked and killed Paules, the final victim. Apparently, Rolling got some of Taboada's blood on him when he stabbed Taboada thirty times, and subsequently transferred some of that blood to Paules's T-shirt.

Next came witnesses who'd examined Danny Rolling's campsite. On August 28, 11:30 A.M., the First National Union Bank, on Archer Road, was held up by two robbers, a black man and a white man. Across the street from another bank, in a fenced, wooded area owned by the University of Florida, Danny Rolling was living in a pitched-tent campsite.

Deputy Sheriff Tim Merrill testified that on August 29, 1990, he'd seen two men, a black man and a white man, walking at 1:30 A.M. Mindful that there'd been a bank robbery earlier that day, committed by a black man and a white man, Merrill questioned why they'd be out so late. He attempted to stop them as they entered a wooded area owned by the University of Florida, through the fence gate. The black man stopped, but the white man ran off.

Merrill called for backup. There was plenty to be had, due to the large numbers of officers patrolling the area at night because of the recent discovery of the three murder victims and the recent unsolved bank robberies.

There was no testimony about the identity of the black man, but the prosecution had no doubt that the murders had been committed by Rolling alone.

Deputy Jim Liddell told of how he'd chased the fugitive white man off the path into denser woods but was unable to find him. A canine tracking unit called to the scene found Rolling's campsite, where officers found a raincoat and dye-stained money on the ground. Knowing that the bank across the street had been robbed the preceding day and that the white male robber had been armed, the officers decided to secure the tent, the witness said.

In it was a tote bag sitting on top of more red-stained money. Liddell searched the bag for a weapon and found a gun box. In the box was a blue steel Taurus handgun. He called crime scene investigators, who after arriving at the campsite began collecting various items.

(The Florida Supreme Court ruled subsequently on appeal against Rolling's contention that the trial court erred in denying his pretrial motion to suppress the evidence seized from the tote bag, on the grounds that his constitutional rights against illegal search and seizure had been violated. The appeals court ruled that the danger to police justified Liddell's warrantless search of the tote bag for weapons.)

Deputy Jack Smith testified about the evidence he'd discovered at the campsite. Six days later, Smith had inventoried the contents of the tote bag. They included a loaded .9mm semiautomatic pistol (which Rolling had used in the bank robbery but not the murders, although he told police he'd had it with him, but had used the knife instead). Also recovered were a screwdriver, headphones, black ninja pants, a tank top, a bag with dye-stained money (from the bank robbery), a pair of gloves and a ski mask. (Rolling told investigators that he'd worn the pants, tank top and ski mask during the murders. He used the screwdriver to break into the apartments.)

These items were turned over to the FDLE and later admitted into evidence. Deputy Smith now identified an audiotape cassette player/recorder that he'd found in a duffel bag at the site, also identifying a cassette tape that had been found in the recorder itself.

Homicide Task Force member Hewitt returned to the stand, showing jurors a map illustrating the proximity of the campsite to the murder sites and a Wal-Mart. He said that Rolling had bought a tent at Wal-Mart, but that he'd shoplifted the screwdriver, tape and gloves.

Hewitt also identified the tape recorder and audiocassette recovered from Rolling's campsite. He said that part of the tape was apparently recorded in a motel room in Sarasota; the remainder was taped by Rolling at the campsite.

The audiotape was then played to the jury. Over an hour long, of poor sound quality, it was the jurors' first look inside Rolling's mind. It began with Rolling addressing his mother, father and brother, Kevin—"the three people I love most."

Rolling says, "All I know is I'm just one man alone in this world, facing the whole world by himself. . . . I'll always love you . . . no matter what anybody thinks about this man, Danny Harold Rolling, I want these three people to know that this is not the road that I really wanted . . . but it is the road that is before me now, and I will walk it like a man. . . . Nothing's ever been easy for me . . . well, I promise you this much . . . no matter what happens in the road ahead of me, at least I'll walk it like a man . . . I'm gonna be all right."

He then urges his family to go on with their lives, despite whatever he may do. "You probably hate me now. . . . I don't blame you for that, but perhaps you'll understand one day; I don't . . . but I know there was once some good in me, and perhaps there is still a little. . . . I hate this; I hate what's happened, the way I have to live. . . . I know that we're all basically evil . . . I don't know what the future holds for me or for anyone. . . . My life is not easy, but I will walk it until the Lord decides to take me home; I will walk the road before me the best I can. . . . I know the judgments of men and how it stinks; man does not judge rightfully or justly . . . no, this world is corrupt . . . civilization is not of the Lord, it's of the Devil . . . y'all pray for me, I need your prayers."

In the tape's next section, Rolling sang some of his songs, his original compositions, while the jury followed along with transcripts of the song lyrics. First came "Let Me Tell You 'Bout It," a country blues tune: "I got the blues/Now, let me tell you 'bout it/The radio plays a sad, sad song/Did you lose your mind?/It comes crashing in."

The song "Boggy Bayou" begins ominously: "Jeanie went down to the creek to fetch a pail of water/She ain't been seen since," and goes on to repeat, "Some people get lost in Boggy Bayou way down in them swamps."

Another song is titled "You Hurt Me More Than I Love Ya."

Next is "Mystery Rider": "Mystery Rider, what's your name?/You're a killer, a drifter gone insane/What's your game?/You're a rebel no one can tame."

At the end of the tape, Rolling once more addresses his family: "I'm making do. I really don't know what to say. I know we can't ever be together, but at least I'm free. . . . I've been stomped by the police I don't know how many times . . . I guess I'll make do; I hope I do . . . it's just the way it is . . . I don't want you feeling sorry for me . . . I'm a big boy, I can take care of myself . . . We're all down here for just a breath, anyway."

Rolling also encourages his brother, Kevin, to kill a deer in his memory: "Aim for the lungs, straight through the rib cage, either there or the heart, but the best thing to do is hit the lungs. It's the best shot for a deer, straight through the lungs. He don't go very far. Don't chase after him when you hit 'em, when you stick him, when that arrow hits him, what you got to do, is you got to just watch which way he goes and when he goes outta sight, listen—you hear him banging into trees and stuff, and then finally you'll hear him either fall down or you hear him stop running."

Prosecutor Smith later remarked, "He talks about this thing with Kevin, in this little thing about, I'll show you how to kill a deer, and you need to know how to kill a deer, and it's not even very masked that what he's really talking about is how he's going to kill somebody."

The recording ends with Rolling saying to his dad, "I wanted to make you proud of me, I let you down, I'm sorry for that. Well, I'm gonna sign off for a little bit, I've got something I've got to do . . . I love ya. Bye."

According to prosecutors, Rolling's sign-off was especially chilling in retrospect, since after ending the recording with that phrase, the defendant went out and committed the Larson-Powell murders.

Also, on the tape, Rolling talks about how much he loves his father, but his entire defense was built around the fact he is mentally ill mostly because his dad treated him badly. In the tape, Rolling says he feels bad about shooting his father.

Special Agent Ed Dix, of the FDLE, described by prosecutor Rod Smith as the man who knew every detail about the case, took the stand to introduce Danny Rolling's videotaped confession, made on February 4, 1993 (the first, audiotaped confession having been given on January 31, 1993).

The videotape was played for the jury. In it, Dix

and two other law enforcement officers, Hewitt and Kramig, talk with Rolling and inmate Bobby Lewis. At one point, Rolling ridicules the officers for being unable to find the knife after he told them where he buried it. (They never did find the knife.)

He says that he didn't know there were two females at the first crime scene. He decided to rape and kill one of the women, but he killed the other one, too, so there wouldn't be any witnesses.

He peeked into Christa Hoyt's apartment before breaking in. He also peeked in at Tracy Paules, and was surprised to find a man in her apartment after he broke in. He says he didn't slash any of the victims' faces—true enough, since decapitation isn't face-slashing. He denied committing sodomy, although one of the victims had been anally raped.

Rolling says that the motive for the killings was his incarceration at the state penitentiary in Parchman, Mississippi, in revenge for the "substandard" conditions under which he was forced to live. He vowed revenge on the society that had imprisoned him there—one victim for each of the eight years he'd spent doing time in prison.

He claims to suffer from multiple personalities, Ennad, who robs and rapes, and Gemini, the evil spirit who kills. "They became a reality to me. One personality is a gentleman named Ennad [almost Danny spelled backward], who is a Jesse James type. He's not a good person, but he's not really an evil person. . . .

"The person I really have struggled against is a person called Gemini. . . . I want to understand it, anybody that's ever known me knows that Danny just wanted to be a good person, a likable person. . . . I can't go back over my life . . . I never wanted to come this way, but I'm here . . . and I ain't got nobody to blame but myself . . . and I want to understand as much as anybody, because I was so bad."

Up to now in the trial, the defense still hadn't cross-examined any of the witnesses. They said they'd offered to stipulate to all this, but the state wanted to present its case piece by piece.

After court, his attorney said Rolling didn't suffer from clinical multiple personalities. He said Rolling thinks he's possessed by demons.

Friday, March 11, 1994, day five. Prosecutors introduced a second Rolling confession, this one on audiotape, which had actually been made before the one shown to jurors the previous day. Rod Smith said the reason he played them backward is so the jury could get used to the format of the session before listening to the tape. He thought they would be confused if they had just heard the tape without seeing the setup in the video first.

Present at the interview were Rolling, Bobby Lewis and three law enforcement officials, Kramig, Hewitt and Dix. The first hour of the tape features Rolling's awkward use of Bobby Lewis. Rolling says, "Bobby is my mouthpiece. He is my confessor. I talk to him, he will speak to you."

The investigators balk at first, because they wanted the confession out of Rolling's mouth, not from some other inmate. Rolling finally wins and Lewis is brought into the room. Bobby Lewis does most of the talking on the three-hour tape.

As the tape begins, Rolling is upset about a

shakedown of his cell, complaining that guards destroyed many of his personal belongings, including a Valentine's Day card he made for his fiancée, Sondra London.

Watching that segment of the tape in the press room, London said that the card wasn't destroyed, that she had it and it had been shown on *Geraldo*.

A detective asks, "August 26, 1990, at the Williamsburg apartment in Gainesville, Florida, there were two female victims killed. Was Danny Rolling responsible for these homicides?"

Bobby Lewis says, "Yes, he was."

Lewis reads Rolling's written confessions to all five deaths. On August 24, at 3:00 A.M., Rolling broke into the Williamsburg apartment, killed Sonja Larson, and raped and killed Christine Powell. Lewis says that Sonja Larson died first: "The whole thing lasted maybe thirty seconds and she died." At the defense table, Rolling sat with his head in his hands.

Lewis says Rolling then crept down the stairs and raped and killed Christine Powell, stabbing her once in the back. "She put up little resistance." After the rape, he wiped and douched her body to destroy evidence.

Due to Judge Morris's earlier ruling on the inadmissibility of testimony regarding the mutilations, the jury did not get to hear that after Powell was dead, Rolling cut off her nipples and put them in a sandwich bag and took the bag with him, later throwing it away.

Rolling told Lewis that on August 25, 10:00 P.M., at the second crime scene, he entered Christa Hoyt's apartment by the rear glass sliding doors.

He moved a bookshelf so he could hide and surprise her when she entered. He finally saw her walking in. Lewis says Rolling thought Hoyt had been playing tennis because she had a racket with her.

She realized he was there, but "it was too late, I [Rolling] was on her." He taped her hands behind her back and took her to the bedroom and took off her clothes, everything but her socks. He "played with her," then turned her over and stabbed her one time through the heart.

What the jury did not hear was that after she was dead, he cut off her nipples. Nor did they hear that he came back an hour before sunrise to see if he'd left his wallet there, and at that time he cut off her head and posed her body.

At the third crime scene, Rolling broke in to kill Tracy Paules. He was surprised a man was there and he attacked Manuel Taboada first. During the fight with Taboada, Paules came out of her bedroom with a curling iron in her hand, which Rolling first mistook for a firearm. After Rolling killed Taboada, he raped and killed Paules. He then wiped the blood off her face.

Also on the tape, Rolling says, "I am a pitiful excuse for what a Christian should be, but I am that."

What the jury did not hear was that he raped Paules again after she was dead.

Rolling told Lewis he killed five victims, one for every year he'd served in prison. But at that time he'd served eight years, not five. Were the three Grissom family members murdered in Shreveport in 1989 part of the body count?

Later on in the tape, Rolling goes on to say that

people don't listen to their Maker anymore, and then rambles on for a bit about demons. Lewis says, damagingly for the defense, that Rolling "knows the things he did was wrong," and that Rolling had problems with his father as a child.

Florida State Prison inmate Russell "Rusty" Binstead had been convicted of twenty felonies and had been in prison for eighteen years. In July 1992, he met Danny Rolling in prison and proceeded to cultivate his acquaintance, figuring he might pick up some information on the Gainesville murders, valuable information to have. Rolling also gave Binstead detailed information about the crimes, including a letter in his own handwriting detailing how he killed Christa Hoyt. Binstead said Rolling relished telling the details as to how his victims died and how their cries were muffled. Rolling had told him that the Ka-bar knife "went in like butter, came out like butter. It went through bone."

Binstead testified that Rolling told him that at the first murder scene (Powell/Larson), he'd found one girl sleeping on the couch and then went upstairs to another girl on a bed. Rolling said he had to kill one and rape the other. He killed the one on the bed, then went downstairs and woke the other girl.

Rolling told Binstead he forced Christine Powell to perform oral sex on him. Binstead said he asked Rolling if he was afraid she would bite off his penis. Rolling said he wasn't worried about it—"She was too scared. She would have done anything to live."

Rolling said he should have raped the girl up-stairs instead, because she had a better body.

Binstead said that one day in prison Rolling compared a nude photo in a porno magazine to the features of victim Tracy Paules. Rolling told him about the Taboada/Paules slayings. He'd entered a bedroom and found the man and knew he had to kill him to get to the girl. He stabbed him while he was sleeping. The man fought hard for his life. Rolling found the girl in the hallway. She ran into the bedroom. Rolling raped her and killed her.

The witness smiled as he told jurors of how he'd stashed away Rolling's handwritten confession about Hoyt's rape-murder. Rolling had given it to him, telling Binstead to tear up the original after Binstead had written out the confession in his own handwriting. He said he'd faked out Rolling into thinking he'd destroyed it.

The jury did not learn that in the letter Rolling said he'd placed Hoyt's head on a bookshelf so those entering the apartment would see it, and that he'd posed her headless body sitting on her bed with her arms at her side.

Binstead said that Rolling told him that the reason Christa Hoyt had been posed was that the killer "wanted to give everyone something to think about."

"He wanted to evoke terror," Binstead said.

Prosecutor Smith later told *Court TV*, "He [Rolling] staged everything, so Danny was leaving these little messages. He had been there and he wanted to make sure this was a signature crime or these were signature crimes. That's consistent—he went back and sexually posed them. It was a sexual fantasy to Danny that he engaged in. So he was leaving messages of that sexual fantasy."

Binstead then read aloud a poem written by Danny Rolling entitled "Gemini," part of which went: "Through the haze it smells your fears/Then . . . it appears . . . /Your nightmare come to life/A maniac with a knife." It goes on to say, "Tonight in the arms of Gemini/A captured butterfly will die," then, later, "No more pain . . . no more fear/Close your eyes, my dear/And sleep." It concludes, "The whisper . . . the cry/Into the night comes Gemini/And tonight . . . you die. . . ."

Rolling explained to an interviewer that "it depicts the mind of murder . . . there's nothing good or pretty about murder."

Binstead was the first witness to be cross-examined by the defense as attorney Barbara Blount-Powell asked him about his efforts to keep Rolling near him in prison. Binstead said he helped Rolling fake suicide attempts to keep him in the psych ward so he wouldn't be transferred to another wing of the prison. But the witness denied having convinced Rolling to make the attempt. Rolling was opposed to suicide, but he didn't want to go to the other wing.

Binstead said he'd overheard some of Rolling's conversations with Bobby Lewis. He said that Rolling knew what he told him would get back to investigators. Rolling also told Binstead that he was high on crack cocaine and alcohol and visited by demons during the murders. He spoke of his mood swings and violence. He said that he'd committed the murders, not Gemini.

In an interview with *Court TV*, Sondra London said that Danny Rolling manipulated the crime scenes to create a message. "Who was the message to? It had nothing to do with the deceased. The action that went on there after these people were already raped, murdered, and the crimes were committed, the next thing that happened was a staging of a tableau. So that those who were to find these terrible crimes would know that something had happened.

"What was the message that he was sending there? According to Danny, he doesn't know what the message is, but if you press him, Gemini's message was that evil lives, that evil walks the earth like a natural man."

Diane McDougal, handwriting analyst with the Jacksonville regional crime lab, said that the confession letter and the poem were definitely written by Danny Rolling.

Prosecutor Jeanne Singer took the direct examination of Dr. William Hamilton, pathologist and medical examiner. He'd examined the bodies of all five victims, concluding that each of them had been stabbed to death. Three of the women were raped. Christine Powell had been stabbed five times; Sonja Larson had eleven stab and cut wounds (including five puncture wounds); Christa Hoyt was stabbed once in the heart and lung; Manuel Taboada had thirty-one stab and cut wounds; and Tracy Paules had been stabbed three times.

Dr. Hamilton said that the pattern of Sonja Larson's wounds didn't tell if Larson was struggling. All the injuries could have happened very quickly, and she would have lost consciousness fast. The witness opined that the same weapon was used on Powell and Larson. An effort had been made to clean up Powell's vaginal area. An examination of Powell's hands at the scene indicated that duct tape had most likely been used to bind her.

A single stab wound to the back killed Christa Hoyt, Dr. Hamilton said, adding that the wounds were consistent with those of Larson's and Powell's. Hoyt's body was moved after she'd been dead for a couple of hours. Semen was found in the victim's body.

Manuel Taboada put up a struggle, but he lost a lot of blood in a short time and couldn't have struggled for very long. The wounds on his hands were defensive wounds. Tracy Paules was stabbed on the bed and then her body was dragged down the hallway. Paules was sexually abused, much like Christine Powell. It seemed as if the area was cleaned up. Rape and sexual assault tests done on Paules yielded sperm cells. Her wounds were consistent with those of the other rape victims.

The state argued that Larson and Taboada put up fights to defend themselves. That could go to proving the murders were heinous, atrocious and cruel, or what is known in Florida as the "hack factor." If a victim is aware of impending death, that makes the murder more heinous, atrocious and cruel, one of the aggravating factors.

Rolling's confessions didn't gibe with the medical examiner's findings at certain points. Rolling said he stabbed Christine Powell once in the back. The medical examiner said she was stabbed five times. Rolling said he did not sodomize Tracy Paules. The medical examiner said she was anally raped. Rolling said all his victims died quickly. The medical examiner said some may have been conscious for a minute or more.

Monday, March 14, day six. The state wrapped up its case, first presenting two FDLE expert crime scene analysts to testify about tools used for the break-ins, establishing that the screwdriver found at Danny Rolling's campsite was used in the break-ins.

The state's third and final witness was Bobby Lewis, a prison inmate with seven felony convictions and eighteen years spent behind bars. Lewis befriended Rolling two years earlier, becoming his jailhouse confessor and confidant. He claimed to have spent hundreds of hours talking to him about the Gainesville murders.

Now, Lewis testified about what Rolling had told him. At the first crime scene, the Powell/Larson apartment, the witness said that Rolling had told him he went upstairs, put masking tape over Sonja Larson's mouth, and started stabbing her. She put up a struggle—"He had to stab her just wherever he could," Lewis said.

He said that Rolling said that all three rapes lasted "a fairly long time," and that he'd kept the victims alive for a "pretty long time." He told the women what he was going to do to them before he did it. He told them he was going to kill them and then he did it.

Later, Lewis offered several possible explanations for the decapitation and posing of Christa Hoyt. "He [Rolling] had a couple of reasons. He was trying to make a statement. He was trying to terrorize the city of Gainesville. He was trying to make himself infamous or famous.

"He wanted to be a superstar amongst criminals."

At the third crime scene, Rolling said Manuel Taboada put up a ferocious struggle. "He [Taboada] called him a bastard and called him a son of a bitch. He was struggling to let the girl in the next room know and give her a chance," Lewis said. Rolling told Lewis that he was terrified of Taboada.

Because of the prohibition on testimony relating to the mutilations, Lewis was not allowed to reveal to the jurors that Christa Hoyt had been decapitated after the murder.

Now the defense put on its case. First up were two relatives of Danny Rolling's. Charles "Chuck" Strozier, Rolling's cousin (their mothers were sisters), said he and Rolling had been close while growing up. He recalled that the relationship between Rolling and his father, James Rolling, "wasn't a very loving relationship. . . . Danny tried to show his dad his love, but his dad wouldn't accept it. His father was very demeaning. . . . He didn't show any love to him, there was no love there."

The witness said James Rolling didn't show affection to anyone in the family, and even beat his two sons. "James Harold wanted to be in control of his boys."

Strozier claimed to have heard the two Rolling brothers being beaten by their father. "James Harold was very conscientious about not letting anyone else see the discipline of Danny and Kevin. It sounded like maybe a belt, strap, fists, knuckles, slapping them around—weakness was not allowed."

Defense counsel Johnny Kearns asked the witness about Danny Rolling's mental stability. Strozier said that Kevin Rolling, the defendant's brother, had voiced his concern that both Danny and James Harold Rolling needed help.

After Danny Rolling's marriage ended in divorce, "he was devastated," the witness said, "because that was the only structure he had. His wife gave him that structure that he needed. When the divorce was over with, it was like a failure for Danny."

He also recalled conversations he'd had with the defendant about "spirits, demons and devils." "Rolling would talk about visions of demons, people in his dreams beating him, torturing him, demons gnawing at him, an individual or figure would beat him, torture him."

Strozier said that Rolling would draw pictures of these demons, and said that the defendant told him that he could see the spirits. But he never suggested Rolling see a psychologist, because "all his life he's been told he's been a failure. I didn't want to bring any more negativity to Danny."

On cross-examination, Jim Nilon got the witness to admit that he'd only occasionally seen James Rolling beat his sons, Strozier claiming that verbal abuse from the father was much more common. He conceded that Kevin Rolling continued to stay in contact with his father, and that Kevin, unlike Danny, had never been in any kind of trouble.

Neighbor Bernadine Holder testified about James Rolling's physical abuse of Danny Rolling, including one incident where the beating was so severe she feared James Rolling would kill his son.

The defense counsel said, "Did Mr. Rolling Sr., now, Mr. James Harold Rolling, ever express to you his feelings about Danny?"

The witness said, "He hated him."

"Did he use those words?"

"He hated him, he told me he hated him. He told me he would kill him."

Danny Rolling told *Court TV*: "The Bible says to honor your father and your mother that your days will be long on the face of the earth. Well, I failed to do that. But my dad is still alive, so I really don't want to go into too much about it. I'll only say this much, it wasn't a happy house. It wasn't a happy house."

The defendant's mother, Claudia Rolling, too ill with liver cancer to testify in person, testified via videotaped deposition. Although she testified that James Rolling was abusive as a husband and father, she still lived with him. (He was not in the house when the deposition was made.)

She said that James Rolling was domineering, a control freak, and critical of young Danny in every way. The boys were terrified of him. She had to always feed them first, because in their father's presence they would get nervous and often drop something, which could provoke a beating. She described a life full of beatings and verbal abuse. The boys would beg her to leave him. She and her husband would sometimes separate for a time, but they always got back together.

She said the kids never had birthday parties, and Christmas was horrible because James Rolling always ruined it. He once beat fourteen-year-old Kevin until he wet his pants. Danny tried to get his father's attention, while Kevin learned to avoid him. "It almost seemed as if Danny did everything to draw attention to himself in front of his dad. It was almost as if, 'if you won't hug me, hit me.' "

Once, after fifteen-year-old Danny and his father had a fight in the backyard, and James Rolling beat him, Danny went inside the house, scrawling in lipstick on the bathroom mirror: "I tried, but I just can't make it." Then he went to a drive-in, making a botched suicide attempt with a razor.

James Rolling once had Danny arrested for coming home late and drunk. Danny spent between two and three weeks in jail.

Then there was the more recent incident, in May 1990, when Danny Rolling had shot his father. An outdoor fight escalated and moved indoors, with the defendant shooting his father in the face. (Danny Rolling was never convicted of any crime relating to the shooting.)

Claudia Rolling claimed there was a history of mental illness in the Rolling family. She said that as a child, James Rolling saw his grandfather kill his grandmother by slitting her throat from ear to ear. One of James Rolling's uncles killed himself by shooting himself in the mouth with a shotgun; another uncle died in a mental institution. She said that James Rolling's mother appeared to be schizophrenic—"That's the disease that I was told the family had," she explained.

Evidence of a hard childhood is not a statutory

mitigating factor, but it was admissible in court nonetheless.

Claudia Rolling's videotaped testimony stretched over into Tuesday, March 15, day seven. In this section, she said that Danny Rolling had never held a job, because every time it looked like he might get a promotion, he'd quit or get himself fired.

She said that she'd seen Danny Rolling's "other personality" come out once. She didn't remember the name he'd given her then, but she said that a definite change came over him. His voice was harsh and his face and demeanor were much different. "If I didn't know Danny so well, I wouldn't have known it was him."

Lillian "Bunnie" Mills, a country-western singer and record producer, first met aspiring singer-songwriter Danny Rolling in 1988, when James Rolling invited her over to the house. Prosecutors would claim that this helped prove the senior Rolling wasn't as bad as the defense had painted him—he had called a record producer and invited her over to meet son Danny and listen to his music.

In 1988 and 1989, Mills and Danny Rolling were romantically involved. During this phase of direct examination, the witness appeared unhappy about having to testify about the relationship, reluctantly conceding that she and the defendant had had a sexual relationship: "We dated," she said.

Mills said that Danny Rolling seemed nervous all the time and appeared to be suffering from acute anxiety. "He was very nervous, he couldn't be still. His attention span was very short . . . but he and

I had lots of talks. Danny would tell me lots of things, but when I talked back to him, his attention span was very short."

He said he and his father didn't get along. He always cried when talking about his relationship with his dad.

She related an incident that Rolling had told her, in which a fight with his girlfriend led to James Rolling's having him arrested. She said that she became friendly with Claudia Rolling, and that she tried to get Danny Rolling into counseling a couple of times. "I begged him [defendant] to go. He told me he was afraid that if he got treatment his dad would kill him, if his dad found out what he told the psychiatrists . . . he didn't want somebody to pick his brain."

Mills said that Danny Rolling had told her of an incident during his marriage, when his father and mother burst into his home, storming into his bedroom, where his dad pulled the covers off him and held a knife to his throat for no reason. He said he was naked and embarrassed to be nude in front of his mother.

On cross-examination, the state pointed out that the incident where his father had him arrested took place after Danny came home drunk after being expelled from school. The state's version of the marriage incident was that James Rolling had burst into his son's apartment because Danny was skipping work again and his father thought that was the only way to get through to him.

Arthur Carlisle, a Mississippi attorney who'd helped in Danny Rolling's defense on a 1985 armed robbery (his third), told of calling the Rolling home to let them know of their son's whereabouts (jail) and to see if they'd send him any money for cigarettes and whatnot.

He said that James Rolling "responded in a very volatile manner. He proceeded to cuss me out and call me every name in the book, and [told me] to not ever call his house again concerning his son the SOB."

The witness said he'd never before experienced that kind of verbal abuse. When he told Danny Rolling what had happened, the defendant said, "I told you that's how my daddy is."

The state suggested that the reason James Rolling had responded so violently was that he was tired of seeing Danny screw things up.

Now came the defense expert witnesses who'd testify about their findings on Rolling's mental state. Since there was no insanity plea, the experts were not required to have face-to-face interviews with the defendant, but instead relied on the state's records and reports.

First on the stand was Dr. Harry Krop, a Gainesville clinical psychologist and veteran expert witness from many criminal trials, who spent twenty-two hours evaluating the defendant and interviewing him and several members of his family. His first interview with Rolling was on January 26, 1991, months before Rolling was named publicly as the prime suspect.

He diagnosed Danny Rolling as suffering from borderline personality disorder, antisocial personality disorder and personality disorder not otherwise specified (which included narcissism, obsessive/compulsive and histrionics). He also found that Rolling suffered from alcohol and substance abuse. Rolling was immature, unstable, narcissistic, angry and unable to maintain intense interpersonal relationships.

Krop opined that Danny Rolling's primary diagnosis was paraphilia: "[It's] a sexual disorder in which there is recurrent, intense sexual urges and/or sexually arousing fantasies, generally involving other individuals.

"In this case, the sexual disorder is voyeurism—he's a Peeping Tom, and it's of a severe nature."

Krop explained how Rolling said that when he was fourteen or fifteen, he spied on a neighborhood girl getting out of the shower. "Once he engaged in that particular act, it almost became a compulsion with him. It became extremely strong, and he started prioritizing his life around finding opportunities to start looking in windows."

As the defendant got older, the peeping compulsion got stronger, occurring with ever-greater frequency. He liked to masturbate while peeping in windows at women, but also had difficulty in achieving orgasm.

Krop said Rolling told him he used to pray God would come and take his father away. He said he'd witnessed years of spousal abuse, with his mother being beaten and slapped around.

Danny Rolling had a tremendous love-hate relationship with his mother, Krop said. He felt betrayed by her because she wasn't able to completely protect him from his father's violence. He saw her as being weak, and he couldn't respect that in anyone.

Dr. Krop had also interviewed Kevin Rolling, but he didn't have those kinds of memories. He'd interviewed James Rolling, who denied ever beating Danny Rolling. James Rolling said, "I never whupped him, but I raised hell. I never treated him like my father treated me."

On cross-examination, Dr. Krop received something of a roughing-up from prosecutor Rod Smith, who pointed out numerous inconsistencies in the stories that Danny Rolling had told through the years. Smith said Rolling has always blamed everyone else for his troubles.

He pointed out that James Rolling sometimes bailed Danny out of trouble; for example, when he'd fixed it so the defendant could live out his parole from Mississippi while living at the family home in Louisiana. He showed that despite complaints from the neighbors, James Rolling didn't beat Danny for being a Peeping Tom until he actually caught him at it.

Danny Rolling had never mentioned Gemini or Ennad, his multiple personalities, to Dr. Krop. "He has not tried to suggest someone else is in control of him," Krop said.

Krop said he remembered Rolling telling him that he wanted to kill the two police officers who chased him into the woods that night his campsite was discovered in Gainesville, but it was so dark that he couldn't find his campsite, where his gun was. Rolling said he would have gotten his gun and killed the lawmen if he'd been able.

Rolling told the doctor that his reason for the murders was to get revenge for all the injustice dumped on him during his life.

The state chose not to call James Rolling as a witness even though he'd been attacked in court. He was blind in one eye and had worn a hearing aid since Danny shot him. The prosecution also said he suffered from brain damage.

The defense chose not to call the defendant's brother, Kevin Rolling. They didn't think he could help them much. Apparently, his memories of the Rolling family's home life differed markedly from Danny's.

The state's response to the defense's case was to show that Danny Rolling had control over his decision-making processes, and that he chose to commit murder. His father didn't make him; his mother didn't make him. It was *his* choice.

Wednesday, March 16, 1994, day eight. The defense case resumed with the reading in court of a deposition from Agnes Mitchell, Danny Rolling's aunt. Mitchell, hospitalized in intensive care in Louisiana, was deposed on October 13, 1993. She detailed years of abuse, beginning even before Danny Rolling was born. She'd seen James Rolling shove wife Claudia down the stairs while she was pregnant with Danny. When Danny was born, his father said in the hospital that he wasn't taking the baby home with him because Claudia was too immature to raise a child. He said he didn't want any kids and that he would never be proud of Danny.

She said that during Danny's and Kevin's boyhood years, she'd seen them frequently beaten by James Rolling. Sometimes the beatings would draw blood. Once, she saw the boys sitting in the hall with pots on their heads, while their father beat the pots with a spoon. James Rolling sometimes tied the boys up or handcuffed them out in the yard during the summer. She'd seen the boys blindfolded at meals a couple of times, too.

Danny was a troubled child who was always having problems. Once, the witness caught him cutting up a dress and a scarf with a razor because he said he saw bugs on them. James Rolling stopped all efforts to get counseling for Danny.

Gainesville clinical psychologist Dr. Elizabeth McMahon had examined Danny Rolling for about twenty-nine hours, essentially reaching the same conclusions as Dr. Krop. She opined that he was not insane, not schizophrenic, not manic-depressive, that he was in contact with reality. He was immature, insecure and unable to empathize with others. He was filled with rage and anger.

She said that he had a borderline personality disorder with antisocial disorder features. His voyeurism crossed the line into violence, she said. He had a "possession disorder" and had spoken of Gemini, one of his multiple personality alter egos. He couldn't accept the rage within him, so he compartmentalized it as Gemini.

"It's out here, it's somebody else, it's not me, it's 'Gemini,' " the witness said. "So he will say that it's Danny that's the voyeur, Danny that robbed, Danny that raped, but it's Gemini that killed. Because that's what he cannot accept."

Dr. McMahon said Rolling told her that Gemini came to him while he was in prison in Parchman,

Mississippi. He said a bird died outside his prison cell and lights flickered, so he knew it as a sign, a portent of his diabolical destiny.

But Gemini held dangers for the defense. The prosecution argued that Rolling had gotten the idea from the movie *Exorcist III*, in which the villain is named the Gemini Killer and a priest finds a dead bird while lights flicker. In August 1990, *Exorcist III* was showing in Gainesville near the Wal-Mart where Rolling had gotten his tent and supplies. He told Dr. McMahon that he went to see the movie around the time of the murders.

Prosecutor Smith later told *Court TV*, "I believe his [Rolling's] worldview is not biblical as much as it is Miltonic. I think that Danny sees these spirits and sees that these spirits are competing for what he does, and when he does bad, when he sees himself as acting badly or misbehaving all the way up to vicious acts of murder, which he did here and in Shreveport and the rapes that he's done all over, [he'll claim it] wasn't me. Wasn't me, it was one of these other spirits that possessed me, but it's also cheap theatrics and it's also copied right out of the movie."

Dr. McMahon, who told the court she'd been previously unaware of the similarities between the film and Danny Rolling's Gemini alter ego, said that knowing the similarities between the movie and Rolling's Gemini character didn't change her diagnosis. She ascribed the parallels to Rolling's susceptibility to suggestion.

The state maintained that Rolling never mentioned Gemini to anyone until 1993, years after the murders. Rolling said Gemini first appeared in the mid-1980s. Yet when he was interviewed by a mental health expert in 1989, he said he had never had any visions or heard voices.

After court, at a press conference, prosecutor Rod Smith told of waking up earlier that morning, thinking about the movie *Helter Skelter,* the narrative of the Manson murders where much is made of Manson's obsession with the Beatles' songs and lyrics. He remembered that Rolling had told his psychologists he'd been to see *Exorcist III* while he was in Gainesville. Smith had an assistant rent the movie and skipped the first part of the trial on Wednesday so he could see it. He said he nearly fell out of his chair over the similarities.

Defense attorney Rick Parker said Smith's mention of the movie was another theatrical move by the prosecution that could prejudice the jury.

Thursday, March 17, 1994, day nine. Court resumed with the testimony of Philadelphia psychiatrist Dr. Robert Saddoff, who'd met with Danny Rolling for eight and a half hours in 1993, and had extensively reviewed all the case reports and expert analyses before reaching his conclusions.

The witness said that Rolling repeatedly said he loved his father despite the years of abuse. He said his father was a war hero "who made Audie Murphy look like Mr. Magoo." James Rolling's service records showed that he'd earned a Purple Heart, an honorable distinction, but nowhere near the war record of Murphy, America's most-decorated serviceman in World War II.

Danny Rolling continues to need for his father

to love him, Dr. Saddoff said. He said that Rolling had created his two alter egos, Gemini and Ennad, as a way to deal with the rage bottled up inside him. Rolling can't accept that he can have so much anger bottled up, so he says Gemini is the evil one.

The witness agreed that in 1990, at the time of the murders, Danny Rolling went to see *Exorcist III*, which includes a demon character named Gemini. "Seeing the movie confirmed for him that the sign was right, that this was what had happened to him, and there it is in the movie. . . . He can then say, 'It's real; Gemini is my sign.'

"Most of us would take that as a coincidence, but not the magical thinking of the borderline Danny Rolling."

Dr. Saddoff continued, "[Danny Rolling] is mostly rational, but there are times when I think his thinking is not rational; it's based on fantasy, wish fulfillment, unreasonable expectations—not so rational.

"He has a very serious illness."

He opined that the defendant was suffering from a serious emotional disturbance and lacked substantial capacity to conform his conduct to the requirements of law at the time of the murders.

On cross-examination, Jeanne Singer got the witness to admit that Danny Rolling knew right from wrong in each of the homicides. That was the crux of the state's case. Each of the defense witnesses acknowledged that Rolling never lost sight of right or wrong.

Defense experts agreed that Rolling had a borderline personality disorder and was antisocial.

There was no evidence of any organic brain damage.

The state pointed out that many people have borderline personality disorders and are not murderers.

There was a bizarre incident involving Rolling and a juror during the day's session. The defendant and juror were reportedly making eye contact and smiling at each other. Another juror wrote the judge a note about it, but after consulting the attorneys, the judge decided not to take any action about it. The defense attorneys told Rolling to stop it.

Friday, March 18, 1994, day ten. The state called two witnesses in rebuttal. First was Danny Rolling's ex-wife, O'Mather Lummus. They first met at the United Pentecostal Church, marrying six months later. They were both nineteen years old. They were married from 1974 to 1977. A daughter was born in 1976. The witness was now married to a Louisiana police officer.

The state put Lummus on the stand primarily to rebut testimony about the abusive relationship between James Rolling and his son Danny. Lummus looked only once at the defendant, when she identified him as her ex-husband.

She said that she and the defendant had spent lots of time at his parents' home, calling the father-son interaction "normal." She said that James Rolling treated her well, that Danny Rolling never complained about the way his father treated him. She never saw them fight. James and Claudia Rolling were very supportive of the marriage, the father trying to use his contacts to get Danny a job. Whenever the couple was short of money for groceries, James Rolling was the one who came through for them.

After O'Mather had a baby, Claudia Rolling came to the hospital and gave her some money from James Rolling. Claudia Rolling said that her husband told her to tell Lummus that he wasn't the kind who sends flowers, but that he wanted her to have the money.

She recalled an incident that had happened during her pregnancy. Danny Rolling came home late at night, saying that he'd gone to an apartment and a woman came to the door wearing only a shirt. Later that night, two police officers came to the Rolling house looking for Danny. They said he'd been peeking in windows.

Lummus said, "Naturally, it upset me very much. It was embarrassing and humiliating. It didn't sit very well with me. I admit it."

She told of an incident where Rolling struck her when she confronted him about his erratic behavior, giving her a black eye. She said Rolling was using marijuana at that time.

The prosecutor said, "Did you ever hear Danny or anybody in his family talk about demons or being visited by demons or anything like that?"

Lummus said, "I never did."

"Did you ever hear anything about anybody named Gemini or Ennad or any other name given to a spirit?"

"No, I didn't." Asked about the breakup of their marriage, O'Mather Lummus said, "The reason I left or decided to leave was that he threatened my life with a shotgun."

Kearns, on cross-examination, set out to show that there was a lot about the Rolling family that she never knew, such as that Claudia Rolling had had a nervous breakdown, that she and James Rolling had separated fifteen or twenty times, and that Danny Rolling had tried to commit suicide as a teenager.

Lummus said that she tried to talk to Rolling about his problems and that he never told her about any childhood abuse. She conceded that while she had never heard James Rolling abuse Danny, she had never heard him say anything positive to or about Danny, either. Defense counsel established that James Rolling had never come to visit her in the hospital, although she had just birthed his first grandchild. The witness also recalled an incident in which Danny Rolling went into a back room of his parents' home and wept uncontrollably.

After testifying, Lummus was immediately whisked out of the courtroom, her husband holding her arm.

Defense attorneys said later that Rolling was upset at seeing his ex-wife, of whom he'd once said that he prayed and prayed for a wife, and God sent him O'Mather Lummus. But he was upset more because she had brought back memories of his past family life than because she used to be married to him, they said.

At the time of the trial, there was some speculation that O'Mather Lummus may have resembled Danny Rolling's female victims, all of whom were petite brunettes. Apart from that, most observers said, there didn't seem to be any striking resemblances between them. But one of the defense psychologists testified that Danny Rolling told him he was stricken by how much Christa Hoyt looked like his ex-wife. Christa Hoyt was the only one of his victims that he decapitated. (Another suggestion was that Rolling had seen Hoyt's ASO cap in her apartment, thus marking her as a law enforcement agent and therefore a special target for his ire.)

After Lummus's testimony, Danny Rolling, under close watch, left the courtroom for a few minutes—whether because he was upset at seeing his ex-wife, or because he was having a tiff with Sondra London, or some other reason, is unknown.

Sondra London was absent from the courtroom when O'Mather Lummus testified.

Special Agent Ed Dix returned to the stand, to refute some of Rolling's statements regarding conditions at Parchman prison in Mississippi. Dix said they weren't nearly as bad as Rolling said.

Later, prosecutor Smith said he was pleased with the Lummus testimony and thought it gave the state everything it needed in rebuttal.

On Monday, March 21, 1994, day eleven, the state presented its own expert psychiatric witnesses, to counter those of the defense. Tampa psychologist Sidney Merrin had interviewed Danny Rolling briefly in 1991 when asked to determine his competency in another case. Merrin had since studied the documents in the Gainesville student murders. He concluded that Rolling was not a borderline personality, was not mentally ill, but he was antisocial. The Rolling family was dysfunctional, but others come out of similar backgrounds without killing five people they don't know.

He said, "You can come out of a dysfunctional family and know full well what the requirements of the law might be. Danny Rolling knew the rules of society. He also knew how to break the rules."

Many of Rolling's actions appeared to be controlled and measured. He hid outside of a couple of apartments, ducking down when someone walked by, before breaking in. He went back to Christa Hoyt's apartment to see if he'd left his wallet there. That showed he was thinking and was aware that such information could hurt him.

The witness said of Rolling, "He has what I would refer to as a kind of a Swiss cheese sort of a conscience. That is, sometimes it holds, and he drives children to church. But most of the time, it just goes right through the holes."

Merrin said he found "uncanny parallels" between Rolling's accounts of Gemini and the movie *Exorcist III*. He disputed the defense claims that Rolling suffered from paraphilia (Peeping Tomism) to the point of obsession. Rather, Rolling rearranged his life to give himself opportunities to peek at women because he got sexual pleasure from it. The witness compared it to eating ice cream a lot: you do it because you like it and it gives you pleasure, not because you are compelled to do it because of some force inside you.

Tampa psychiatrist Daniel Sprehe generally concurred with Merrin's diagnosis, saying that Rolling did not have a real mental illness, that he had the ability to make choices to conform his conduct to the confines of the law, but he chose not to.

In defense rebuttal, Dr. Elizabeth McMahon returned to the stand, saying that it was possible for Danny Rolling to have numerous psychological afflictions at the same time.

In all, the state called thirty-one witnesses and the defense called ten witnesses, with the state calling four witnesses in rebuttal and the defense one.

On Tuesday, attorneys met with the judge to set the jury charge. On Wednesday, March 23, 1994, at 9:30 A.M., court reconvened for closing arguments. First was Rod Smith for the state, who began by asking jurors to focus on the core of the case: whether the state of Florida had established aggravating factors and whether the defense had proved mitigating factors to counter them.

Smith said, "You've seen the evidence, you know the case. Remember your duty . . . duty's an easy concept to talk about, but sometimes an unwelcome thing to do. As long as you approach your duties today in light of the evidence, this case is not a particularly difficult decision."

Smith said that the aggravators had been proven beyond a reasonable doubt. He said that this case was not about Danny Rolling's troubled past—it was about a man who wants to rape and kill people. There are some crimes that are so horrible that the law requires a recommendation of the death penalty.

He reminded the jurors that they were making a recommendation, not the final decision. He said

Rolling's troubled background didn't even approach the severity of the murders. The aggravators far outweighed everything else, and therefore required a recommendation of the death penalty.

"He wanted to be the superstar of crime," Smith said. "Now he's committed five murders and I guarantee you nobody committed worse murders than these. These are legendary murders. These aren't just murders you hear about or read about. These are murders you never forget about."

Johnny Kearns urged the jury to choose life for the defendant. "You have to choose between a recommendation of life and a recommendation of death. Life in this case is one hundred twenty-five years . . . life in this case is punishment, because it's a sentence to Mr. Rolling of life without hope.

"It is the absence of hope that is the punishment. Mr. Rolling is going to die in a small room behind a brick wall . . . he's going to die in that prison."

Kearns argued that the abuse the defendant had suffered from his father was a mitigating factor in the case. Danny Rolling was regularly abused by his father during his formative years.

He said, "We know instinctively this is going to have a harmful effect on the child. This will have long-term repercussions . . . as the twig is bent, so grows the tree.

"For every action, there is an opposite and equal reaction. You had an opportunity to see the reaction of what happened in Gainesville in August 1990."

Summing up, Kearns noted that Danny Rolling had admitted his guilt in the case, claiming that this was a mitigating factor in favor of life imprisonment over death. "He [Rolling] is unable to mature. He is inconsistent with his chronological age. He does not function socially age-appropriately.

"There's a lot going on here . . . it's not as simple and as clear-cut as people would like you to believe. Danny Harold Rolling is a seriously disturbed and ill individual; he has been for a long period of time. But there are reasons why he should live, because from this type of environment, with these types of problems, you get these types of results. Remember, he did not choose to be this way."

On Thursday, March 24, 1994, after approximately five hours of deliberation, a jury of nine women and three men returned with their advisory sentencing verdict in the case, which was read aloud by the court clerk.

"We the jury, by a vote of twelve to zero, advise and recommend to the court that it impose the death penalty on Danny Harold Rolling."

By a vote of twelve to zero in each case, the jurors advised the court that Danny Rolling receive the death penalty for each of the five murder counts to which he had pleaded guilty.

On March 29, 1994, at a presentencing hearing, the court was shown a videotape of Claudia Rolling pleading for her son's life. At the same hearing, Danny Rolling got to address the court, stating that there was a lot he'd like to say, "about our world, my beliefs and the destiny of man . . . whatever I might have to say at this moment is overshadowed by the suffering I've caused.

"I regret with all my heart what my hand has

done. For I have taken what I cannot return. If only I could bend back the hand on that ageless clock and change the past. Ah, but alas, I am not the keeper of time, only a small part of history and the legacy of mankind's fall from grace.

"I'm sorry, Your Honor."

Later, Rod Smith observed, "You know, the other thing that's interesting about Danny is he's very bright, very verbal. There's a strange myth out there that Ted Bundy was this superintelligent guy and that Danny Rolling's kind of a less intelligent marginal guy. I might be wrong, but I believe that Danny's stated I.Q. is slightly higher than Ted Bundy's was or about the same. His verbal aptitude is as high or higher, which is amazing given the fact that he has very little formal education. . . .

"Danny is very histrionic, narcissistic, he knows how to act. He could meet you somewhere and actually charm you; nothing unusual about that. He can play roles. He has a vicious role, he has a nice role. He has this meek and mild, poor Danny role. I mean, you watch him sometimes shuffle in the courtroom, people honestly never realized Danny's a big man . . . he had mannerisms that would kind of make him look smaller, he would almost shrink up. Danny's a big guy, [a] big strong guy."

On April 20, 1994, Judge Stan Morris formally sentenced the defendant. Accepting the recommendation of the jurors, Judge Morris officially sentenced Danny Rolling to death for each of the five murder counts against him.

"You having been said sentenced; I remand you to the custody of the division of corrections. May God have mercy on your soul," the judge intoned.

As Rolling was led away, Manuel Taboada's brother Mario stood up and shouted at him, "You're going down in five, you hear that!—" Going down to the execution chamber in five years is what he meant.

Later, Mario Taboada said, "I wanted him to know I was there . . . I just wanted to have the last word, I guess." At a press conference, he said, "This man [Rolling] has yet another court to attend and it's greater than all of us. I want him to get there as soon as possible."

Rolling had been held at the Florida State Prison in Starke, a small town in northern Florida between Jacksonville and Gainesville. He returned there after being sentenced to death, after first being processed through the Northern Florida Reception Center under his new sentence. At Starke, he was admitted to his 7' x 8' death row cell, equipped with a TV and radio. He was one of about twenty men on death row at Starke. While inmates new to death row go to Starke for processing, inmates who are a threat to escape tend to stay there. With a previous escape from a correctional institute on his record, Rolling fit that profile. The other 300-plus men on death row in Florida were held across the river in Bradford County, in Union Correctional Institution.

Prisoners on death row are allowed to leave their cells only to shower every other night, to exercise twice a week for two hours each time, for legal and medical appointments, and to receive visitors from 9:00 A.M. to 3:00 P.M. on Saturday and Sunday. All meals are eaten in the cell.

On March 20, 1997, Danny Rolling's first mandatory appeal was rejected by the Florida Supreme Court. The appeals process continues, and it is estimated that Rolling will not be issued an official execution date until sometime around 2002. The average amount of time spent on Florida's death row between sentencing and execution is 9.4 years.

As for the Grissom murders in Shreveport, Louisiana, police uncovered enough evidence indicating Danny Rolling was the killer that for all intents and purposes, the case is considered closed.

Danny Rolling told *Court TV*, "There was a demon in me. I believe I was possessed. Period. I've seen it face-to-face, I know it's real . . . and you know something—when you leave here, believe it or not, there's demons that are out to get you.

"Somebody wrote me once, 'Does darkness swallow the light?' If you let it, it will.

"Light is goodness. Demons, you know, they like the dark. They can't stand the light. 'Cause then they're revealed and demons don't like to reveal theirselves. Only on rare occasions does a spirit, whether evil or good, reveal itself. Sometimes they do. But very rarely."

In 1994, Sondra London was filmed reading aloud a statement that Danny Rolling had penned in her defense. It said, "I [Rolling] have something to say, there's a loosely used misconception about Sondra London and Danny Rolling at this point and [it's] time I feel it necessary to refute these slanderous allegations. Number one, Sondra London is not using her charms to squeeze a product out of me, namely literary and artistic endeavors she and I are involved in.

"Hell, I want the girl to use me, I want her to be successful and to make money, damn right, she's paid her dues, earned her place in the media and literary world.

"Number two, Sondra London did not just jump up one day and decide to love Danny Rolling, it didn't happen that way. We shared correspondence over many months before she and I grew close enough for love. We want to get married, we want to visit like any other couple given that privilege here at Florida State Prison. Love has no boundaries, it reaches across the oceans, traverses the universe and even finds its way into the dark corners of a prisoner's heart locked away beyond the sight of humanity."

When she'd finished reading it, a misty Sondra London said, "That Danny, what a guy."

London offered Rolling's drawings and paintings for sale to private collectors with a taste for esoterica. "Killer art is mostly something that is engaged in by collectors. They wish to have a little piece of history. They like to have something they can hold in their hands that has been touched by the hands of a killer. A lot of people are interested in acquiring Danny Rolling's artwork for this reason. I make it available. . . . People that write to me wish to obtain some of Danny Rolling's artwork;

it's possible to work out terms and they can buy some pieces of artwork." She said his paintings start at $300 and have sold for up to $800. Drawings range from $50 to $75.

A partial survey of Danny Rolling's artworks includes: painting of man slaying dragon; painting of Devil in cave at gate to hell with frightened women and Grim Reaper in the background; painting of Sondra London as a Goddess of Discordia; painting of bound naked woman being attacked by dragon; picture of mermaid; painting of Elestria the Death Angel; painting of long-haired man with bloody knife with "fuck you" on his lips, spelled backward; picture of cloaked skeleton riding black horse, entitled *Rider.*

Sondra London explained, "He [Rolling] sees me as an angel. He's portrayed me as Elestria, which is an angel that he dreamed will welcome him and help him transition through to the other side upon his death. It was an angel that he calls Elestria and he said she looks like me. He also sees me as my evil twin Horenda, and so he would portray both. There is no middle ground. Either goddess or demon."

She noted that Danny Rolling was born under the sign of Gemini, the Twins.

She said, "I would just like to say that the relationship that I have with Danny is not a normal relationship and it doesn't compare to a normal relationship. He's never getting out of prison, we're never going to go home together. I'll never have to wash his dirty laundry, we'll never have to have any fights, he is never going to beat me up, he's never going to get in any fights with me about his jealousy and my independence. So all these things are not going to happen.

"I compare it to a parent who has a disabled child who is developmentally retarded or who has a fatal disease . . . there is still a love there . . . and I'm not going to quibble about what the meaning of the word 'love' is. . . .

"Certainly, I have respect for Danny as a human being. . . .

"When it comes to Danny Rolling, I think a lot of people think because he is a serial killer, a man, and I am a woman, that quite naturally that he is manipulating me and that he wants me to work his psychopathic will and I'm under his spell. If anything, the opposite is true. If anyone is manipulating anyone, it's me controlling Danny Rolling."

Asked if she played a kind of gatekeeper role, she said, "That is true, he would not have been able to write a book without me. Danny Rolling had the idea that he wanted to tell his story before he met me. He had already begun writing before he met me. He was going to do it one way or another. But he himself has said that it would not have been possible for him to complete the project without me there pushing beyond the limits that he was able to do."

Janet Frake said she was raped by Danny Rolling in Sarasota, Florida, in early August 1990, just weeks before the killings in Gainesville. Her attacker wore a ski mask and carried a knife. He bound her with duct tape and also used it to cover her eyes. Then he took her into the bathroom and raped her. She talked to him, humoring, flattering him, doing what it took to keep herself alive. Later the tape was removed from her eyes and the attacker showed himself without the ski mask before leaving.

When she saw Danny Rolling on TV, she was certain he was the one who'd attacked her. Police matched DNA from the crime to Rolling. Frake wanted Rolling prosecuted for the rape, but the Sarasota State Attorney's Office declined because of Rolling's five death sentences. She filed a million-dollar civil suit against Danny Rolling. He wouldn't talk about the suit in his *Court TV* interview.

In September 1994, Judge Stan Morris ruled that $20,000 to be paid by the *Globe* tabloid to Sondra London and Danny Rolling for a three-part series of Rolling's version of the Gainesville murders be placed instead under a temporary injunction, with the money to be held in a trust fund until the Son of Sam statute issue was resolved. London protested the violation of what she deemed her constitutional rights, and charged that State Attorney Smith's office was conducting a "vendetta" against her.

She told *Court TV,* "I am a journalist; I got a story; I published it; it belongs to me. No money goes to Danny Rolling, not because of the lawsuit, but because he was voluntarily stepping forward and writing and signing and notarizing an agreement [that] he voluntarily forgoes what should be his right under the law to accept a profit from accounts of [the] crime and under contract he's not going to accept any profits from accounts of [the] crime, anyway."

She also wanted to make a statement about the

families involved in the litigation. "The families of the victims of the Gainesville student murders have all accepted thousands of dollars in return for their accounts of the dead children. On the other hand, they have threatened to kill me for publishing my account of what really happened in Gainesville and why.

"I [brought] out the facts of what happened in those crimes and answering the questions that the families had asked repeatedly, *Why did this happen?* For my efforts to uncover why and reveal why, I have been rewarded with a concerted campaign to destroy my credibility and to attack me on any front possible."

Later, she said, "I do not write, what you call, straight true crime books. I am more interested in facilitating the communication directly from the offender without intervening by taking a supposedly neutral position in which I stand to one side and assert my judgmental distance from what the offender is saying.

"I don't think that the point of view of the offender is ever going to be fairly represented unless the person that is facilitating that communication is willing to allow them to take the lead and say, this is your message and I want to present it from your point of view."

Rod Smith declined to comment on Sondra London and her ideas because he was in litigation with her. "I think it's safe to say that I professionally, intellectually and personally disagree with Sondra London, and there's no way that I could characterize what I think she's done in this and other cases other than [as] the lowest form of opportunism."

On December 3, 1995, John Gerard Schaefer, the litigious "Sex Beast," was found stabbed to death in his cell at Florida State Prison at Starke, stabbed and slashed with a handmade shank knife. Ft. Lauderdale homicide sleuths who'd been examining cold case files in the twenty-year-old disappearances of three young area women had found evidence they believed pointed to Schaefer as the perpetrator. They expressed frustration that he'd gone to the grave with his secrets untold.

Schaefer's killer was inmate Vincent Rivera, serving two life sentences for two murders in Tampa in 1990. Investigators theorized that the motive was related to money that Schaefer had collected as a jailhouse lawyer.

In June 1996, Danny Rolling and Sondra London became "un-engaged." Here was a romance that had started out so hot it could only cool off. Rolling decided that he liked another female pen pal better.

Sondra London said, "We both agreed and signed an agreement that we would no longer be engaged. Our personal relationship continues the same. . . . We still continue to correspond regularly and we write each other at least three times a week. I'm still his only confidante, he still relies on me for advice."

In 1997, the state of Florida, acting under the Florida Civil Restitution Lien and Crime Victims' Remedy Act of 1994, attempted to seize the amount, somewhere between $15,000 and $20,000, that Sondra London allegedly made from the sale of Rolling's story to the *Globe* tabloid, as well as royalties and advances on two books, one of which, *The Making of a Serial Killer*, was cowritten by London and Rolling.

Sondra London described it as "basically a two-hundred-page book of which fifteen pages are accounts of the crimes of which we speak. That leaves 92.5 percent of the book to account for why it happened and to allow you to get into the mind of the serial killer."

Danny Rolling told *Court TV*, "Maybe there's something I can say to help somebody. I don't know. I spent about three and a half years writing a book, tearing my heart out and slapping it on a page for people to read."

In the book, published in 1996 by Feral House, a section entitled "Appendix B: A Pack of Lies," lets Danny Rolling vent and set the record straight as he sees it (or wants it to be seen). He forthrightly declares that he is not a Satanist, proclaiming in capital letters, NO! I AM NOT INTO THE OCCULT! He concedes that the medical examiner found evidence of anal rape on Tracy Paules's body, but says that he doesn't recall sodomizing her, that he doesn't even believe in sodomy.

He says "Bobby Lewis is a pathological liar," and maintains that it was Lewis who was always talking about Ted Bundy, not Rolling. Rolling says that he's not a fan of Ted Bundy. Contrary to Lewis's claim, Rolling says he never had a séance with the spirit of Ted Bundy in the woods.

He denies defense psychiatrist Dr. Harry Krop's contention that he (Rolling) had difficulty in achieving orgasm, claiming that he enjoyed sex immensely and just liked to prolong the pleasure. He spends most of a page vehemently denying that he's gay: "I AM NOT A BLASTED BLOODY QUEER!"

The state contended that the fact that Sondra London and Rolling were having a personal relationship removed the "objective reporter" label London might otherwise have been able to claim entitled her to the money.

London insisted that her personal relationship with Danny Rolling was irrelevant to the matter. She asked the court to find that the Florida Son of Sam–type statute was unconstitutional as a restraint of free speech.

In September 1997, under pressure from the governor of Wyoming and victims-rights advocate Mark Klaas (whose daughter Polly was abducted from her own house and murdered), and a threatened boycott, America On Line agreed to take down Sondra London's Web site featuring the writings and drawings of Danny Rolling and other serial killers. The governor was particularly upset by the Web pages devoted to convicted triple-killer Keith Hunter Jesperson, who'd committed murder in Wyoming.

On December 31, 1997, in the matter of the *Globe*'s payment for Rolling's story, Judge Martha Ann Lott found for the plaintiff, the state of Florida. Two years later, on December 2, 1999, Judge Elzie Sanders ruled that the $15,000, which had been held in trust, should be dispersed to the families of Rolling's victims. Some family members expressed reservations about accepting what they called "blood money." It was suggested that the funds could be used to build a park in Gainesville, or perhaps create a college scholarship or some similar life-affirming projects.

In the anthology *Apocalypse Culture II,* published by Feral House in 2000, a short essay by Sondra London, "Murder Lite," is appended by this editor's note: "Due to frequent death threats, Ms. London has given up her true crime career."